SYSTEMATIC READING INSTRUCTION

SYSTEMATIC
READING
INSTRUCTION

Gerald G. Duffy
George B. Sherman
MICHIGAN STATE UNIVERSITY

HARPER & ROW
PUBLISHERS

NEW YORK   EVANSTON   SAN FRANCISCO   LONDON

for our families

Acknowledgments / It is impossible to acknowledge all the many people who have assisted us in one way or another in the development of this book. However, we wish to acknowledge our particular indebtedness to Drs. Clyde Campbell, Howard Hickey, Bettye Jennings, and Anne Nagel, of M.S.U.'s Mott Institute for Community Improvement, whose work on the *Mott Expanding Notebook for Teaching Reading Skills* provided the genesis for our efforts.

SYSTEMATIC READING INSTRUCTION

CONTENTS

PREFACE

The authors believe that a primary cause of reading failure rests with teachers who, through no fault of their own, do not know the skills of reading. Not knowing the skills, they are unable to teach them. Even when a teacher does know the skills, her instruction may be haphazard and inefficient. She lacks a strategy for determining what skill each learner needs at any given moment and for systematically teaching that skill.

This problem is even more evident with paraprofessionals, who now frequently assist in teaching reading. These nonprofessionals, as well as the professionals, need a systematic guide for planning and teaching the basic reading skills.

Systematic Reading Instruction meets this need. Its structure emphasizes the skills of word recognition and comprehension necessary to attain a level of functional literacy. Its style and format appeal to volunteers and paraprofessionals as well as to teachers. Its content provides a strategy for efficiently diagnosing and systematically teaching the basic reading skills.

This book has a broad range of use. In a structured basal program it can provide diagnostic information and corrective treatment. In partnership with a language experience approach or an individualized reading program, it can provide the necessary structure and sequencing for supportive skill development. It can be used with Head Start, kindergarten, and primary age children, with remedial readers, and with adults. It can be used with individual learners in tutorial situations or with groups in a regular classroom. Finally, it provides

a source for the experienced teacher and an invaluable guide for the trained paraprofessional or volunteer tutor who lacks the educational background and/or experience to provide an appropriate sequence of basic reading skills.

It is distinctive from other books on reading instruction in five ways. First, it focuses on the skills of reading, stating each of these in performance terms. Second, it provides an instructional strategy for mastering these skills, including alternative techniques for teaching each skill and specific devices to determine when these have been learned. Third, it focuses on the teaching-learning act itself and not on any theoretical considerations. Fourth, it clarifies technical reading terminology so that paraprofessionals, as well as professionals, can use it easily. Finally, it serves as a resource that paraprofessionals and professionals can use both in their preservice training and in their actual teaching of reading in the classroom.

Although the book has a broad range of utility and a number of distinctive features, *it is not intended to provide all the answers in reading instruction.* Instead, its focus is on the skills (or the mechanics) of reading. The importance of teacher-pupil relationships, interests, attitudes of both the learner and the teacher, vital creative learning experiences, and the role of literature is recognized and suggestions are made relative to these, but the book's *unique* contribution is its systematic skill development program.

Gerald G. Duffy
George B. Sherman

CHAPTER ONE /
SYSTEMATIC
READING
INSTRUCTION

In recent years increased emphasis has been placed on reading instruction. The federal government has made literacy a priority goal, massive programs have been initiated to provide every citizen with the "right to read," and paraprofessionals, as well as teachers, have become deeply involved in reading instruction.

This is as it should be. Reading is the most crucial of the fundamental skills, for a learner's success or failure in both school and society depends largely upon his skill as a reader. Consequently, reading instruction must be of the highest quality.

However, neither a massive federal campaign nor increased manpower in the form of volunteers and paraprofessionals can by themselves eradicate reading disabilities. If we are to eliminate reading failure, we must systematically teach reading skills to all learners.

A system for teaching reading skills must possess certain characteristics. It must reflect what is known about reading and how we learn to read. It must be easy to apply and must produce the desired achievement. It must specify what is to be taught, how to teach it, and how to determine what learning has occurred. It must enhance and encourage diagnosis and individualization of instruction. It must be easily adaptable to both group and tutorial situations, as well as to the various reading materials and methodologies currently being used in classrooms. Finally, it must be easy for both the professional and the paraprofessional to use. This book provides such a system.

READING IS A SKILL

Reading is a skill. More specifically, reading is a group of skills that extend in a hierarchy from the simple to the complex. The successful reader can perform each of the skills in this hierarchy. A person who is unable to read cannot do one or more of the things that a successful reader does because he lacks one or more of the skills of the successful reader.

Reading skills are learned. Although occasionally a child may learn to read by himself, the typical learner must be taught. The purpose of reading instruction, therefore, is to teach reading skills.

This book is based on three premises. The first is that reading instruction is successful to the extent that it provides learners with reading skills. Consequently, a major portion of the book is devoted to identifying a hierarchy of reading skills and to stating these skills in performance terms—in terms of what a person can do when he possesses these skills.

The second is that instruction in reading skills must be systematic. The skills are ordered from the simple to the complex, and a learner must not be moved into a skill until he has mastered the prerequisite skills. Consequently, for each skill identified in this book, a simple test of mastery is included.

The last is that reading skills must be *taught*, and that certain instructional strategies and activities have more utility and efficiency than others. Therefore, for each skill identified, specific instructional strategies and activities are provided.

■ WHAT ARE THE READING SKILLS? Reading is a developmental process beginning with the first acquisition of oral language and continuing throughout life. A complete listing of reading skills would include all those that the mature reader needs and would be tremendously extensive. In this book, however, we focus instead on those skills the reader must possess in order to attain a level of functional literacy—that is, the level at which he can independently handle reading materials of fourth-grade difficulty.

The skills required for functional literacy have been organized into three major categories. The first category, found in Chapter 4, emphasizes the important prerequisites to decoding printed language. These are frequently called the "skills of readiness" since mastery of these skills indicates that a learner is ready to read. The skills included in this category are divided into two sets. The first teaches learners visual discrimination: what to look at in examining letters and words and how to differentiate among them. The second teaches auditory discrimination: what to listen to among the sounds of letters, word parts, and words, and how to differentiate among them.

The second category of skills, found in Chapter 5, builds on the prerequisites developed in Chapter 4 and emphasizes the decoding act itself. The learner is taught to recognize some words instantly and to use problem-solving techniques for identifying others. These are called the "skills of word recognition" because students learn to identify and remember written words. They are divided into two sets. The first teaches instant recognition of selected words, and the second teaches the analysis of unknown words. Included in this latter set are techniques for blending the sounds of words together, of noting word parts, and of using sentence sense or context.

The final category of skills, found in Chapter 6, focuses on how to get meaning from what is read. The emphasis is on understanding, and the tasks described are called the "skills of comprehension." These skills are divided into three sets. The first teaches individual word meaning, the second teaches the organization cues in meaning getting, and the third teaches how to infer meanings.

Possession of the skills included in these three chapters is essential for successful reading of fourth-grade materials. Further, they form the crucial foundation upon which continued growth in reading is based. Consequently, a person's success as a reader—and ultimately, his success in school and society—is dependent upon his mastery of these fundamental skills. They must be carefully taught and thoroughly learned.

■ HOW ARE THE SKILLS TAUGHT? To make certain that the skills are thoroughly learned, this book describes a three-step instructional strategy that emphasizes systematic appraisal of learner needs, specific instruction, and demonstrated mastery of skills.

In teaching a learner to read, first it must be determined which skills he needs. This is accomplished by administering a series of simple pretests. If the learner performs at or above the established criterion level for the pretest at the lowest level, assume he has already mastered that skill. Go on to the next skill, administering the pretest and comparing the learner's performance to the criterion level established for that skill. If the learner once again performs at or above the established criterion, you assume he has mastered this skill and move on to the next. This process continues until the learner encounters a skill he cannot perform. Thus, the first step in the strategy is that of data gathering. Time is not wasted teaching the learner a skill he has already mastered, and effort is not wasted teaching him a skill that is too difficult for him.

After determining the individual skill needs of each learner, the second step is to provide direct instruction designed to develop these skills. The lessons are highly intensive and direct. There is no misunderstanding about what needs to be taught, nor is the skill left to develop naturally or as a result of generalized reading lessons. Your objective for the lesson is clear; your instruction specific.

The third step is the administration of the posttest to determine whether the instruction has been successful. This procedure is similar to the first step. Once again, you give the learner a series of tasks testing his ability to perform the specific skill he has been taught. If he performs at or above the established criterion level, the instruction has been successful, the skill has been mastered, and the learner can be moved to the next skill. If, however, he fails, you must assume that the instruction has not been successful, and another lesson designed to develop this skill must be planned and taught. Thus, the third step in the strategy insures that each skill in the sequence is mastered in turn and that no learner is moved on too quickly. The posttest prevents us from assuming that the skill was learned simply because it was taught. The criterion for determining the success of instruction is the learner's ability to actually perform a reading skill in a specified manner.

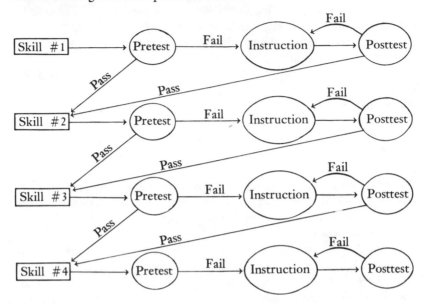

The instructional strategy can be diagramed as shown in the figure. As can be seen, a learner proceeds through the skill hierarchy in a sequential fashion, from the simplest to the most complex. For each skill, he takes a pretest. If he passes the pretest, he needs no instruction in that skill, and he moves to the next skill and takes that pretest. If he fails a pretest, he must be taught that skill; he is provided with instruction, and his performance is then tested again. If he passes this posttest, he moves to the next skill. If he does not, he receives additional instruction in the skill until he demonstrates his mastery on a posttest.

The instructional strategy for teaching reading skills is systematic. It provides a pretest for each skill so that instructional time is spent only on what needs to be mastered, instruction that is specifically planned to teach the skill needed, and posttests to insure that no learner moves from one skill to another until the prerequisite has been mastered.

SOME WORDS OF CAUTION

What we offer is a highly effective strategy for developing reading skills. When used well, it eliminates much wasted motion in skill teaching while insuring a greater measure of success among learners. However, it must be clearly stated that *the book does not do everything.*

First, although it does provide a systematic approach to teaching reading skills and some suggestions for applying these skills in daily reading, the major responsibility for application is left to the teacher. Skills are fundamental to reading success and must be learned, but once learned they must be put to work in appropriate settings. The best way to do this is to provide learners with much reading that is important and meaningful to them (see the final chapter), but the exact mechanics of accomplishing this are left to you.

Second, we also leave largely to you the task of developing the creative and affective aspects of reading. Activities that help learners express themselves concerning what they read and that develop appreciation for reading are important parts of a good reading program. Although Chapter 7 mentions this aspect of instruction, it is not a major emphasis of the book.

Third, we leave to you the task of creating an exciting and vital school day that focuses on the development of important ideas and activities. A vital curriculum will support the skill program described here by providing learners with an appetite for learning, a desire to read, and a place to apply the skills. Again, however, this facet of reading instruction is outside the scope of this book.

Finally, we leave to you the most influential aspect of any reading program—the degree of commitment you bring to your work. Instructional success is always influenced more by the attitude of the teacher than by any other single variable. Successful teachers have a patience and love for their students, they are determined to teach in spite of all difficulties, they examine themselves and their techniques when instruction fails, and they consider it their responsibility to see that learning occurs. In short, successful reading programs demand teachers who are dedicated, tenacious, persistent, and extremely hard workers. Is this a description of you?

Our position, then, is clear. A child cannot read unless he possesses the skills of reading. We provide a strategy for systematically developing these skills. However, though learners must learn the skills if they are to read, *a skills program is not all that is needed*. There must be a supportive program that includes much reading of interesting material, constant pursuit of a broad spectrum of learning in a vital manner, and the development of the creative and affective, as well as the mechanical, aspects of reading. In addition, there must be a teacher who is committed to the development of effective readers and who possesses the human characteristics that foster communication with learners. When the strategy we describe is put to work in any instructional situation, the probability of its success is high. But this probability will be even higher when it is put to work in a setting possessing both the supportive program and the teacher that all good programs need.

SUMMARY

Early in this chapter, we stated that a system for teaching reading skills must have certain characteristics. This is an appropriate time to evaluate our strategy in terms of those characteristics.

First, we stated that such a program must reflect what we know of reading and how reading is learned. Since the book is based on a sequential development of reading skills within a framework of individual progress, it accounts for both the developmental nature of reading and the individual nature of learning. Hence, the strategy we describe considers the nature of reading and learning and fulfills the first criterion of a fundamental skills program.

Second, we stated that a fundamental skills program must be easy to apply while producing the desired achievement. This book is easy to apply because it is highly structured and is organized so that a teacher can use it with a minimum of confusion. The book meets the criterion of being thorough in its effectiveness because the strategy utilizes a system of pretests and posttests to insure that each learner masters each skill in sequence before moving on to more difficult skills. The authors' experience in using the strategy supports this.

Third, we stated that the program must specify what is to be taught, how to teach it, and how to determine that learning has occurred. This is the focus of Chapters 4, 5, and 6.

Fourth, we stated that the program must enhance and encourage diagnosis and individualization of instruction. The pretests are diagnostic, determining specifically what instruction the learner needs at any particular time. By selecting learners with similar skill difficulties for short skill lessons, instruction can be individualized. Hence, the criteria of diagnosis and individualization are met in this program.

Fifth, we stated that the program must be easily adaptable to both group and tutorial situations and to the various approaches to reading instruction commonly used in classrooms. Our program meets this criterion because it can be used as a supplement to any other program, and it can be used with one learner or with a group of learners having the same skill deficiency.

Finally, we stated that the program must be easily used by both the professional and the trained paraprofessional. The format of the book and its step-by-step organization make it possible for both groups to use it with a minimum of orientation.

In sum, the strategy we describe provides a systematic structure for developing the crucial skills a learner must possess to attain functional literacy. The program is clear, sequential, and easy to follow. Its use requires a minimum of background and preparation time, but at the same time provides for diagnosis and individualization of instruction. It has a high degree of utility because it is planned for any classroom in which the beginning skills of reading need to be taught. Like any program, it is most effective when used by a dedicated teacher who conducts an exciting school day, but in any situation it will provide for a more systematic and efficient development of the foundation skills essential for reading success.

CHAPTER TWO / A
READING SKILLS
PROGRAM

This book is designed to be a tool you can keep at your desk for ready use during the planning and teaching of reading skills. To reap its full benefits, however, you must be aware of the resources it offers and be oriented to its uses.

If you teach children in Head Start, kindergarten, or the primary grades, you will find this book extremely helpful in teaching the crucial beginning reading skills. However, its use is not limited to these groups. It can also be adapted for use by upper elementary and secondary teachers faced with the task of helping disabled readers in their classes, by teachers of special summer or extraschool reading programs, by remedial reading teachers, and by teachers of adult literacy classes.

If you teach in a regular classroom, you may use this book as the basis for your skill instruction. Pretest each learner on each of the skills, group together those needing a particular skill, use the suggested activities to plan skill lessons, and use the posttests to assess the effectiveness of your instruction. In this manner, you provide efficient and systematic skill instruction with a minimum of effort and time.

Similarly, if you use volunteer teachers, paraprofessionals, or student teachers to assist you with individual and small-group instruction, you can give them this book and direct them to follow the specifications for pretesting, teaching, and posttesting that are provided in Chapters 4, 5, and 6. The need for elaborate supervision of the trained volunteer or paraprofessional is largely eliminated; we provide ample structure to insure the acquisition of skills.

Finally, the book can be put to work in combination with any approach to reading. For example, if you want to use a basal text, provide directed reading lessons from that source and use this book to systematize instruction in the skills. If you wish to use the language experience approach, have the learners dictate, write, and read their own stories and again use this book to provide the foundation in reading skills. If you prefer the individualized reading approach using trade books, reap the benefits of self-selection and pacing inherent in that approach while using this book to provide the fundamental skills each learner must develop to progress satisfactorily. Similarly, what we propose can be combined with any other approach to reading. The point is that the reading skills are universal, they do not change, and they must be taught. Therefore, no matter what method or material is used, we provide a systematic base for this skill development.

The book, then, is very useful. It can be particularly helpful to Head Start, kindergarten, and primary-grade teachers, but it also provides a structure for teaching the basic skills to readers of all levels and in all situations. It can be used with individual learners, with small groups, and as a basis for large-group instruction. Finally, it can be combined with any approach to reading instruction that you desire to use.

HOW THIS BOOK IS ORGANIZED

The first three chapters are introductory in nature. The first explains the rationale for systematic skill instruction, the second provides a step-by-step strategy for implementing a skills program, and the third provides suggestions for teaching skill lessons and for managing instruction.

Chapters 4, 5, and 6 represent the heart of the book in which the specific skill objectives, the pretest and posttest materials, and the suggested instructional activities are detailed. Of these chapters, both the fourth and the fifth are concerned with word recognition, while the sixth deals with comprehension.

You should view Chapters 4 and 5 as one large group of sequential skills, since the first of these teaches the prerequisites to word recognition and the next teaches the word recognition skills themselves. Because of the volume of skills contained in these chapters, both are divided into *clusters* for easy management. Within each cluster, the skills are again divided into two sections. The first emphasizes the skills a learner must master to recognize words instantly, and the second teaches the problem-solving techniques needed to analyze words. Hence, each cluster of skills in Chapters 4 and 5 is divided into sets of visual, or recognition, skills (A) and sets of analysis, or problem-solving, skills (B). It should be noted that the division of skills into clusters is purely arbitrary, and you must not equate the completion of a particular cluster with a particular level of reading achievement or force a learner to progress through a set number of skills in a single school year.

Chapter 6, emphasizing comprehension, has also been divided into clusters. The arrangement in this chapter is slightly different, however, since this division is based on the type of skill being taught rather than on the difficulty of the skill. Whereas in word recognition it is possible to describe a certain number of discrete skill units, it is not possible in comprehension because the thinking skills required depend largely upon the specific content being used, and they are infinite in number. Consequently, Chapter 6 is organized into three generalized clusters of word meaning (Clusters IA and IB), organization (Clusters IIA, IIB, and IIC), and inferential skills needed for comprehension (Clusters IIIA and IIIB), with the suggestion that these be taught on a spiral basis rather than as a strict sequence. For example, at a low level you can teach an inferential thinking skill orally based upon the word meanings and organization skills the learner has in his oral language at that time, while the same skill can be taught later in a reading setting when the more sophisticated word meaning and organization prerequisitics have been taught. Each comprehension objective is a resource that you return to again and again to teach the same general skill at a higher level and in conjunction with the particular demands of the material currently being used by the learner.

Chapter 7 describes a strategy for transferring the skills taught in isolation to the daily reading of books. The emphasis here is on the development of a recreational reading program that provides both meaningful application of the reading skills and an atmosphere in which learners develop the habit as well as the skills of reading. It is important that you note the content of this chapter carefully in order to place skill instruction in its proper perspective.

The appendix provides a number of resources to aid you in teaching reading skills. A complete listing of the objectives taught in this book is provided. There is a list of commercial practice material suitable for use in teaching the skills, as well as sources for obtaining trade books for use in a recreational reading program. A detailed week-by-week plan for organizing your class along the lines of the management suggestions described in Chapter 3 is provided. This is followed by a test that places learners in appropriate skill clusters. An analysis of the difference between teaching and testing, a model skill lesson, and a checklist are available for use in evaluating your skill lessons. There is also a model for applying comprehension skills in content materials. Also included is a series of three diagnostic charts describing various reading deficiencies and the objectives in the book that would be most appropriate in correcting these deficiencies. Finally, a glossary is included to help you clarify the meaning of any terminology used in the book. These appendixes will help you implement a skills program, and you are urged to familiarize yourself with them.

■ NUMBERING SKILL OBJECTIVES   For ease of management and convenience in teaching, the skills have been divided into sections called clusters. Each cluster comprises a group of related objectives. In numbering objectives, the roman numeral at the left indicates the cluster number, the upper-case letter in the middle indicates skill classification, and in Chapters 4 and 5 the arabic number at the right designates the sequence of the objective in that skill classification. For example, in Chapter 4, Objective IIIA 4 is the fourth objective in Section A, "What the Learner Looks at," of the third cluster, and Objective IVB 2 is the second objective in Section B, "What the Learner Listens to," in the fourth cluster.

The following is a list of all the clusters and their skill classifications in Chapters 4, 5, and 6. This will help you interpret the coding system used. For a more detailed listing of the separate skills contained in each cluster see Appendix A.

Chapter 4:

Cluster IA	1 through 8	What the Learner Looks at
Cluster IB	1 through 7	What the Learner Listens to
Cluster IIA	1 through 8	What the Learner Looks at
Cluster IIB	1 through 12	What the Learner Listens to
Cluster IIIA	1 through 10	What the Learner Looks at
Cluster IIIB	1 through 9	What the Learner Listens to
Cluster IVA	1 through 10	What the Learner Looks at
Cluster IVB	1 through 3	What the Learner Listens to

Chapter 5:

Cluster IA	1 through 3	Sight Words
Cluster IB	1 through 13	Word Analysis
Cluster IIA	1 through 3	Sight Words
Cluster IIB	1 through 13	Word Analysis
Cluster IIIA	1 through 3	Sight Words
Cluster IIIB	1 through 9	Word Analysis
Cluster IVA	1 through 3	Sight Words
Cluster IVB	1 through 7	Word Analysis
Cluster VA	1 through 3	Sight Words
Cluster VB	1 through 8	Word Analysis
Cluster VIA	1 through 3	Sight Words
Cluster VIB	1 through 7	Word Analysis
Cluster VIIA	1 through 3	Sight Words
Cluster VIIB	1 through 10	Word Analysis

Chapter 6:

Cluster IA		Content Word Meaning
Cluster IB		Function Word Meaning
Cluster IIA	1 through 3	Meaning Relationships
Cluster IIB		Classification Skills
Cluster IIC		Main Idea and Detail Skills
Cluster IIIA		Fact Skills
Cluster IIIB		Inference Skills

■ KEY OBJECTIVES   Certain objectives in some clusters are designated as *Key Objectives,* meaning that this is the first appearance of a skill that will be repeated in more sophisticated form several times throughout the book. These objectives contain a thorough description of the skill and a storehouse of activities for teaching it. When the same skill reoccurs in more sophisticated form later in the book, you are referred back to the Key Objective to refresh your memory concerning the crucial attenders and to select appropriate instructional tactics. The list of Key Objective skills on the inside front cover of this book will make it easy for you to locate these objectives quickly.

IMPLEMENTING THE PROGRAM

Effective teaching of reading demands a committed and dedicated teacher who works extremely hard to make certain that her learners achieve success. If you possess these characteristics, this book provides the other raw materials you need to guide your learners to functional literacy. The following step-by-step plan will aid you in successfully implementing an effective program.

   Step 1 / Your first step is to organize your class for efficient instruction. Unless the routines of effective management have been clearly established and both you and your learners understand what is expected at any given time, your skills program will bog down in the quicksand of aimless wandering and constant threats of disciplinary action. To avoid this contingency, read carefully the suggestions regarding management of instruction in Chapter 3 and follow the week-by-week plan for organizing your class described in Appendix D. Do not rush into a skills program. Instead, take sufficient time to firmly establish the needed routines and to acquaint the learners with your way of doing things. It is much better to delay the skills program for six weeks to be sure that it functions smoothly for the remaining thirty-four weeks than to rush into it only to have it fall apart periodically because of management difficulties.

   Step 2 / Your second step is to determine the level at which each of your learners is currently reading. It is essential that you provide each learner with reading material commensurate with his ability. Your skill program will surely fail if you demand that learners read material which is too difficult for them, since they will then become frustrated with reading and build all sorts of elaborate defense mechanisms justifying why they *should not* learn to read. To determine reading levels, use the suggestions on page 31 in Chapter 3.

   Step 3 / Once you know the level at which each of your learners is currently reading, you can begin to collect materials for a recreational reading program. The suggestions provided in Chapter 7 will be helpful, as will the source list of trade books found in Appendix C. As you gather these materials, you should also be attending to the atmosphere of your classroom, making certain that it reflects an emphasis on books and reading. Also at this time begin implementing some of the Chapter 7 suggestions regarding room environment and activities that support the development of an interest in reading.

Step 4 / As you begin to organize your classroom and as your recreational reading program gets under way, you can start administering the pretests provided in this book. If you are working with a learner who cannot read at all, or who reads very poorly, begin with the objectives in Chapter 4. If he can read but not fluently, begin with the objectives in Chapter 5. If his difficulty is limited to comprehension, check his performance on the objectives in Chapter 6. In each case, start with the lowest level skill and administer the pretest for that skill. Note whether he performs at or above the criterion for mastery as stated in the pretest. If he does, take him on to the next skill and repeat the process, continuing until he encounters an objective that he is unable to perform satisfactorily. It is at this point that your skill instruction for that learner will begin. This initial skill testing can be shortened by using the placement test provided in Appendix E prior to beginning individual pretests.

Several cautions should be noted about pretesting. First, you should do your best to make the situation as nonintimidating as possible. The best way to do this is to explain frankly that you are trying to find out how best to help each learner. You must also minimize the tendency of learners to compare their performances with each other by conducting the pretests in a routine, matter-of-fact, and casual manner. Second, you should be sure that the items in each pretest are appropriate for the experience backgrounds and dialects of your learners. Although attempts have been made to caution you to these differences as the objectives occur, it is impossible to foresee all the situations in which the pretests will be used. Therefore, you should not hesitate to use the model pretest as a basis for building a more appropriate test for your learners if you feel this is necessary. Third, some pretests can be given to groups of learners but others must be individually administered. Those that you administer to groups should be conducted in such a way as to make certain that you are truly determining the learner's ability to perform the task and not his ability to follow the lead of another, more competent, peer. Finally, you are cautioned to take nothing for granted on the pretests. If you have any reason to doubt the learner's mastery of a particular task, it is always better to teach the skill and insure mastery than to make a faulty assumption that will handicap him later when he encounters more sophisticated skills for which this one is a crucial prerequisite.

Step 5 / As soon as you begin pretesting, you will need a record-keeping device. Efficient record keeping is a crucial aspect of the management of instruction, particularly if you are truly committeed to teaching each learner the skill he needs when he needs it. The suggestions provided on page 32 in Chapter 3 will aid you in developing an efficient and manageable record system.

Step 6 / Once the initial pretests have been concluded and recorded, you must examine your record-keeping device to determine your initial skill groups. This is described on pages 32–33 in Chapter 3; you should use the procedure as a model for establishing your own skill groups.

Step 7 / You are now ready to initiate skill instruction. Using the skill groups identified in Step 6 above, select one group for instruction. Locate in this book the page containing the objective that needs to be taught. For each objective, there is a heading titled "Directing the Learner's Attention." Examine this paragraph carefully to determine what the learner must attend to in order to master the task, and make specific plans regarding how you will direct such attention.

Objectives that appear in similar form throughout the book have been keyed to the original description of the task. If the objective you are teaching is one that has been taught in similar form previously, the description under "Directing the Learner's Attention" will direct you to the original Key Objective. Turn to that objective, read "Directing the Learner's Attention," and examine the "Model Activity." As the name implies, this activity has been carefully written to provide you with a model for teaching a particular skill, and your chances of teaching it successfully will usually be enhanced if you follow this model rather closely. If this is the first time the skill has been taught in the book, of course, there will be no Key Objective for you to refer to, and you will use the model activity described right there. In any case, the model activity, as you teach it, must include the instructional conditions of *presentation, response,* and *reinforcement* as explained in Chapter 3.

Once you have used the model activity to present the skill, select one of the alternates listed under "Suggestions for Reteaching and Practice" to build a practice exercise. Most of the suggestions provided do not require any special materials other than those you can construct yourself. If you wish, however, you may refer to Appendix B and use some of the commercial practice material listed there. You are cautioned, however, to make certain that whatever material you select does indeed practice the skill you have taught.

Step 8 / Once the practice has been completed, administer the posttest provided in the objective to make certain that the learner has now mastered the skill. The guidelines outlined for the pretests in Step 4 above are appropriate for this task.

Step 9 / Once the learner has successfully completed the posttest, you still are faced with the crucial task of making certain that he applies this skill in his daily reading. This means that in the days following the skill lesson, you must consciously structure experiences that help the learner put to use the skill he has been taught. For example, he can be given a short story containing the skill and directed to read it silently in preparation for oral reading to a group of children, or he can be shown how the skill is used in today's social studies assignment. In any case, the skill must be transferred from the isolated skill lesson to the learner's reading.

Step 10 / This step requires the most flexibility on your part. Learners being learners, you know that in any skill instruction some will learn and some will not. This poses a severe problem of organization, since some are ready for the next skill and some are not. However, it is a problem you can handle. First, but least desirable, you can hold back the ones who mastered the skill until you have retaught it to those needing extra help, at which time the whole group proceeds on as a body. Second, you can move along those who mastered the skill, holding back those who did not until they can join another group needing that skill. Finally, your best option is to create new groups as your learners exhibit different rates of achievement. In any case, the situation requires a good deal of flexibility and organization on your part, as well as a commitment to accurate record keeping. Although it will seem a nuisance at times, the success of individual skill instruction demands that you teach each learner what he needs to know at the time, and not that you keep him with a particular group regardless of whether he has mastered the skill or not.

■ WHAT HAPPENS WHEN A LEARNER FAILS A POSTTEST?   As was stated above, a learner will sometimes fail a posttest despite your best efforts to make certain that he does not. The first step in handling this problem is to acknowledge that it will happen, that it is human not to succeed at everything the first time, and to determine how best to handle the situation. There are a number of concrete steps you can take.

First, you must check to make sure that the learner has indeed mastered the crucial prerequisite skills. If you have any doubts about this, it is best to return him to the prerequisite.

Next, you must face and accept the fact that you will have to reteach the skill, since it would be disasterous to assume that "he'll pick it up somewhere along the line." The fact is that he usually will not, and this failure will be the cause of other failures among the succeeding tasks having this skill as a prerequisite.

Before you begin your reteaching, examine the attenders listed under "Directing the Learner's Attention" in the objective and evaluate your instruction in terms of the checklist provided in Appendix H. If the learner is not mastering the skill but possesses all the prerequisites, the cause of his failure either will be that he is not attending to the crucial aspects of the task or that you are failing to teach him effectively. The two sources cited above, as well as the material contained in Chapter 3, will assist you in identifying the difficulty.

Next, plan a new lesson to reteach the skill, modifying the model activity provided in the objective or selecting a simplified version of the skill as stated in the "Suggestions for Reteaching and/or Practice," making your presentation and administering another drill exercise that directs the learner to practice and retrieve the desired response. You are cautioned, however, against simply repeating verbatim the original skill lesson. Such a practice is tedious both for the learner and for you and does not make much sense. Since the original lesson failed to teach the skill, it is unlikely that a repetition of the same thing will result in success.

Once the skill has been retaught, repeat the posttest provided in the objective or structure another posttest to assess mastery. Do not assume that learning has occurred simply because you have taught it twice. As discouraging as it may sound, it will sometimes be necessary to teach a skill four or five times before mastery results. Only if we systematically teach each skill can we be assured that the learner will achieve the reading proficiency we desire for him.

SOME COMMON CONCERNS

Several common questions are frequently asked by teachers regarding the use of the strategy described in this book. These questions, together with answers, are presented below.

1/Question Must the directions for the pretest be followed precisely?

Answer It is best to do so. However, teachers in special environments, such as remote rural areas or inner-city ghettos, may wish to substitute local vocabulary that more closely fits both the language and experience backgrounds of the learners while still fitting the skill being tested.

2/Question Most of the pretests appear to be designed for administration to one child at a time. I don't have that much time in my class. I have too many pupils to be able to pretest each one separately. Is it possible to give the pretests in groups?

Answer Most of the pretests were designed for individual administration because of the fundamental belief that teachers *must* focus on individual achievement. However, if you feel you cannot give individual pretests, you can use the placement test provided in Appendix E or adapt the pretests for group use. You are urged, however, to observe certain cautions. First, before going to group testing, make absolutely sure it is not possible to operate at the individual level. Second, if you must give the tests to groups of children, make the groups small. Third, when using group tests, be sure you are testing the same behavior stated in the objective. Finally, when giving tests to groups, guard against children who copy the answer from peers rather than perform the task individually.

The most difficult tests to adapt will be those that require individual auditory responses, such as that specified in Objective IIB 4 in Chapter 4 where the learner is directed to match spoken words beginning with the same sound. This could be adapted by replacing your oral presentation of words with pictures that have the same beginning sound characteristics. Now the task is to supply each learner with sets of four pictures, naming each picture in the set and directing the learner's to draw a line from the picture at the left to one of the other three with a name that sounds the same at the beginning. Hence, you have retained the oral characteristics of the task while adapting it for group administration.

3/Question The teaching suggestions for each skill do not specifically mention the principles of presentation, response, and reinforcement described in Chapter 3. Should we ignore these principles when teaching from this book?

Answer Absolutely not. Each teaching suggestion is, for all practical purposes, a suggested presentation. In addition, it is essential that the teacher elicit responses from learners during the course of the instruction and that appropriate reinforcement be provided throughout.

4/Question In the model teaching activity, the exact words of the teacher are sometimes provided. Is it necessary to use the exact words as they are written?

Answer No. Exact words are provided simply as a model for you to follow if you wish.

5/Question The wording for most objectives refers only to the singular form, *learner*. Does that mean that each child must be taught in a tutorial situation?

Answer No. The skills can be taught to individuals or to groups of learners all needing the same skill. The authors have simply reserved the plural to indicate those suggestions that *require* more than one learner.

6/Question Is it all right to teach a learner first a skill from one set in a cluster and then a skill from another set in the same cluster, or must we take him through all the skills of one set before starting on the skills for the next?

Answer It is perfectly all right to do both simultaneously. However, it is suggested that all the skills in *one cluster* be mastered before moving on to a more difficult cluster.

7/*Question*   What if one of my students goes more quickly through one set of skills than he does through another?

Answer   This is perfectly all right. In fact, it is natural for some students to learn more quickly through visual modalities than through auditory, or vice versa. Again, however, it is usually wise to stay in one cluster until the skills of that cluster are mastered.

8/*Question*   What should I do if one of my students gets stuck on one skill? Should I skip it?

Answer   No. The skills are built in a hierarchy, with the successful acquisition of one skill depending upon the learner's ability to perform the skills that precede it. If a learner gets stuck on a skill, try all the alternate suggestions. If he still has difficulty, go back and reteach the prerequisites to that skill. If all that fails, call in the reading specialist for consultation. In any case, do not skip it. Keep after it, because the learner will need that skill in order to perform subsequent skills.

9/*Question*   Am I limited to the teaching suggestions provided, or can I make up my own?

Answer   By all means, you are encouraged to make up more or to alter those provided to fit your particular style or preference. However, be sure that the activities you devise do indeed teach the skill that you want taught. The model activity should provide you with a good guide in this regard.

10/*Question*   The suggested activities sometimes specify certain materials to be used. Can I substitute other material that is easier for me to obtain?

Answer   If other material will do the job just as well, use it.

11/*Question*   Some of the activities are essentially the same from skill to skill and seem to be a bit mechanical. Can I alter them somewhat?

Answer   Creative adaptation on the part of the teacher is encouraged and can only enrich the learning situation. However, once again, you must be careful that in adapting you do not lose sight of the specific skill you are attempting to teach.

A WORD OF CAUTION

The skills included in this book are essential and must be learned. Without them, a learner will fail in reading. However, despite the crucial importance of these skills, the well-rounded reading program should also include other activities that support the learner's general development as a reader. Such supportive activities should be planned daily to build oral language proficiency, to expand experience backgrounds, to develop concepts, and to promote sound social-emotional growth. Although it is not the purpose of this book to describe these supportive activities in detail, the following may serve to suggest appropriate activities to accompany a skills program.

1   Provide for much oral sharing of experiences through activities such as "Show-and-Tell."
2   Develop games that involve learners in oral language activities.
3   Read and discuss story books with children frequently.
4   Have many picture books and other interesting reading materials scattered about the room, and encourage learners to use these.
5   Take field trips and encourage children to share their experiences with each other.
6   Use films and other media to expand the learners' horizons and to develop new concepts.
7   Play games requiring learners to manipulate concepts such as *up, down, big, small, tall, short, bright,* and *dull.*
8   Encourage learners to tell each other about the picture books or stories they have particularly enjoyed.
9   Dramatize favorite stories.
10   Make puppets of favorite story characters or make up stories to go with the puppets.
11   Let learners make up and tell their own stories.
12   Do much reading of rhythmical, rhyming poetry.
13   Encourage a group of learners to make up riddles and stories together and share these with other groups.
14   Devise choral speaking activities, especially with rhyming poems, riddles, etc.
15   Do much role playing of common social situations.
16   Re-create difficult human situations and discuss appropriate emotional responses for these situations.
17   Do much artwork, especially as it relates to reading (illustrate favorite stories or write and illustrate stories made up by individuals or by the class).

SUMMARY

This chapter serves as your orientation to the use of this book. It provides you with a global view of the resources offered and with a specific, 10-step strategy for implementing a skills program using these resources. It also answers frequently asked questions about systematic skill instruction and cautions you again to make your reading program broad enough to include reading activities other than skill instruction.

CHAPTER THREE / THE ART OF TEACHING IS THE SCIENCE OF INSTRUCTION

In the previous chapters, the strategy for systematically developing reading skills was described, emphasizing the pretest, teach, posttest sequence. This chapter answers the question How do you make the teaching segment of the strategy a success? by describing how principles of learning theory and efficient classroom management can be used with this book.

THE TEACHER'S ROLE

What makes a teacher a teacher? What makes a teacher, for example, different from a doctor, a social worker, a disc jockey, a psychologist, or a parent? It isn't focus of interest, because all these people are interested in children. Doctors are interested in children's health, and so are teachers. Social workers are interested in the social environments of children, and so are teachers. Disc jockeys are interested in entertaining children, and so are teachers. Psychologists are interested in the mental development of children, and so are teachers. Parents are interested in the total well-being of children, and so are teachers.

Teachers are different from these other people because they are *instructors*. Their prime responsibility is to act as a connector between children and learning by knowing what to teach and by controlling the conditions that lead the child to make the appropriate response. In the first case we know what response we want our learners to make, and in the second we control the conditions that lead to the child's successful accomplishment of that response. This is the most credible difference between teaching and any other child-centered task. Teachers wear many hats, but the instructional role is uniquely theirs, and they must be experts in this function.

THE INSTRUCTIONAL TASK

To provide instruction that leads the child to make the appropriate responses, you must know what it is you are teaching—that is, the response desired or the skill to be taught. This is provided for you in Chapters 4, 5, and 6 and in Appendix A. Second, you must provide activities and materials for the learner. This information is provided in Chapters 4, 5, and 6 and in Appendix B. Finally, you must know how to control and direct the learning situation so that the skill is learned as efficiently as possible. This is the core of the instructional act, and knowledge about this task is the focus of this chapter.

Often, you may know what you want to teach and you may plan exercises designed to produce the desired achievement, but the end result of the instructional episode is failure; the learner has not learned, or has only partially learned, what you taught. Nonlearning, or partial learning, results when we control the learning situation inadequately. Instruction must result in total learner mastery of the taught skill; consequently, the instructional task is to control the learning situation so that the desired response *does* result.

■ GUIDES TO EFFICIENT INSTRUCTION   To lead the learner to the appropriate skill response, you must control and direct the learning situation. Although the specifics of accomplishing this vary slightly depending upon the skill to be taught, learning theory provides a series of benchmarks to guide us in creating efficient instructional episodes. These benchmarks include the conditions of attention, presentation, response, reinforcement, practice, and application.

Attention / When we talk about attention in the instructional situation, we do not mean sitting up straight in the seat with arms folded. On the contrary, we are concerned with both physical and psychological conditions in the classroom and in the learner. To adequately direct the learner to the task to be learned, we must be certain that the learner possesses an appropriate psychological set for learning the task and that he is attending to the salient features of the task to be learned. Let's look first at the psychological conditions.

Attending behavior on the part of the learner is often the result of his interest in the learning task. Although this psychological condition is to be desired and strived for, it is not always possible. If your skill in creating attending behavior is limited only to those activities that interest children, you will be a failure in teaching the many tasks that simply are not interesting. We suggest that you should strive for interest whenever possible, but that you should always be sure that the learner attends to the task at hand, interesting or not. Insuring such attention is the first essential step in the creation of efficient instructional episodes, and is dependent upon your skill in establishing an appropriate psychological set in the learner.

Every teacher uses different techniques to achieve this condition. Some approach the task to be learned by issuing a challenge: "Hey, listen to what I can do. I'll bet you can't do this!" Others use a question, "Do you really think you can learn to read the word *dinosaur*?" Still others pair their verbal attenders to physical movements and gestures that catch the eye and ear simultaneously. Whatever techniques you develop, you will probably find learners who dodge them, who in spite of your best efforts remain inattentive to the learning task. Usually, these are learners who have experienced a long history of failure and confusion in learning what adults want to teach. They have found that teachers invariably put them in positions where they can't perform, where they can't find the answer or make the correct response. Therefore, in self-defense, they refuse to play the teacher's games, which they always lose. Such a learner views himself as "dumb," because he is made to feel dumb every time he joins a learning activity, and as a defense mechanism, he will not be proven dumb again by a teacher whose instructional skills do not allow him to learn. For such learners, you must pay special attention to the psychological conditions of learning. One suggestion follows.

The act of learning is the act of changing behavior. What can't be done or isn't done can be described as a block to a desired behavior change. For example, if the beginning reader doesn't recognize the word *the*, he has a block to the learning of the word. If this word was known by the reader, or if it didn't exist, there would be nothing to learn and therefore no block to challenge him. But it does exist, and so long as it remains unrecognized, it is a block to a desired behavior change.

When the reader can read a word, he has overcome the block and conquered the word. This is a difficult task, and acknowledgment of this difficulty by the teacher is a very appropriate and powerful attending technique. In practice it works something like this.

Suppose I bake a pie and invite you to eat it with me. You taste the first bite and exclaim over its flavor and my skill in pie baking. "I wish I could bake a pie like this," you say. Now the principle of blockage comes into play. Your present behavior does not include the skill of pie baking—a block exists regarding the baking of pies. If I am a poor teacher, I will say to you, "Fine. Pie making isn't hard, so let's learn to make a pie." In my efforts to give you the necessary confidence, I may even say, "Anyone can bake pies." With these two encouragements, I have probably spoiled your opportunity to learn to be a successful pie baker by removing the challenge to the learning of pie baking. Let's see what happens.

You take the recipe and my directions, and you proceed to bake a pie. When it is finished, you take the first taste and the pie is delicious. You are a successful learner of pie making. But wait. Is this anything to be proud of? Didn't I explain that pie making was easy and anyone could do it? Now, do you feel like a successful pie maker if you know that the task is easy and that anyone can perform the skill? The answer is obvious.

Let's back up a minute and see what happens if your first pie-baking effort is a failure. You take the first bite and it tastes terrible. Now, what can you say about yourself? You were told the task was easy, but you couldn't do it. "Anyone can bake a pie," I said. What does this make you? Do you suppose you will try baking pies again? Probably not, because by failing to acknowledge the difficulty of the learning, I cancelled your success as a learner. If you do the performance successfully, it really isn't worth doing in the first place because it was so easy, whereas if you fail the first time, it is because of a defect in you, since everyone else can do it. You are damned if you learn, and damned if you don't.

How does a good teacher capitalize on the principle of blockage? When you indicate interest in baking a pie, the good teacher recognizes the block that exists. He knows that pie baking is not easy or sure-fire. He expresses these reservations to you. He says, "I will give you the recipe and careful directions, but pie baking is not easy. You can do everything right and still not bake a good pie. Not everyone can bake a good pie the first time." The task is now realistic. The block to your learning to bake a pie has been established. The difficulty of the task has been acknowledged.

What happens when you bake a pie and it is delicious? You feel much success about yourself as a pie baker. Chances are you will bake other pies and go on to other successful learning performances. The task was a difficult one, but you did it. Your self-concept as a learner receives great reinforcement.

But suppose the pie is poor? What happens then? Well, you had been forewarned that the task wasn't easy. You had been told that not everyone can bake a good pie the first time. Is this damaging to your self-concept? No. It was not you that was defective, it was the task itself that was difficult. You can try again knowing that failure is no stigma when the task is hard.

The recognition that a block can exist, and the sensitive acknowledgment of the difficulty of the learning task, is an important aspect of efficient instruction; it assists in establishing an appropriate psychological set for the learner. A wise teacher recognizes that learning, whether it be pie baking or a reading skill, is seldom a one-shot deal, that failure will probably occur more often than success, and that recognition of the difficulty of the task to be learned is essential if the learner is not to feel personal failure.

One important ingredient of establishing attending behavior on the part of the learner is that of creating an appropriate psychological set. This is, however, only half the job. Attention must also be physical. To direct the learner to the task, you must be certain also that he is looking at and/or listening to the salient features of the task to be learned— that he knows what to pay attention to and that he is indeed paying attention to those things.

Let's look at the task of baking a pie again. What must the learner pay attention to if he is to succeed in baking a pie? What are the salient features of baking a pie? If we analyze it, we would probably find that to bake a pie successfully the learner must visually or aurally note the ingredients used, the quantity of these ingredients, the sequence in which they are mixed, the physical movements used by the baker as he mixes them, and the length and temperature of the baking process itself. If, during the time he is being taught to bake a pie, the learner fails to attend to each of these features, the chances are good that he will not be able to bake a successful pie himself when the instruction is completed.

The same attention to the salient features of the task must be exercised when learning a reading skill. For example, if he is learning to read his name, the student must *listen* to the sound of his name and simultaneously *look* at the spelling of his name. If he is not using these two senses simultaneously, a pairing of his name with the written form of his name will only occur by accident. If he is listening but looking at a fly on the window, conceivably he could pair his name with the fly. This is an exaggerated illustration, but it should put you on guard. If you do *not* control the input to the learner's senses, both visual and aural, no learning of the desired pair can result.

As teachers, we are always saying, "Now, pay attention." Unfortunately, this is all too often the sum total of our instructional repertoire for creating attending behavior in learners. This is not enough, for it does not tell the learner what specifically he must attend *to* in order to attain the task. Attention needs specific cues, both verbal and physical. For example, you might say, "We are going to learn to read Tom's name. Look at my finger. See where it points. Now it is pointing at Tom's name. This word says *Tom*." Both the verbal cue and the pointing cue serve to direct the learner's attention to the goal to be achieved and to looking at and listening to the paired inputs. It is no longer necessary for the learner to wonder what he has to do to learn the task, and the guessing game element of learning is removed.

Presentation / Once you have made certain of the learner's attention, both from the standpoint of establishing a psychological set and of accounting for the salient features of the learning, you are ready for the second step in instruction, the presentation step. This means simply that once the learner is attending, you must "take him by the hand" and lead him to the appropriate response. For example, in pie baking you may say to the learner, "Now watch what I do and then copy me." In teaching a child to read his name, the presentation might consist of saying to the learner, "I have my finger on your name. I am going to say your name. It is *Tom*. I am going to take your finger and put it on your name. Now you say your name." Problem-solving tasks might require much more complex presentations.

The criterion for judging your skill in presenting learning is whether the learner makes the desired response. If he does, you have presented the learning well. If he does not, the fault lies not with the child but with your presentation of the learning. The implication is that you must now repeat the presentation, adjusting it to compensate for the aspect of the task that caused his lack of understanding in the first presentation. In repeating a presentation, always use a different and simplified form.

Three kinds of models can be used to make the presentation clear. The first consists of *telling* the learner what it is you want him to learn. For example, if you want him to note the differences between Tom and Tim, you can say to him, "Look at these words. See the word *Tom*. Look at the middle letter in the word. It is *o*. Now look at *Tim*. Look at the middle letter in the word. It is *i*. The difference between the words *Tom* and *Tim* is the *o* in Tom and the *i* in Tim."

The second model for making presentations clear to children sets conditions for the learner to generalize the learning himself. For example, instead of *telling* the learner the differences between *Tom* and *Tim*, you can say to him, "Look at these words. See the word *Tom*? Look at the middle letter in the word. What is it? Now look at *Tim*. Look at the middle letter in that word. What is it? Now, what is the difference between the words *Tom* and *Tim*?"

Although the second model is preferred because it involves the learner more completely, both models are effective, providing that the learner attends to the task and clearly understands what it is he must do to perform it. In the illustration above, the learner must note that to differentiate between *Tom* and *Tim* one must "see" the middle letter. As long as the presentation makes this clear, it has been a success.

If neither of the above approaches results in success, you may wish to employ a third technique, called *modeling*. This is simply a matter of demonstrating the task for the learner, talking through the steps aloud as you do so. You then direct the learner to "do as I did." He models his behavior after yours and through such imitation learns to perform the task.

Additional assistance in structuring the presentation is provided in Appendixes F and G. Details are provided regarding techniques for clarifying and dramatizing the pieces of a skill puzzle, for using crutches to assist the learner, and for gradually leading him to perform the desired task independently.

In any case, the heart of the instructional episode is the presentation. It is here that teaching takes place. The extent to which a learner masters a skill—makes the desired response—depends upon how clearly the task is presented to him in this second step of the instructional episode.

Response / The third condition of learning is the response. It is to this that all your efforts in the first two steps of instruction have been directed. The whole purpose of your instruction has been to lead the child to learn—that is, to make the desired response. This response is the evidence that he has learned, or not learned, the skill you are teaching. If the response is appropriate, you have taught; if inappropriate, you have not.

Up to the response stage, *you* have been doing most of the work. However, learning does not take place without an expenditure of energy on the part of the learner, and this energy is spent in responding to your presentation.

The good teacher calls for frequent response during the presentation. She might say, "This word says *Tom*. I can look at the word and say *Tom*. Can you look at the word and say *Tom*? Follow my finger. Who can say *Tom*?" Since repetition is a necessary part of all learning, at this stage the creative teacher will find many ways to elicit responses without making them boringly rote. "See, I can stand on one leg, look at the word *Tom*, and say *Tom*. Can you?"

When the instructional episode started, your goal was to lead the learner to the appropriate response. When he makes that response, you have succeeded in the crucial first steps of instruction. Now your instructional task is to make certain that the response is available to the learner the next time he needs it.

Reinforcement / The fourth condition of learning is reinforcement by the teacher of the desired response on the part of the learner. Appropriate reinforcement will tend to help the learner retrieve the response when he needs it.

Reinforcement goes by many names. Some call it reward, others bribe. As teachers, we too often view the condition of reward as an intrinsic state where success at the task is internalized by the learner, and he learns for learning's sake. This is fine for the learner who has such a reward system but, unfortunately, many children come to school never having learned what it means to be praised for doing something well. The successful learner is one who has a reward system. The poor learner is the one who hasn't yet learned how to accept reinforcements. Your first task in using reinforcement is to judge each learner individually and to choose reinforcers appropriate to him.

At the lowest level, these reinforcers are physical—an apple, a token that buys a toy plane at the end of the week, some M&M candy, a box of raisins, or even S&H Green Stamps. This looks like bribery, but it can be the start of a reward system. The next step above physical rewards is a touch or movement reward. Here you pat a shoulder or shake a hand when the response is properly performed. At a still higher level, you gradually replace the touch or movement with a word or two of verbal praise. Your objective here is to help the learner find satisfaction in the learning task, moving him through the levels of reinforcers as he progresses. As he moves, you help him extinguish the lower rewards, replacing them with words and gestures. To learners who ultimately develop sophisticated reinforcement systems, a smile or a nod on your part is sufficient reward. In any case, the reward or reinforcer must be appropriate to the learning and to the learner's reward system.

Your second task in regard to reinforcement is providing the reward immediately following the correct response of the learner. Delayed rewards work only after the learner has learned to delay them. At the early stages of learning, especially, children need immediate feedback regarding their success or failure in making the correct response.

Reinforcement, then, provides a reward for the learner when he makes the desired response. The reward must be appropriate to the learning and to the learner's reward system. It should use levels of reinforcers with the intent of moving learners from bribes to intrinsic rewards, and should immediately follow the correct response in order to provide the learner with immediate feedback regarding his success or failure with the task.

Practice / The fifth condition of learning is providing practice in performing the newly learned response. Such practice serves two functions. First, it gives the child experience in retrieving the response that heretofore he has made only with your assistance. Now he is asked to practice the response independently in a variety of contexts. Second, in the process of making this retrieval he will establish the response as a habit. In effect, he solidifies the learning so that it is in his head and can be retrieved without effort. As a teacher, you must provide this review. What is learned today must be reviewed tomorrow. What is learned in one episode with one set of conditions must be reviewed in other episodes with contrasting conditions. This will insure that what your children learn will not be isolated responses to isolated skill drills.

Practice can take many forms. For example, the learner may be given a game or written exercise that requires him to retrieve the response he has just learned. It must be cautioned, however, that practice material does not teach. Workbooks, Ditto sheets, games, and other devices are useful only as a means of habituating the response developed during the previous presentation step. Learners given practice materials without the benefit of teaching are likely to learn nothing or, worse yet, learn the wrong thing.

Application / The sixth condition of learning is application, a stage that occurs after the actual skill lesson has been concluded. Application focuses on the transfer of the skill to the actual reading situation. The skill lesson itself is an isolated activity divorced from the reading of books, magazines, and other matter. If the skill taught in this isolated situation fails to transfer to the reading situation, the instruction has failed. Consequently, you must make every effort to make certain that the transfer is made.

The best way to do this is to regularly structure reading activities that make use of the skill you have taught in isolation. As the learner participates in these activities, you direct his attention to one place where he can use the skill he has just learned and encourage him to look for similar instances. In addition, any device that involves the learner in the reading of a multitude of books or other materials enhances the application process and insures that the learner not only performs the skill in isolation but uses it in his daily reading.

An Illustration / The object of instruction is to teach the learner to make the desired skill response. The overall strategy of this book provides a pretest, teach, posttest sequence to learning that insures a systematic presentation of a hierarchy of skills. In the teaching phase of the strategy, you should use the conditions of attention, presentation, response, reinforcement, practice, and application. In operation, these principles would look like the following.

The learner is Sam. The teacher has been taking Sam through the various pretests in the hierarchy of reading skills. On one pretest, he is unable to distinguish between the words *where* and *there*. Consequently, the teacher plans an instructional episode that will result in Sam's distinguishing between these two words. She first acknowledges to Sam the difficulty of the task, explaining how hard it is, noting the difficulty that many children have with it, and generally establishing the condition of blockage. She then devises ways for Sam to attend to the task at hand, saying, "Look at my finger. It is pointing at *where*. This word says *where*. Look at the first two letters of the word. What are those letters? Are they the same as the first two letters in *there*?" As attention is established, the teacher makes a presentation designed to clarify for Sam the crucial difference in form between *where* and *there*. She says, "Look at *where*. Now look at *there*. What is the same about these two words? What is different about these words? What part of the word must you look at most closely to distinguish between *where* and *there*?" Sam responds to these questions, and each time he makes a correct response, the teacher immediately reinforces him. The type of reinforcement used depends upon the sophistication of Sam's reward system, but the teacher strives to have him ultimately rely more heavily on intrinsic than on physical rewards. Next, the teacher provides practice in the task being learned, perhaps flashing the words *where* and *there* on cards, giving Sam only an instant to examine the words before saying them. When Sam's responses indicates he can retrieve the skill, the teacher administers the posttest, checking his performance against the criterion level for success. If he has mastered the skill, the teacher moves him on to the next skill. If not, they return to the same skill and repeat the process with a different activity until the teacher feels that Sam has learned and is once again ready for the posttest. On the following day, the teacher directs Sam to note the presence of *where* and *there* in his social studies assignment as a means of helping him to apply and use this skill.

This, then, is the instructional act. It consists of six crucial conditions.

When present in the teaching situation, they tend to increase the incidence of successful instruction and decrease the amount of repetition needed for the learning. The instructional tasks specified in Chapters 4, 5, and 6 provide suggestions regarding attenders, presentations, and practice which should help you apply the conditions of learning as you use this book.

MANAGING INSTRUCTION

If you had only to concern yourself with one learner at a time, then the instructional model proposed above would probably be sufficient. With some degree of creative adaptation on your part, the six conditions could be structured, and learning would take place. However, the normal classroom does not have just one learner. Another set of behaviors is needed in order to manage and control those learners who are not in direct contact with you at any given time.

Many attempts, both pedagogical and administrative, have been made to handle the problems of class size and variability of achievement. Thirty fourth-grade children neither look alike physically nor are their reading achievements homogeneous. Typically, such a class will show an achievement differential of six grades, spanning from the first- to the seventh-grade levels, but all housed and taught in a fourth-grade room.

You have many options regarding your answers to this teaching problem, but all are based on the firm assumption that it is not possible to teach all these learners the same reading skills at the same time and with the same materials. There must be differential instruction.

A basic premise of this book is that the best method for dealing with individual skill differences is to group together those learners who need the same skill. For example, if on the pretest, six or eight learners failed to meet the criterion measure for IIB 7, they would be grouped together to receive instruction on that skill. In this way, you can teach to a smaller number, making it easier for you to control the six learning conditions.

The problem with this premise is not what you do with the reading group you are directing, but rather how you manage those learners who are not in your group at any given time. If the small-group instruction is to be successful, there can be no interruptions from the rest of the class. Minimizing interruptions depends upon the skill with which you can manage your classroom. Efficient classroom management includes the principles of planning, directions, relevancy, a buffer, and a safety valve.

Planning / Let us suppose that, on a given day, you have four groups of learners needing specific skill help. These groups have been formed as a result of their failure to perform adequately on the pretests for some skill. You are going to give each of these separate groups 20 minutes of direct instruction. This means you plan to have 80 minutes of reading. However, you cannot terminate your planning once you have planned the four skill lessons, because this does not include the planning you must do to free yourself from the three groups you are *not* working with at any given time. Your task, then, is not only to plan the four skill lessons, but also to plan activities that can be used by the learners not directly involved in the group you are teaching. Unless they are working independently, you will not be able to teach your small skill group effectively. Planning for those working independently, then, is the first essential aspect of managing group instruction.

Directions / When you have planned and know what you want all the learners to do at all times, you must be capable of communicating this information. This communication may be written or oral, but it must be totally understood by the class. Each learner must know what he is expected to do during his time away from you, and he must be able to determine when he has satisfactorily completed it. This is extremely important. Unless each learner knows exactly when he has accomplished the task, grouping will fail. Some learners will decide that they have finished after only a few minutes, and with time on their hands, they will become the "devil's workshop," disrupting the class, particularly the reading group that is working with you. Consequently, the second crucial aspect of successful group management is thorough direction giving.

Relevancy / The term relevancy is meant to be a generalized statement of the condition that is the opposite of busywork. When you plan, you must create independent work that is not just so many problems or "fill in the blanks". Such busywork invariably *creates* disrupting behavior in children. Whatever the learning task, it must have a motivating relevancy for the child. If it does not, it will fail to hold his attention and will create a double failure, leaving his meaningless work undone and disrupting you as you instruct the reading group. Independent work tends to be relevant if the learner knows it is important or if he knows it will be used in some important way. For example, some teachers achieve relevancy by sending independent material home regularly for parental inspection. In any case, successful group management depends upon each learner having independent work that he considers worthwhile.

Buffer / Grouping can fail in spite of good planning, directions, and relevant work for the independent groups simply because there is no mechanism in the classroom for handling routine matters while you teach the small group. When learners work independently, situations will always develop that demand attention and decision. Your time must be totally free to work with the small skill group, so you need to create a buffer between yourself and the children working independently. This buffer can be a learner who is appointed by the week to be the expert or teacher during reading period. Any problems, from assignment directions to toilet turns, are his responsibility. He is the only person designated to converse with you while you are working with the small group, and then only in an emergency. Children soon learn that you take the reading groups seriously and that they must respect the time set aside for them. A buffer, then, is a crucial factor in successful group management.

Safety Valve / Finally, you must recognize that the learners who are working independently will never finish their work at the same time. You must have safety valves that can be used by learners when they have finished their individual work. Again, they soon learn that such projects are rewards for attending to business during reading periods, and it is a simple matter for you to use these safety valves as rewards for proper work habits. The safety valve is the fifth crucial consideration in managing reading groups.

Teaching is at least as much art as science, but managing instruction is one area that requires a particularly high degree of art. If you use grouping in reading and find that you are constantly distracted in your work with the small groups, you can be assured that the problem is not in the idea of grouping per se, but rather in the degree of art you bring to the management problem. While the principles of planning, directions, relevancy, a buffer, and a safety valve are essential to effective management of groups and should be an integral part of your thinking when you work with your group, your success or failure in using these principles will depend upon the way in which you put them to work.

A PROGRAM IN ACTION

What does a classroom look like, physically and in terms of learning, if both the strategy described in this book and the principles in this chapter are being used? Let's examine one such classroom, but before we do let us caution that this classroom is only a model. Other teachers may wish to use the skills program with a strict basal text approach to instruction, with a language experience approach, or with some other approach that fits the local teaching conditions and style of the teacher.

The situation described is a fourth grade in a disadvantaged section of a midwestern city. There are 25 pupils in the class, all of whom are reading at first-grade level or below. The children have experienced three years of failure, and their attitude toward school in general and reading in particular is poor.

The children's attitude, as illustrated by their aggression and general behavior difficulties, is rooted in three sources. First, they are trying to perform tasks in reading that are too difficult for them. Like the beginning swimmer who develops an aggressive attitude toward swimming instruction when he is thrown into an advanced swimming class, these beginning readers developed an aggressive attitude toward reading instruction when required to perform at fourth-grade level with first-grade tools. Second, they are reading material having little meaning or interest to them. Finally, they have poor self-images and little confidence in their ability to handle independently any reading task, a fact attributable to their lack of reading skills.

We will examine this classroom in four ways; we will look at the teacher's overall strategy, at the physical setting, at the whole class as it operates during the reading period, and at a skill lesson in operation.

The Teacher's Overall Strategy / To meet the reading needs of the children in this class, the teacher instituted a three-step program. First, she determined the level at which each child was currently reading in order to provide reading matter suitable to his individual abilities. Second, she provided each child with material that he was interested in and that was at his reading level. Finally, she instituted the program of systematic skill instruction developed in this book.

The teacher used two simple techniques to determine each child's reading level. First, she selected representative passages from various basal texts, ranging in difficulty from a preprimer level to a third-grade level. She then asked each child to read these passages to her, noting the child's errors as he read. The important errors noted were omitting words, adding words, and miscalling words. If the child made fewer than one of these errors in 20 words and if he could correctly answer four out of five questions about the passage after he read it, the teacher assumed that he could adequately handle a book of that difficulty. If, however, the child made more than one error in 20 words or failed to answer at least four out of five comprehension questions, the teacher assumed material of that difficulty was too hard for the child to handle.

Second, the teacher selected representative passages from various basal texts, ranging in difficulty again from preprimer to grade three, and made mimeographed copies of these, with every seventh word represented by a blank space. She then asked the child to read each passage silently and write in the blank a word he thought should go there. If the child correctly supplied 45 percent of the omitted words, the teacher assumed that the child could handle that level material. If, however, the child supplied fewer than 45 percent of the omitted words, the teacher assumed that the material was too difficult for him.

The teacher then compared the child's performance on the two tests. If it was essentially the same, the teacher concluded that this was the child's reading level. If it was different, the teacher repeated the tests, using different materials until she obtained enough information to correctly place the child. Once the teacher determined each child's reading level, she knew the range of reading material needed. In the class being described, this material ranged from picture books to first-grade reading level.

In selecting the material to be used, the teacher operated from the view that children in school seldom have an opportunity to read what interests them and, consequently, they do not learn that reading can be enjoyable. To eliminate this problem, material that children find stimulating, enjoyable, and important was begged, borrowed, and bought from all available sources and collected in the room. These materials included comic books, illustrated magazines, children's magazines, hard and softbound picture books, selected stories cut from old basal texts and stapled together, old *Weekly Reader* stories, material written by the class (about field trips, social studies projects, science investigations, and other activities), hard and softbound easy-to-read books, popular magazines such as *Sport* and *Cycle,* materials written by the teacher, stories dictated or written by the pupils themselves, stories written by children in higher grades, and anything else obtainable that could possibly interest the class.

These materials were displayed around the room in an attractive fashion, and children were urged to look at and read any that interested them. They were not tested on what they read, they were not required to make book reports, and they were not required to read completely everything they picked up. They were, however, encouraged to share a good story with the rest of the class, and time was provided to develop projects relating to the books they read, to prepare puppet plays, to dramatize enjoyable stories, to make up scrapbooks relating to a particular theme in their reading, and to generally spread the good word to their peers whenever an enjoyable piece of reading material was encountered. As a result, the class became enthusiastic about reading.

Once the children started reading materials of their own choice, the teacher began to teach the reading skills systematically, following the procedures described in this book. The total class was given the placement test described in Appendix E, and then each child was pretested on the skills appropriate to his level, with the results being recorded in a notebook. As shown in the table, by looking in the notebook and noting which children had not yet successfully completed the pretest for a particular skill, the teacher could select those children needing instruction in that skill. While the rest of the children were occupied reading their individual material and performing other tasks, the teacher would teach a 15- or 20-minute lesson on a particular skill for those children who needed it. For example, she would get Bert and George together

		Skill 1	Skill 2	Skill 3	Skill 4	Skill 5
	Bert	OK	No	No	No	No
	Susie	OK	OK	OK	OK	No
	Tom	OK	OK	No	No	OK
CLUSTER IA	George	OK	No	No	No	No
	Mike	OK	OK	OK	OK	No
	Andy	OK	OK	No	OK	No
	Anne	OK	OK	OK	No	No

for a lesson on skill number two. She would give a posttest at the end of instruction to determine whether the children had mastered the skill, noting the results in the notebook. In the next 15- or 20-minute segment of time, the teacher would draw out another group needing instruction in another skill. This process continued, except during those times when the children either were sharing their books or the results of their creative activities, or when the teacher was working with a particular child to help him apply a learned skill to his individual reading.

The teacher's strategy met the particular needs of this group of children. With each child reading individual material matched to his reading level, the aggressive attitude toward reading that had grown from frustration with material that was too hard was eliminated. With each child selecting his own material, a viable reason for reading was provided that helped him become more enthusiastic about reading generally. Teaching the skills in a systematic fashion provided the children with the mechanics needed to read more and more difficult material and to improve their self-image and confidence in handling the reading act.

The Physical Setting / The time is 8 A.M. We see the teacher in the classroom preparing for the reading period, which is the first activity of the morning. At this time, she is determining which children will need specific skill instruction by noting their progress on the skill chart in her notebook, and planning the independent activities that the other children will pursue while she is working with the groups.

As we enter the classroom, we notice that the west side of the room contains a number of science experiments. For example, an aquarium is set up, a number of books about fish and fish care are nearby, and there are specific instructions for experiments relative to fish life and care that the children may wish to pursue. In the same section of the room there is a terrarium and an incubator with books and Dittoed instructions regarding specific reading activities to be completed relative to these activities.

Near the northwest corner are a number of shoe boxes, each having the name of one of the children printed on the side. Inside these boxes are corrected papers and special assignments that the teacher has prepared for each child. These are used as part of the independent activities to be carried out by each child when he is not involved in a skill group.

The northeast corner of the room has been walled off by large bookcases to leave a space that is physically separated from the rest of the class. Here the reading skill lessons are taught.

Against the east wall is a recreational reading center. It is composed of a small table with many attractive books scattered about on it, a bulletin board describing favorite books, a small scrap of rug on the floor, and some throw pillows. Here the children come to select and read books of their choice.

In the southeast corner and extending down the south wall is a long table and 10 small chairs. On the table is a tape recorder and a set of 10 earphones. Here the children come when assigned to do independent listening activities.

The children's desks are set up in irregular clusters in the center of the classroom. The teacher's desk is near the southwest corner of the room. Just behind her desk is an activity bulletin board relating to the class study of regional geography. This bulletin board also invites pupil participation; it lists specific directions regarding independent activities the children can perform.

The Reading Period / The children arrive at 8:45 A.M. Following the short opening exercises, the teacher begins the reading period.

As the children enter the room, they find packets of materials on their desks. The teacher has planned this in advance as part of the independent work she wants completed while she teaches skill groups. In the packets are activities relating to general reading tasks or mathematics and social studies that everyone completes. For certain children the packets may also contain special materials planned to provide practice in a skill taught to them the day before. In any case, in accordance with the management guidelines described above, the assignments have been carefully planned by the teacher and are relevant to the children.

The teacher first gives directions for the independent activities. Rapidly, but thoroughly, she goes through the common material found in the packets and describes what should be done and what can be learned or practiced. She also provides instructions regarding any special assignments she may have included for specific individuals. She reminds the children of who the buffer is for the week, and she indicates some of the safety-valve activities available around the room, such as the current projects in science, regional geography, listening, and recreational reading noted above. She also reminds the children that they may use this time to work on projects relating to the sharing of books they have been reading, as well as checking their shoe boxes for the special activities included there.

The teacher then calls the names of Bert and George, and takes them to the reading corner. She immediately sets to work teaching these children skill number two.

Meanwhile, the rest of the children begin work on the assignments found in their packets. There is general movement around the room, but it is purposeful rather than aimless. If questions arise, they are directed to the buffer. When a child comes in late, the buffer goes over to the latecomer and explains what is to be done in the independent activities. The children do their independent work in no particular order, but they work through it steadily. As they complete assignments, they select one of the many safety-valve activities and continue to work diligently.

The Skill Lesson / While we have been observing the independent activities, the teacher has been working with Bert and George on skill number two. Having completed their lesson, they return to their seats and begin their independent work. The teacher then calls the names of four other children who need help with another skill. Because the pretest was completed previously, the teacher begins immediately with the principles of the instructional act described earlier. The principle of blockage is established as the learners are directed to attend to the crucial elements of the task; the teacher makes a presentation, elicits responses, and provides appropriate reinforcement; practice is given; the posttest administered; and the learners are provided with specific suggestions for applying the skill.

SUMMARY

The purpose of this chapter was to develop an understanding of and an appreciation for the instructional function and the elements in a learning situation, especially as they fit within the strategy for skill development proposed in this book. Six conditions of instruction that should be used when teaching the reading skills were explained, and suggestions for organizing the class to implement a skills program were given. Finally, an illustration of the program in action in one classroom was provided to help you visualize how it can work.

CHAPTER FOUR / IF THE LEARNER CANNOT READ AT ALL

Skill Objectives for Teaching
Word Recognition Prerequisites

This chapter provides the fundamental skills a beginner must master to succeed in identifying words. These are readiness skills; they prepare the learner for intensive study of the word recognition techniques in the following chapter. If you work with beginning readers of preschool, kindergarten, or first-grade age, or with older children or adults who are so severely disabled as to be considered nonreaders, start them at this chapter.

SKILLS TAUGHT IN THIS CHAPTER

Word recognition is the label given to the large body of skills a reader uses to identify words on the printed page. These skills are divided into the two major categories, *recognition* and *analysis*. A reader memorizes some words—learns to instantly identify them at sight—and this is a recognition skill. His ability to do this depends primarily on his skill in discriminating among visual symbols and his repertoire of visual memory techniques. Other words—those the reader does not know at sight—must be examined for known elements and then pronounced. This is an analytic or problem-solving task. The ability to do this depends primarily on the reader's skill in using auditory cues to identify the phonetic and structural elements in words. This chapter and Chapter 5 provide skills of recognition and skills of analysis.

Consistent with the recognition and analysis aspects of word recognition, skill clusters in this chapter are divided into two major categories.

The first, "What the Learner Looks at," teaches the prerequisite skills of visual discrimination and visual memory. The second, "What the Learner Listens to," teaches appropriate auditory discrimination tasks.

Included in this chapter are objectives teaching the concept of *different* as it relates to visual and auditory cues; *sequencing*, in terms of first and last symbols and sounds, and left-to-right progression; *discrimination* of gross and fine differences in visual and auditory cues; *connection* of visual symbols (letters) with the sounds normally associated with these symbols; the use of *context* to anticipate unknown words; and *visual memory* techniques for recognizing specific words at sight.

Learners who master the skills of this chapter will be able to:
1 Differentiate between letters and words similar in shape.
2 Differentiate among the sounds of *m, d, s, h, l,* hard *c, t, b, p, w, r, f, g, k, j, h, sh,* and the voiceless *th* at the beginning of words; and match these sounds with their corresponding letters.
3 Differentiate among the sounds of *m, d, l,* and voiceless *s* at the end of words and associate the sounds with their corresponding letters.
4 Name the letters of the alphabet (both upper and lower case).
5 Examine words from left to right and pages from top to bottom.
6 Recognize at sight 54 words, including 10 chosen by the learner himself.
7 Use a combination of oral context and initial consonants as a means for anticipating unknown words.

USING THIS CHAPTER

This chapter and the following chapter are related, with both focusing on the skills of word recognition. They should be viewed as one continuous hierarchy of sequential skills.

The specific skills to be taught if a learner cannot read at all begin on the next page. Refer to Chapter 1 for an overall description of the strategy employed in using the objectives, to Chapter 2 for specific guidelines in using this book, and to Chapter 3 for techniques of instruction and management. The test provided in Appendix E should be used to determine each learner's approximate placement in terms of the skills taught in this chapter. Inserted at random among the objectives are reminders designed to help you develop a well-rounded total reading program.

IA **1** KEY OBJECTIVE

■ THE PERFORMANCE OBJECTIVE Given three geometric figures that are exactly alike and one that is clearly different, the learner marks the one that is different.

■ THE PRETEST Direct the learner to indicate (mark or point to as appropriate) which figure in the following sets is different. Criterion for mastery is 80 percent.

SET I ○ ○ □ ○   SET VI ⬭ ◯ ○ ⬭

SET II □ ○ □ □   SET VII ▽ △ △ △

SET III △ ○ ○ ○   SET VIII □ □ ▱ □

SET IV ○ ▱ ▱ ▱   SET IX ▱ ◇ ◇ ◇

SET V ○ ○ ○ ○   SET X □ □ □ □

■ DIRECTING THE LEARNER'S ATTENTION The purpose of this task is to teach the learner the concept of *different*. His future success as a reader will depend on his skill at spotting the visual differences that exist between words. He must first understand what is meant by different and the visual characteristics that make one figure or letter or word different from another. At this beginning level, you must provide him with the concept of different and show him how to look at printed forms in order to determine what makes one different from another. You must be certain that the learner attends to your oral directions and to the form of the figures in each set.

Key objective for developing skill in noting visual differences.

■ TEACHING ACTIVITIES / *The model activity* Prepare a duplicated handout in which each of the pretest figures (or letters or words) is enlarged. Take the learner's finger, point to each figure, letter, or word in succession, and ask the question, "Does this look like this?" When the response is, "No," you respond, "You're right. This one is different." Once the correct answer is achieved, have the learner repeat the same procedure for each of the remaining sets, independently pointing to and verbalizing the response, "This one is different."

If the learner is unable to perform the task in this way, add to your sequence of questions, "Look at each figure in turn and tell my *why* one is different." If he is still confused, model the behavior for the learner by asking questions for him such as: "Does this look like this? Here is a straight line, here is a straight line, but here is a curved line. This one is different." Encourage the learner to respond by mimicking your words and actions.

/ *Suggestions for reteaching and/or practice*

1 Place three children's chairs and one teacher's chair in a row. Have the learner examine each chair in sequence. Ask the same questions as in the model activity above.

2 Use the same activity as the above, varying the objects. For example, use all round objects with one square object, all red objects with one yellow object, etc. Ask the same questions as in the model activity.

3 Have the learner match geometric forms, letters, and words. He takes a form, letter, or word from a grab bag and matches it with individual cards he has in front of him.

4 Provide simple puzzles of common objects and forms, or provide for experiences in assembling blocks to duplicate patterns you have pictured for him.

5 Make up a jigsaw puzzle in which the pieces to be fitted are commonly confused forms, letters, or words. The learner must match the pieces shaped as letters to the appropriate place in the jigsaw puzzle.

6 If the learner has particular difficulty noting differences between specific forms, letters, or words, do tracing activities with him. For example, using a tray of sand, draw the forms, letters, or words the learner is confusing and have him trace them, verbalizing the differences as he does so.

7 Use sets of attractive pictures, of which all but one are the same. Place these on the chalk tray with one of the similar pictures clearly apart from the others on the left-hand side. Ask the learner to look at the picture at the left and to find the picture in the row which is different. When he finds it, encourage him to verbalize the difference, saying, "This ball is different from this ball because this one is red and that one is blue."

8   Forms, letters, or words can be written on the chalkboard in arrangements similar to the following:

b   b   b   d   b

The learner is asked to find the one in the set that is different from the one to the left, and to verbalize the way in which it is different.

9   The same activity as described in No. 8 can be varied by using different mediums. For example, alphabet blocks, sandpaper letters, and tagboard letters can be used to give the learner tactile, as well as visual, clues in assessing the differences which exist in the letters.

10   Learners can be helped to attend to the visual differences in forms, letters, and words by teaching them to write these forms, letters, and words. As you teach the learner to use the straight lines and circles associated with the printing of the letters, for example, you can simultaneously be cueing him to the fact that one letter is different from another by saying, "This curve faces to the right and this curve faces to the left."

11   Using two frequently confused forms, letters, or words, list them on the chalkboard in this fashion:

was	saw
saw	was
saw	saw
was	was
was	saw

Direct the learner to circle all the words in the two columns that are just like the first word in the left column and to draw a line under each word that is just like the first word in the right column.

12   Use a list of words such as the following and direct the learner to draw a line under all the words in the list that are exactly alike except for the first letter:

cold   take   cook   make   sake   rake   fade

13   In an exercise similar to No. 12, use a list of words such as the following and direct the learner to draw a line under all the words on the list that are like the first word except for the last letter:

him   hat   hit   have   his

14   Have the learner find the form, letter, or word in a written series that is unlike the other words in the series.

15   Provide the learner with two parallel columns of words, letters, or forms in which the same words, letters, or forms are used but in a different order. Direct the learner to draw lines connecting the like words, forms, or letters in the two columns.

■ THE POSTTEST   Same directions and criterion for mastery as on the pretest.

SET I □ □ ○ □   SET VI △ △ △ △

SET II ○ △ △ △   SET VII △ ▽ △ △

SET III □ □ ▽ □   SET VIII ○ ○ ◯ ○

SET IV ▭ ▭ ▭ ▭   SET IX □ □ ▯ □

SET V ○ ◿ ◿ ◿   SET X ◇ ◇ ◇ ▱

KEY OBJECTIVE IA ■2

■ THE PERFORMANCE OBJECTIVE Given a few seconds to examine a geometric figure, the learner reproduces from memory a figure just like it, to the satisfaction of the teacher.

■ THE PRETEST Prepare four flash cards, one with a square, one with a circle, one with a triangle, and one with a diamond. Flash each for the count of "1000, 1001, 1002, 1003." Then direct the learner to reproduce each shape. Criterion for mastery is teacher judgment concerning accuracy of lines and angles for each reproduction. Size is not a criterion.

■ DIRECTING THE LEARNER'S ATTENTION The purpose of this task is to develop the learner's visual memory. The successful reader carries word images in his head; he remembers what words look like. This is the beginning task to create the memory skill. You must be certain that the learner attends to your oral directions and to the salient features of the visual form for as long as it is shown.

> **Key objective** for developing skill in visual memory.

■ TEACHING ACTIVITIES / *The model activity* Prepare flash cards of the figure, letter, or word to be remembered. Explain to the learner that he will have to remember what is on the card and that he must look carefully. Care must be taken to eliminate all distractions so that he will take the entire three seconds for his examination of the figure, letter, or word. Directions such as, "Look carefully at this picture for as long as I let you," would be appropriate. When the flash card is put down, say, "Now hold the picture of what you saw in your mind. Take your pencil and draw exactly what you saw."

When the learner is unable to perform the task in this way, simplify the memory task for him. For example, ask him to "hold a picture in your mind" of a one-line figure rather than a three-line figure. When he can reproduce the single-line figure, increase the difficulty by asking him to produce a two-line figure, and finally a three-line figure so that he is able to perform the task as stated in the objective.

Are your learners coming to school excited and eager to start a new day?

/ Suggestions for reteaching and/or practice

1 Familiarity training with the shape of the figure, letter, or word to be remembered will help the learner with this memory task. This can be done by having him trace with his finger the shape of the figure, letter, or word that is used in his memory training. He can also be encouraged to trace block figures or to trace in sand. This should be done from a model with no memory involved.

2 Give the learner an outline of a triangle superimposed on a square. Flash him either a square or a triangle, and ask him to trace the figure that matches the one on the flash card.

3 Give the learner four cards on which is drawn one of four figures, letters, or words. Flash one to him, and ask him to match the flash with the correct card from in front of him.

4 Display two objects for the learner. Cover one and direct him to identify which one you hid. Increase the difficulty of the task by increasing the number of objects.

5 Display a picture for the learner. Direct him to examine it. Then remove it and have the learner tell all he remembers about the picture. Increase the difficulty of the task in subsequent sessions by using more complex pictures.

6 Make a design from blocks, pegboards, or bead chaining. Direct the learner to examine the design. Then remove the design and direct the learner to reproduce it from memory.

7 Play a game with several learners in which you touch an object; the first learner touches that object and one more; and the next learner touches both previous objects and one more, and so on, with each learner in turn touching all the objects that were touched before adding a new object.

8 Play a game like television's "Concentration." Figures, letters, or words are placed on a table and covered up. The learner draws a card containing a figure, letter, or word from a box in front of him, and he must remember where the matching pair is located on the table. Begin by using just a few possibilities, adding other figures, letters, or words as the learner becomes more proficient.

9 Place a group of figures, letters, or words on the chalkboard. Direct the learner to examine these and then to turn away from the board. You erase one figure. When the learner turns back, he must reproduce the figure, letter, or word you erased. Start by using just two possibilities, increasing the number as the learner becomes more proficient.

10 Using a tachistoscope or flash cards, show the learner a numeral and direct him to reproduce it from memory. If he can, repeat the process using two numerals in a sequence. Continue to increase the number of numerals he is asked to reproduce as he succeeds at each level.

■ THE POSTTEST   The pretest may be used as the posttest.

IA ▪3

■ THE PERFORMANCE OBJECTIVE   Given three letters that are exactly alike and one that is clearly different, the learner marks the one that is different.

■ THE PRETEST   Direct the learner to indicate (mark or point to as appropriate) which letter in the following sets is different. Criterion for mastery is 80 percent.

SET I	g	g	w	g	SET VI	x	x	x	c
SET II	S	a	a	a	SET VII	d	r	d	d
SET III	e	y	e	e	SET VIII	o	o	j	o
SET IV	m	m	m	l	SET IX	z	z	z	v
SET V	b	v	b	b	SET X	s	s	S	s

■ DIRECTING THE LEARNER'S ATTENTION   The purpose of the task is to teach the learner the concept of different as it applies to letters. This is basically the same task as IA 1, but with finer discriminators. Use the storehouse of suggestions found in IA 1 and adapt those activities to this task. Remember to be certain that the learner attends to the visual form of the letters.

■ THE POSTTEST   Same directions and criterion for mastery as on the pretest.

SET I	t	t	T	t	SET VI	v	b	b	b
SET II	b	b	b	i	SET VII	l	l	l	m
SET III	u	u	j	u	SET VIII	y	e	y	y
SET IV	r	d	r	r	SET IX	a	s	s	s
SET V	c	c	c	x	SET X	w	w	q	w

IA 4

■ THE PERFORMANCE OBJECTIVE Given a few seconds to examine a letter, the learner reproduces the letter from memory, to the satisfaction of the teacher.

■ THE PRETEST Prepare 10 flash cards, each card having one letter of the following sequence.

p　　w　　s　　a　　e　　y　　m　　l　　v　　b

Flash each in turn for a count of three, and then direct the learner to reproduce it. Criterion for mastery is teacher judgment concerning the accuracy of each reproduction. Size is not a criterion.

Are you planning ahead?

■ DIRECTING THE LEARNER'S ATTENTION The purpose of the task is to develop the learner's visual memory for letter forms. This is basically the same task as IA 2, but the learner is being asked to remember letters rather than geometric figures. Use the storehouse of suggestions found in IA 2 and adapt those activities to this task. Remember that you must be certain that the learner attends to the letter to be remembered for as long as it is shown.

■ THE POSTTEST The pretest may be used also as the posttest.

IA 5

■ THE PERFORMANCE OBJECTIVE Given three numerals that are exactly alike and one that is clearly different, the learner marks the one that is different.

■ THE PRETEST Direct the learner to indicate (mark or point to as appropriate) which numeral in the following sets is different. Criterion for mastery is 80 percent.

SET I	2	2	1	2	SET VI	9	2	2	2
SET II	0	9	9	9	SET VII	6	6	6	7
SET III	8	3	8	8	SET VIII	5	4	5	5
SET IV	5	4	4	4	SET IX	0	3	3	3
SET V	1	1	1	6	SET X	7	7	1	7

■ DIRECTING THE LEARNER'S ATTENTION The purpose of this task is to teach the learner the concept of different as it applies to numerals. This is basically the same task as IA 1, but the learner is to note differences in numerals rather than in geometric forms. Use the storehouse of suggestions found in IA 1 and adapt those activities to this task. Remember to be certain that the learner attends to the visual form of the numerals in each activity.

■ THE POSTTEST Same directions and criterion for mastery as on the pretest.

SET I	1	1	7	1	SET VI	6	6	6	1
SET II	3	0	0	0	SET VII	4	5	5	5
SET III	4	5	4	4	SET VIII	3	8	3	3
SET IV	7	7	7	6	SET IX	9	0	0	0
SET V	2	9	9	9	SET X	1	1	2	1

IA 6

■ THE PERFORMANCE OBJECTIVE Given a few seconds to examine a numeral, the learner reproduces it from memory, to the satisfaction of the teacher.

■ THE PRETEST Prepare 10 flash cards, each card having one numeral in the sequence from 1 to 10. After you flash each for the count of three, direct the learner to reproduce it. Criterion for mastery is teacher judgment concerning the accuracy of each reproduction. Size is not a criterion.

■ DIRECTING THE LEARNER'S ATTENTION The purpose of the task is to develop the learner's visual memory for numerals. This is basically the same task as IA 2, but the learner is being asked to remember numerals rather than geometric figures. Use the storehouse of suggestions found in IA 2 and adapt those activities to this task. Remember that you must be certain that the learner attends to the numeral to be remembered for as long as it is shown.

■ THE POSTTEST   The pretest may be used also as the posttest.

IA 7

■ THE PERFORMANCE OBJECTIVE   Given three words that are exactly alike and one that is clearly different, the learner marks the one that is different.

■ THE PRETEST   Direct the learner to indicate (mark or point to as appropriate) which word in each of the following sets is different. Criterion for mastery is 80 percent.

SET I	yes / yes / no / yes	SET VI	he / elephant / he / he
SET II	I / and / I / I	SET VII	here / here / at / here
SET III	the / was / was / was	SET VIII	come / come / come / of
SET IV	in / to / to / to	SET IX	it / he / he / he
SET V	of / of / my / of	SET X	up / up / up / come

■ DIRECTING THE LEARNER'S ATTENTION   The purpose of this task is to teach the learner the concept of different as it relates to words. This is basically the same task as IA 1, but with more complex discriminators. Use the storehouse of suggestions found in IA 1 and adapt those activities to this task. Remember to be certain that the learner attends to the visual form of the words.

■ THE POSTTEST   Same directions and criterion for mastery as on the pretest.

SET I	come / come / come / up	SET VI	my / my / of / my
SET II	he / it / it / it	SET VII	to / in / in / in
SET III	of / of / of / come	SET VIII	was / the / the / the
SET IV	at / at / here / at	SET IX	and / I / and / and
SET V	elephant / he / elephant / elephant	SET X	no / no / yes / no

IA 8

■ THE PERFORMANCE OBJECTIVE   Given a few seconds to examine a short word, the learner reproduces the word from memory, to the satisfaction of the teacher.

■ THE PRETEST   Prepare 10 flash cards, each card having one word of the following sequence:

yes   no   and   the   was   in   to   of   my   he

Flash each for the count of three. Then direct the learner to reproduce it. Criterion for mastery is teacher judgment regarding the accuracy of each reproduction. Size is not a criterion.

■ DIRECTING THE LEARNER'S ATTENTION The purpose of the task is to develop the learner's visual memory for word forms. This is basically the same task as IA 2, but the learner is being asked to remember words rather than geometric figures. Use the storehouse of suggestions found in IA 2 and adapt those activities to this task. Remember that you must be certain that the learner attends to the word to be remembered for as long as it is shown.

■ THE POSTTEST The pretest may be used also for the posttest.

WHAT THE LEARNER
LISTENS TO

IB **1**

■ THE PERFORMANCE OBJECTIVE When directed to close his eyes and listen to a sound produced by the teacher or from the immediate classroom environment, the learner names the sound.

■ THE PRETEST Prepare a tape recording having the following sounds: a car motor, a bell, a door slamming, footsteps, a bird song, a guitar, a fire siren, laughter, a dog barking, and a dripping faucet. Direct the learner to listen to each sound and name it. Criterion for mastery is 80 percent. The sounds used may be adjusted by the teacher to meet the specific environmental conditions of the learner. For example, rural children might be asked to identify a preponderance of farm sounds.

■ DIRECTING THE LEARNER'S ATTENTION The purpose of this task is to develop in the learner careful listening habits. You must be certain that he attends to the specific sounds produced.

■ TEACHING ACTIVITIES / *The model activity* Prepare a group of pictures of sound producers, such as cars, airplanes, and animals. Have the learner identify an object and create the sound related to it. Then pair learners who have created various sounds and have them identify each other's objects by the sound they produce.

/ *Suggestions for reteaching and/or practice*

1 Make up a game that requires the learner to identify the sounds of common objects. For example, gather a group of pictures, hold up one at a time for the learner to examine, and have him respond by producing the sound that identifies the object.
2 Direct the class to concentrate their ears by closing their eyes. Any learner who wishes can then name any sound that is present in the immediate environment and direct the class to the sound by reproducing it.

■ THE POSTTEST Create a new tape recording using sounds that were not used on the pretest. The procedure and criterion for mastery is the same. *Caution*: The teacher must be ready to accept reasonable interpretations of sounds.

IB **2**

■ THE PERFORMANCE OBJECTIVE   Given sounds in pairs that are either the same or different, the learner identifies the pairs as being the same or different.

■ THE PRETEST   Prepare 10 groups of paired sounds, such as knuckles rapping on the blackboard and a foot stamping on the floor. Pair the sounds and produce each pair in turn. Direct the child to say "Same" if the pair is the same, and to say "Different" if the pair is different. Criterion for mastery is 80 percent.

■ DIRECTING THE LEARNER'S ATTENTION   The purpose of this task is to teach the learner the concept of different as it relates to sound. You must be certain that the learner attends to the oral directions and to the sound pairs.

■ TEACHING ACTIVITIES / *The model activity*   Improvise sound pairing from your immediate environment. For example, two taps on the blackboard should produce the same two sounds. The learner's response would be "Same." One tap on the blackboard and one on a cabinet should produce a learner response of "Different." Direct the learner with questions such as, "Are these two sounds the same?" When the response is correct, say, "You're right. The sounds are the same (or different)." Be sure that you start with two sounds that are clearly different, working gradually to sounds that might be more easily confused. If the learner has difficulty with the first pair of sounds, you must find two sounds that are so clearly different that he can distinguish the difference. Once he succeeds at this level, move him immediately to other sounds that are not quite so different.

/ *Suggestions for reteaching and/or practice*

1 Return to IB 1 and select sounds that have previously been identified. Pair these sounds and have the learner indicate whether they are the same or different.

2 Using a group of learners, select one to assist you, and direct the rest of the group to close their eyes and listen. Move around the room, making sounds such as tapping or moving objects. The assistant follows you and either matches what you did or makes small modifications. The listeners identify the two sounds as being same or different. Keep changing assistants every three patterns.

■ THE POSTTEST   Prepare 10 groups of paired sounds on the same order of the pretest. Procedure and criterion for mastery are the same.

IB 3

■ THE PERFORMANCE OBJECTIVE   When directed to close his eyes and listen to tapped rhythms produced by the teacher, the learner reproduces the rhythms.

■ THE PRETEST   Using a fist on a tabletop, produce the following rhythm patterns which correspond to regular Morse code signals. A tap followed by a pause is a dash; a tap without pause is a dot. Criterion for mastery is 80 percent.

dot/dot	dot/dot/dash/dot
dash/dot	dot/dash/dot/dot/dot
dot/dash	dash/dot/dash/dot
dash/dot/dot	dot/dash/dash/dot
dot/dot/dot	dash/dash/dot/dot/dash

■ DIRECTING THE LEARNER'S ATTENTION   The purpose of this task is to help the learner create an auditory memory. You must be certain that the learner attends to the oral directions and to the pattern of rhythms. In giving directions, initially you may have to model the response for the learner.

Have you ordered the practice material (see Appendix B)?

■ TEACHING ACTIVITIES / *The model activity*   Direct the learner to watch and listen as you clap your hands in a simple rhythm. Then take his hands and repeat the same pattern, saying "See. Here is how I did it." Then direct the learner to repeat the clapping pattern by himself.

/ *Suggestions for reteaching and/or practice*

1   Use familiar songs with a definite rhythm. As the songs are sung or

listened to, clap in time to the words and music and direct the learners to do the same.

2 Choose two familiar songs and give the titles of the songs to the class. You might even sing one or two lines from each. Then direct the class to listen as you tap out the rhythm of one of the songs. The class duplicates the rhythm and identifies the song.

3 Using rhythm band instruments, give the learner a rhythm and direct him to reproduce it on his instrument.

■ THE POSTTEST   Procedure and criterion for mastery is the same as on the pretest.

dot/dash	dot/dash/dot/dot
dot/dot	dot/dot/dash/dot
dash/dot	dot/dash/dot/dash
dot/dot/dash	dot/dash/dash/dot
dot/dot/dot	dash/dash/dot/dot/dot/dash

IB **4**

■ THE PERFORMANCE OBJECTIVE   When directed to close his eyes and listen to three words spoken by the teacher, the learner reproduces the words in the sequence in which they were spoken.

■ THE PRETEST   Direct the learner to close his eyes and listen. Say, "Listen carefully to the words I say. When I stop I want you to say them just the way I did." Produce the sets of words in the following sequence. Criterion for mastery is 80 percent.

school/bell/playground	grass/house/rug
elephant/dog/cat	Ford/sky/donkey
desk/chair/table	window/hydrant/card
pencil/pen/eraser	fight/run/tree
red/blue/yellow	laugh/church/sign

■ DIRECTING THE LEARNER'S ATTENTION   The purpose of this task is to help the learner create an auditory memory. You must be certain that the learner attends to the oral directions and to the sequence of words spoken.

■ TEACHING ACTIVITIES / *The model activity*   Provide the learner with a single word and say, "Can you say this?" When the learner responds correctly, create a two-word pattern, using the word given previously. Say, "Now, can you say this?" When the learner responds correctly, follow the same pattern with a three-word sequence.

/ Suggestions for reteaching and/or practice

1   Arrange two objects in front of the learner, such as a book and a pencil. Point to each and name it, directing the learner to name the objects after you. Then add a third object, producing the sequence of three words, and again ask the learner to name the objects. Then direct the learner to close his eyes as you say the words. Finally, without the visual clues, direct the learner to repeat the words in sequence.

2   Repeat the above activity using action words, such as *smile, hop,* and *walk.* Remember to end whatever activity you use with a purely oral presentation and auditory response from the learner, without other memory clues.

■ THE POSTTEST   Same procedure and criterion for mastery as on the pretest. Repeat the pretest, reading each set backwards.

IB **5**

■ THE PERFORMANCE OBJECTIVE   When directed to close his eyes and listen to three words spoken by the teacher, the learner repeats the first and the last words.

■ THE PRETEST   Use the words provided in the previous pretest (IB 4). Read each of the sets in turn, directing the learner to close his eyes and listen carefully. After each set, ask him to tell what the first word was. If he is correct, ask him also what the last word was. Criterion for mastery is 80 percent.

■ DIRECTING THE LEARNER'S ATTENTION   The purpose of this task is to familiarize the learner with sound position in time (first and last). This is a difficult concept to teach because the last word provided is the closest to the learner in time; and invariably he picks it as the first word heard. You must be certain that the learner follows the oral directions and attends to the voice cues delivered by the teacher.

■ TEACHING ACTIVITIES / *The model activity*   Provide the learner with two words. As you say the words, direct him with the oral cues, "First word, elephant. Last word, car. Elephant, car. What was the first word?" Then add a third word and repeat the procedure above, omitting any position reference to the middle word.

/ Suggestions for reteaching and/or practice

1   Repeat the procedure described in the model activity, but use finger cues (one finger for first, two fingers for last) as a further aid to the learner.

2 Place three objects in front of the learner. Point to each object in turn saying, "First, pencil; paper; last, book." Then ask the learner which object is first and which is last. Repeat the names of the objects in sequence without the object cues, asking the question, "Which word is first, which is last?"

3 Line up three or more learners. Say, as you indicate each learner in turn, "First, Tom; Betty; John; Sam; Tim; and last, Mary." Then repeat, saying, "First, Tom, last, Mary." Finally, ask the learner who is first and who is last in the line.

Note: The preceding practice activities use visual cues as mediators for the desired listening behavior. *This skill is a listening skill, and if visual mediators are needed, they must be used only as a transition. Prior to posttesting, the learner must be performing with auditory cues only.*

■ THE POSTTEST   Use the words provided in the previous pretest (IB 4), reversing the order in which they are spoken. Repeat the pretest procedures. The criterion for mastery remains 80 percent.

IB **6**

■ THE PERFORMANCE OBJECTIVE   Given a multisyllable word spoken by the teacher, the learner tells the number of syllabic units in the word.

■ THE PRETEST   Direct the learner to listen carefully to the words you say. Produce each of the following words, direct the learner to mimic you, and then ask him to tell you the number of sound units heard. *Caution:* Speak the words slowly, accenting each syllable. Example: "Ba-by." Criterion for mastery is 80 percent.

table	ice cream	elephant	pencil	umbrella
snowman	tree	bushes	book	helicopter

■ DIRECTING THE LEARNER'S ATTENTION   The purpose of this task is to help the learner create an auditory memory in preparation for instruction on beginning and ending sounds in words. You must be certain that he attends to the oral directions and to the number of sounds heard in each word.

Do your learners see you as a positive person or as a negative person?

■ TEACHING ACTIVITIES / *The model activity*   Using a two-syllable word, say the word and clap for each syllable. Then clap without speaking the word and say, "How many times did I clap? How many sounds in the word?" Give another two-syllable-word, hold the learner's hands, and repeat the above process. Repeat with another two-syllable word and let the learner independently clap the number of sounds heard. Finally, provide a two-syllable word and ask the learner to tell the number of sound units without the aid of clapping.

/ *Suggestions for reteaching and/or practice*

1   Direct the learner to listen as you say a two-syllable word. Have him say the word with you. Say it together again, using your fingers to indicate the number of sound units in the word. Then have the learner say the word alone, indicating with his fingers the number of sound units. Finally, have him say the word and tell the number of sounds without using his fingers.

2   Direct the learner to listen as you say the word. Then have him say the word while you orally count each sound he produces by saying, "One, two."

3   Say a word, nodding your head for each sound unit in the word. Then have the learner repeat the word, nodding his head for each unit.

■ THE POSTTEST   The procedure and criterion for mastery is the same as for the pretest.

begin	bingo	policeman	hippopotamus	flashlight
fishhook	bee	apple	pen	baseball

IB 7

■ THE PERFORMANCE OBJECTIVE   Given multisyllable words spoken orally by the teacher, the learner repeats the first sound unit and the last sound unit in each word as directed.

■ THE PRETEST   Direct the learner to listen carefully to the words you say. Produce each of the following words, have the learner mimic you, and then ask him to say the first sound unit (syllable) and then the last sound unit in the word. Criterion for mastery is 80 percent.

patrol	storybook	hopping	bubble	policeman
treehouse	eraser	telephone	gymnasium	astronaut

■ DIRECTING THE LEARNER'S ATTENTION   The purpose of this task is to help the learner transfer the concept of *first* and *last* to individual word units.

You must be certain that he attends to the oral directions and to the auditory cues inherent in each word.

■ TEACHING ACTIVITIES / *The model activity*   Using a three-syllable word, say the word and clap for each syllable. Then say the word again, but clap only for the first and last syllables. The learner repeats the word, and you hold his hands as he claps for each sound. Then hold his hands as he claps for only the first and last sounds. Finally, have him say the word and tell the first and the last sound. As soon as he is able to do this, give him a three-syllable word and direct him to tell you the first and last sounds without the aid of clapping.

/ *Suggestions for reteaching and/or practice*

1   This activity remains the same as the model activity, but you substitute other cues besides clapping. For example, you may use finger cues or head noddings in the manner described in previous objectives, or you may use any other physical cues you wish.

■ THE POSTTEST   Procedures and criterion for mastery are the same as in the pretest.

about	drugstore	beginning	cultivator	televison
bicycle	happiness	subway	machinery	Sesame

IIA **1**

■ THE PERFORMANCE OBJECTIVE   Given a manuscript model of his own name, the learner makes an acceptable copy, as determined by teacher judgment.

■ THE PRETEST   Give the learner a lined paper on which you have printed his name. Direct him to print his name directly under the model. Criterion for mastery is your judgment regarding the accuracy of the reproduction.

■ DIRECTING THE LEARNER'S ATTENTION   The purpose of this task is to acquaint the learner with the printed form of his name and to teach the specific visual-motor skills necessary to the formation of the letters in his name. This task, plus the following task, will result in the learner's being able to read his name, thereby giving him the first word that he can recognize and read instantly. This word is taught first because it is the most important word to him. When teaching this skill, you must be certain that he attends to the oral directions and to the visual model of his name.

■ TEACHING ACTIVITIES / *The model activity*   Prepare a black-and-white copy of the learner's name in standard, upper-case manuscript form at least three inches high. Using your index finger as a pointer, model the strokes used in each letter formation. Direct the learner to match your strokes with his finger and then to make a pencil copy of the letter directly underneath it. You may wish to name the letters as you trace them, and you can encourage the learner also to do this.

/ Suggestions for reteaching and/or practice

1 Prepare a handout in which the learner's name has been produced with dotted lines. Direct him to close the dots and print his name. Then ask him to reproduce the name without guides, directly under the first effort.

2 Print the names of a number of pupils on the blackboard. After pointing to and reading each name in turn, direct each learner to come to the board, find his name, and copy it with chalk directly under the model.

■ THE POSTTEST   The procedure is the same as for the pretest.

IIA **2**

■ THE PERFORMANCE OBJECTIVE   Given a list of five names of students in his class, the learner identifies his name by drawing a circle around it.

■ THE PRETEST   Prepare a multiple listing of pupil names in groups of five. Each learner is given a list that contains his name and is asked to point to his name, say it, and draw a circle around it. Criterion for mastery is 100 percent.

■ DIRECTING THE LEARNER'S ATTENTION   The purpose of this task is to teach the learner to recognize the printed form of his name. When teaching this skill, you must be certain that he simultaneously attends to the printed name (use the finger as a pointer) and to the sound of the name.

■ TEACHING ACTIVITIES / *The model activity*   Provide the learner with a name card. Say, "I am going to print some names on the blackboard. Maybe I will print your name. If I print your name, you may stand up, read your name out loud to the class, and then line up for recess (or for some other activity)." Be sure the learner looks at his name card as he says his name.

/ *Suggestions for reteaching and/or practice*

1 Learners having difficulty with this task may need to be redirected to IIA 1 for a repetition of the teaching activities outlined there.
2 Prepare a seat plan, either by rows or by blocks, depending upon the class arrangement, and post each learner's names in each row or block at the head of the row or block. Direct the learner to find his name and read it out loud.
3 When the learners are lining up for games or drinks at recess, print their names in groups of five on the blackboard. Read aloud each name as you print it. Then direct the class to line up in the same order as the names appear on the board. Each learner is then asked to point to his name in the list and read it before the group is sent to the next activity.

4 Provide the learner with old magazines and direct him to form his name by cutting letters from the magazines and arranging them in correct order.

■ THE POSTTEST   The pretest is repeated, but the names are arranged in a different order.

IIA 3

■ THE PERFORMANCE OBJECTIVE   Given a lower-case manuscript model of the words *yes* and *no*, the learner makes an acceptable copy of these words as determined by teacher judgment.

■ THE PRETEST   Give the learner a lined paper on which you have printed the words *yes* and *no*. Tell him to copy the words directly under the models. Criterion for mastery is your judgment regarding the accuracy of the reproduction.

■ DIRECTING THE LEARNER'S ATTENTION   The purpose of this task is to acquaint the learner with the printed form of the words *yes* and *no* and to teach him the specific visual-motor skills necessary to the formation of the letters in these words. This task, plus the following task, will provide the learner with the second and third words that he can recognize and read instantly. *Yes* and *no* are being taught at this time because they are frequently used and because they are relatively easy words to teach. When teaching this skill you must be certain that the learner attends to the oral directions and to the visual model of each word.

■ TEACHING ACTIVITIES / *The model activity*   Prepare a black-and-white copy of the words *yes* and *no* in standard, lower-case manuscript form at least three inches high. Using your index finger as a pointer, model the strokes used in the letter formation of the words. Direct the learner to match your strokes with his finger for each word in turn, and to make a pencil copy of each word directly under it. You may wish to name the letters as you trace them, and can encourage the learner to do this also.

/ *Suggestions for reteaching and/or practice*

The teaching activities noted in IIA 1 can be adapted to this objective.

■ THE POSTTEST   The procedure for the posttest is the same as for the pretest.

■ THE PERFORMANCE OBJECTIVE   Given a list of 10 words of which *yes* and *no* are two of the words, the learner identifies first the word *yes* and then the word *no* as directed.

■ THE PRETEST   Prepare a duplicated handout like the one below. Tell the learner to look at the list of words, find the word *yes*, and draw a circle around it. Then tell him to look at the list of words, find the word *no*, and draw a line under it. Criterion for mastery is 100 percent.

dog	cat	no	come	yet
nut	on	not	yes	yell

■ DIRECTING THE LEARNER'S ATTENTION   The purpose of this task is to teach the learner to identify the printed form of the words *yes* and *no*. When teaching this skill, you must be certain that the learner simultaneously attends to the printed name of the word and to the sound of the name.

When a learner fails a task, does he think the fault lies within him or in the difficulty of the task? If it is the former, you had better reread the section on blockage in Chapter 3.

■ TEACHING ACTIVITIES / *The model activity*   Prepare two cards, one printed with the word *yes* and the other with the word *no*. Take one of the cards, say to the learner, "This word is *yes*. Look at the word. Say the word. What word is this? Say the word." This is simply a matter of rote learning and, for most learners, will require some degree of repetition.

/ *Suggestions for reteaching and/or practice*

1   Learners having trouble with this task should be redirected to the tracing activities described in IIA 3.
2   Make two cards for the learner, printing *yes* on one card and *no* on the other. You now have the materials for innumerable games related to this task. For example, you can direct the learner to put the two word cards on his desk in front of him saying, "Would you like to have a piece of candy? If you would, hold up your *yes* card. If you would not, hold up your *no* card." The game can be kept going for as long as you can think up relevant questions to ask.

■ THE POSTTEST   The procedure is the same as for the pretest. The criterion for mastery is 100 percent.

book	fly	card	now	no
nice	yes	in	yak	yet

IIA ▉5▉

■ THE PERFORMANCE OBJECTIVE   Given a random group of alphabet letters in lower case, the learner points to and names each letter in turn.

■ THE PRETEST   Direct the learner to point to and name each of the following letters. Criterion for mastery is 100 percent, with the rationale being that if the learner can name ten randomly selected letters, the chances are good that he knows all the letters. However, if you note that a learner does not know all the letters despite a 100 percent performance on this task, you should test for all the letters of the alphabet and teach those he does not know, using the suggestions provided below.

m   t   w   a   s   e   l   r   o   y

■ DIRECTING THE LEARNER'S ATTENTION   The purpose of this task is to help the learner differentiate among the various alphabet letters and to associate the correct name with each letter. When teaching this skill, you must be certain that the learner attends to the oral directions, to the visual form of each letter, and to the correct pairing of name to letter.

■ TEACHING ACTIVITIES / *The model activity*   Prepare a deck of cards with all 26 letters printed in lower case. Go through the deck with each learner and put to one side those letters he cannot name immediately. Then take the unknown letters, and teach one letter at a time, not necessarily in the order of the alphabet. Say to the learner, "This letter is *t*. Say it. What letter is this? Say this letter." This is simply a matter of rote learning and, for most learners, will require some degree of repetition. *Caution:* Teach letters that are easily confused (such as *b* and *d*, *m* and *n*, and others) initially at widely separate times.

/ *Suggestions for reteaching and/or practice*

1   The learner can be taught to recognize and name the letters by giving him tracing activities. For example, you can write the letters to be learned in a sand tray, saying the letter name as you write it. The learner then traces the letter form you wrote, saying the letter name as he traces it. He can then be directed to use his tracing as a model for writing the letter independently, again saying the letter name as he prints its form.
2   Games such as "Climb the Ladder" can be played. For each rung on

the ladder there is a letter of the alphabet. The learner "climbs" the ladder rung by rung as he names each of the letters in sequence.

3 Similar games can be devised that make use of other devices, such as adding cars to a train (each car having a new letter) or putting leaves on a tree.

4 Another form of the television game "Concentration" can be played in connection with this task. Prepare pairs of cards for five different letters, mix the 10 cards, and turn them upside down. The learner turns over a card, names the letter, and tries to match this letter by turning over the card that is its duplicate. *Caution:* Make sure the learner names the letter when he turns it over.

5 Learners can be provided with letter cards while waiting to be dismissed or while waiting to begin another activity. Name a letter and say, "All those who have that letter may go now." The game can be altered to include physical activities by saying, "All those who have the letter *t* can march to the music now," or "All those who have the letter *l* can skip to the music now."

6 Games can be played in which letters are placed on bowling pins. The learner rolls a ball at the pins, knocking down as many as possible. However, he counts for his score only those pins whose letters he can name.

7 Place letter cards on the seats of chairs arranged in a large circle. The learners march around the chairs in time to music until the music stops. Then each must name the letter on the seat of the chair next to where he stopped.

8 Seat learners in a circle, with one learner in the middle. Provide all the learners with a letter card. The learner in the center calls out the names of any two or three letters and the learners having these letter cards change seats. The learner in the middle also tries to get a seat, and the one left standing calls the next letters. (If the learner in the center calls a letter that no one has, the other learners remain seated.)

9 Make a pocket chart and provide each learner with letter cards. Hold up a letter card (such as the letter *a*) and say, "This is the letter *a*. If you have a letter *a*, come place it in the same pocket where I put mine, and say the letter name as you do so." When all the pockets of the chart are filled, point to each in turn, directing the learner to examine and name the letter in that pocket.

10 Use the pupils' names to help teach letter names. For example, place the names of the pupils on the chalkboard and say, "How many of our names have the letter *f* in them? Who can find a letter *f* in any of our names?" The learner goes to the board, underlines the letter *f* in as many names as he can find it, and says the letter name each time he underlines it.

■ THE POSTTEST The procedure and criterion for mastery remain the same as for the pretest.

a   s   d   f   e   g   u   h   j   i

IIA 6

■ THE PERFORMANCE OBJECTIVE   Given a random group of numerals, the learner points to and names each numeral in turn.

■ THE PRETEST   Direct the learner to point to and name each of the following numerals. Criterion for mastery is 100 percent.

9   4   1   7   1   13   0   6   19   2   9

■ DIRECTING THE LEARNER'S ATTENTION   The purpose of the task is to help the learner differentiate among the various numerals and to associate the correct name with each numeral. When teaching this skill, you must be certain that the learner attends to the oral directions, to the visual form of each numeral, and to the correct pairing of name to numeral.

Have you taken a field trip lately?

■ TEACHING ACTIVITIES / *The model activity*   Prepare a deck of cards with the numerals 1 to 20 printed on them. Go through the deck with each learner and put to one side those numerals he cannot name immediately. Then take these numerals and teach them one at a time. Say to the learner, "This numeral is 1. Say it. What numeral is this? Say this numeral." This is simply a matter of rote learning and, for most learners, will require some degree of repetition.

/ *Suggestions for reteaching and/or practice*

The activities provided for teaching letter names in Objective IIA 5 can be adapted to teach numerals because the task is basically the same in both objectives.

■ THE POSTTEST   The procedure and criterion for mastery are the same as for the pretest.

20   3   5   16   13   2   6   9   10   11

IIA 7

■ THE PERFORMANCE OBJECTIVE   Given a stimulus lower-case letter, the learner matches it with its upper-case counterpart.

■ THE PRETEST Prepare a duplicated handout as follows. Direct the learner to draw lines between the lower-case and upper-case forms of the same letters. Criterion for mastery is 100 percent.

a	s	e	d	c	g	n	i	o	p
C	A	G	D	P	O	S	I	N	E

■ DIRECTING THE LEARNER'S ATTENTION The purpose of this task is to teach the learner to associate the letter name with both its upper- and lower-case form. When teaching this skill, you must be certain that the learner attends to the oral directions, to the visual form of the letters, and to the names he associates with them.

■ TEACHING ACTIVITIES / *The model activity* We know that the learner knows the lower-case letters from a previous objective. The most obvious reason for not performing on this objective is that he does not know the upper-case letter names. You should let the learner use his knowledge of lower-case letters to help him learn the upper-case letters. An efficient way to do this would be through matching exercises where he is given six cards with small letters on them and six cards with the upper-case forms of these same letters. Direct him to pair the cards, naming aloud the upper-case letter when the pairing is made. In choosing which letters to teach first, it is usually wise to start with those letters in which the lower-case and upper-case forms are similar, such as *W–w*, *V–v*, etc. Save the letters with great differences, such as *q–Q*, *r–R*, etc., until last.

/ *Suggestions for reteaching and/or practice*

1 Another form of the television game "Concentration" can be played in connection with this task. Prepare letter pairs on cards, with one of the letters printed in lower-case and the other in upper-case form. Mix the cards and turn them upside down. The learner turns over a card, names the letter, and tries to turn over another card on which is printed the same letter in its upper-case form. You should make sure the learner says the letter name as he turns the cards over, correcting him when appropriate.
2 Prepare a chart of stiff cardboard or tagboard, with upper-case letters printed down the left-hand side and lower-case letters printed down the right-hand side. Attach a string to each of the upper-case letters on the left. Direct the learner to start at the top left corner and to connect the string for each upper-case letter with its lower-case mate.
3 Name a letter and show its lower-case form on a card. Ask the learner to duplicate the lower-case letter in writing and to create the upper-case form of the same letter.
4 Make two sets of letter cards, one for upper-case letters and the other for lower-case letters. Give each learner five of the lower-case

cards, placing all the other cards in a box. Each learner takes turns naming one of his letters, searching in the box for its upper-case mate, and pairing the two. The first learner to make five pairs wins the game.
5 The learner can be provided with block letters or tagboard letters, including both the upper- and lower-case forms of each letter. These are mixed up in a box. The learner's task is to sort the letters out, matching each lower-case letter with its upper-case mate.

■ THE POSTTEST   Procedure and criterion for mastery are the same as on the pretest.

q	w	r	t	y	u	i	m	v	b
Y	M	B	R	W	V	Q	U	T	I

IIA 8 KEY OBJECTIVE

■ THE PERFORMANCE OBJECTIVE   Given cards with the words *yes, no,* and his name printed on them, the learner, when directed, points to the first letter in each of these words and to the last letter in each of these words.

■ THE PRETEST   Provide the learner with three cards on which are printed the words, *yes, no,* and his name. The learner reads each word and when directed to point to the first and last letter in each of these words, he does so and names the first and last letters. Criterion for mastery is 100 percent.

■ DIRECTING THE LEARNER'S ATTENTION   The purpose of this task is to cue the learner to the left-to-right sequence of letters in words and to the importance and position of the first letter and last letter. To read successfully, the learner must be oriented in terms of the sequence one follows when reading—from the front to the back of a book, from the top to the bottom of a page, and from the left to the right of a word. When teaching this skill, you must be certain that the learner attends to the oral directions, to the visual form of the word, and to the first and last letters in each word.

Key objective for developing skill in sequencing.

■ TEACHING ACTIVITIES / *The model activity*   The teaching activities for this task parallel those suggested when the learner is taught *first* and *last* in relation to spoken words and sounds (see IB 5 and IB 7). Print the word *yes,* ask the learner to read the word, and then say to him, "This letter (pointing to *y*) is first, which letter is last?" The reverse can be done on succeeding words, with the learner doing the verbalizing. Always ask for the first letter first, and cue the learner to the left-to-right movement by a physical left-to-right sweep of the finger under the word as well as by teaching the concepts of first and last.

/ Suggestions for reteaching and/or practice

1   Make separate cards for each letter in the learner's name. Scramble these and direct the learner to put them back in the right order to form his name, saying as he does so, "First letter, other letters, last letter."

2   Write a word on a card or on the chalkboard, leaving off either the first or last letter. The learner is directed to print the missing letter in the proper position, saying, "First letter, —" or "Last letter, —."

3   Help the learner grasp a left-to-right approach to words by taking his finger, pointing it to the first letter in a word, and then guiding it in a sweep to the end of the word. Encourage him to do this with his finger when he examines other words.

4   Any time there is an opportunity to display artwork or other learner products, place them on the chalkboard starting at the left and moving to the right. When discussing them with learners, discuss the one at the left first and progress to the right, emphasizing that movement with a physical motion of your hand in the left-to-right direction.

5   When placing directions on the chalkboard or when writing charts with learners, emphasize both the top-to-bottom sequence and the left-to-right sequence by pointing them out. Look for opportunities for eliciting learner responses. For example, have the learner go to the chart to point to the first word, the last word, the first letter in a certain word, and the last letter in a certain word.

6   When reading stories to children or when sharing picture books with them, point out the front-to-back, top-to-bottom, left-to-right directions and look for ways to elicit learner responses to sequencing as they share these stories with you.

7   Use puzzles in which the learner must trace a pattern following numbers or letters. Always have the pattern in such activities move from top to bottom and from left to right to establish the sequencing response desired.

8   Teach the learner to identify his right and left hand by having him associate it with something on himself, such as the hand on which he wears his ring or the wrist on which he wears his watch. Play games in which the learner must lift his right hand, wave his left hand, pick up something with his right hand, and so on.

9   Make frequent use of a wall pocket chart in which the pockets are arranged in rows. Have children use the pocket chart, making certain that they always begin at the top and move to the right across the rows.

10   Prepare a set of pictures in which direction is clearly indicated.

Direct the learners to find something in the picture that is at the top, at the bottom, going down, or going from left to right.

11   Give the learner sets of pictures in which each picture tells part of a story. Comics are useful for this activity. Scramble the pictures and then direct the learner to arrange them to tell the story. Be certain that he arranges the pictures in a top-to-bottom and left-to-right sequence.

12   Use a calendar to teach the left-to-right system by marking off the days in each week, etc.

■ THE POSTTEST   Repeat the pretest. Criterion for mastery remains at 100 percent.

IIB

WHAT THE LEARNER LISTENS TO

■ THE PERFORMANCE OBJECTIVE Given spoken words in pairs that are either the same or different, the learner identifies the pairs as being the same or different.

■ THE PRETEST Using the 10 pairs of words below, say each pair in turn. Direct the learner to say "Same" if the pair is the same, or "Different" if the pair is different. Criterion for mastery is 80 percent.

dog/elephant	cat/cat	rock/rob	stamp/champ	stand/stone
pet/pit	stair/chair	thick/thank	stumble/stumble	shoe/chew

■ DIRECTING THE LEARNER'S ATTENTION The purpose of the task is to teach the learner the concept of different as it relates to the sounds of words. When teaching this skill, you must be certain that he attends to the oral directions and to the sound of each word.

■ TEACHING ACTIVITIES / *The model activity* Give a single word and ask the learner to repeat the word, saying, "Say this word and listen carefully to what you say." When he responds correctly, provide another word, repeating the above process. Then direct him to say both words one after another, saying, "Listen to the two words carefully as you say them. Are they the same or different?" Then direct *him* to say a word. You then repeat the word, or modify a beginning, middle, or ending sound unit, asking him, "Is this the same or different?" A tease situation can be created if you select a learner and a word that he has just spoken during the course of regular classroom activities. You say, "Did you say ———?" making a modification of either the beginning, middle, or end of the word depending on what is needed by the learner at the time. For example, a learner asks a question that has the word *go* in it. You look surprised and say "Did you say *crow*?" The learner will correct you, and you tease him by saying, "Oh, you said, *toe*." Again the learner will correct you and again you can force his attention to the first sound in a word by saying, "Oh, you said *so?*" This is a very graphic way to motivate children to zero in on sound differences in words.

/ Suggestions for reteaching and/or practice

1 The concept of same and different should be well established by now. If it is not, redirect the learner to previous objectives in Cluster I that directly teach the concept and repeat the activities.
2 The only other variable operating in this task is if the learner fails to attend to small sound differences in words. To teach these differences, follow the model teaching activity, but start with gross differences in word pairs, such as *dog–elephant, dog–dig, dog–bog,* and *dog–tog,* refining the sound differences in this manner. Note which sound positions cause the most difficulty and give concentrated attention to them, following the procedures outlined in the model activity.

■ THE POSTTEST Procedure and criterion for mastery are the same as for the pretest.

car/hippopotamus	horse/horse	girl/swirl	black/black	brown/branch
whine/wine	chug/slug	chair/stair	mitt/met	slack/flack

IIB **2** KEY OBJECTIVE

■ THE PERFORMANCE OBJECTIVE Given spoken pairs of words, the learner says "Yes" if the words begin alike and "No" if they do not.

■ THE PRETEST Using the 10 pairs of words below, say each pair in turn. Direct the learner to say "Yes" if the pairs begin with the same sound and to say "No" if the pairs do not begin with the same sound. Criterion for mastery is 80 percent.

boy/book	desk/chair	cat/cow	dog/dig	lake/last
mine/music	happy/house	snap/kiss	chair/shoot	this/that

■ DIRECTING THE LEARNER'S ATTENTION The purpose of this task is to teach the learner the concept of different as it relates to the beginning sounds of words. His ability to analyze words in terms of their sound elements will depend upon his success in isolating and identifying the various phonetic elements of words, particularly as they relate to the beginning sounds. At this beginning level, you must provide the learner with the concept of different and teach him how to listen to words in order to determine what makes one sound different from another. When teaching this skill, you must be certain that he attends to your oral directions and to the beginning sounds of each pair of words.

Key objective for developing skill in noting differences in the beginning sounds of words and in identifying specific beginning sounds.

■ TEACHING ACTIVITIES / *The model activity*   Give a single word and ask the learner to repeat the word, saying, "Say this word and listen carefully to what you say at the beginning." You may find it expedient at this point to exaggerate slightly the beginning sounds in the word. However, this should not be continued beyond the first example. When the learner responds, provide another word, repeating the above process. Then direct him to say both words one after another, saying, "Listen to the beginnings of these words as you say them. Are they the same or different at the beginning?" Then direct him to say a word and you repeat it, modifying the beginning sound or leaving it the same. Ask him, "Is the beginning sound the same or different?"

/ *Suggestions for reteaching and/or practice*

1   The learner will be helped to develop the skill of noting the beginning sound by learning to say words slowly and then fast. For example, you might select the word *fish* and play the following game. Say, "I'm going to do something today that is very hard. I'm going to say a word, and you must listen for the sound you hear at the very beginning of that word. Listen carefully as I say the word slowly. F——ish. Now I'll say it fast. Fish." After modeling the activity for the learner in this way, have him repeat the task, making the same statements you made. Repeat the same process with other words. Ask him to respond by telling you whether the pair of words is the same or different at the beginning. *Caution:* Always put the word back together quickly so the learner gets in the habit of viewing the word as a whole and not as isolated sounds.

2   Have learners bring to class pictures cut from magazines, with each picture or series of pictures showing something that begins with the same sound.

3   Bring in a group of magazine pictures yourself, directing the learner to name what each picture shows and to sort the pictures according to the common beginning sounds. For example, all the pictures that begin with the same sound heard at the beginning of *kite* go in this pile, all the pictures that begin with the same sound heard at the beginning of *top* go in this pile, etc.

4   A learner who has difficulty in learning this task can be helped by teaching him how the beginning sound of a word is formed with the mouth. For example, you can provide him with a mirror and help him to note how he forms the sound heard at the beginning of the word *fish* as compared to how he forms the sound heard at the beginning of the word *man*.

5   Paste a number of pictures on a large piece of tagboard. Direct the learner to match smaller pictures to the pictures on the tagboard on the basis of common beginning sounds.

6 A form of bingo can be played that will reinforce the learning of beginning sounds. For example, the learner can be provided with a bingo-like playing card with pictures in the squares. Say, "Do you have a picture on your card whose name begins with the same sound you hear at the beginning of *dog*? If you do, you may cover that square with a marker." The first learner to cover every picture in a row wins the game.

7 A group of picture cards can be placed on the table. Learners take turns matching pairs of pictures having names which begin with the same sound. Learners with the most pairs win.

8 Provide the learner with an oral listing of words, such as *boy, bat, ball, bingo, tall*. Direct him to name the word that begins with a different sound.

9 Spread a group of pictures on the floor. Direct the learner to point to a picture having a name that begins with the same sound he hears at the beginning of the word you are about to say to him.

10 Play games with learners that follow this pattern: "I'm thinking of something on your desk that begins with the same sound heard at the beginning of the word *pig*. What am I thinking of?"

11 Play a fishing game with learners, in which pictures are paper clipped or stapled to paper fish. Give the learner a pole with a magnet tied to the end. As the learner catches each fish, direct him to say, "I caught a fish that begins with the same sound as ———."

12 As learners are waiting to be dismissed or to move to another activity, you can say, "If you can tell me a word that sounds the same as ——— at the beginning, you can go."

13 Pass out picture cards. Hold up another picture card, saying, "Who has a picture whose name sounds the same at the beginning as the name of my picture?" Direct the learners to hold up their cards if they have such a picture.

14 After a common activity such as a field trip, you can direct the learner to think of all the things he saw that sound the same at the beginning as ———.

15 Direct the learner to "show and tell" something that begins with the same sound as is heard at the beginning of the word ———.

■ THE POSTTEST   Procedure and criterion for mastery is the same as for the pretest.

money/mama	dip/tip	dinosaur/doll	lamp/camp	Sunday/ceiling
huddle/happen	hit/bit	turtle/burp	bicycle/boomerang	ring/water

IIB **3** KEY OBJECTIVE

■ THE PERFORMANCE OBJECTIVE   Given spoken words in pairs that either rhyme or do not rhyme, the learner says "Yes" if the pair rhymes and "No" if it does not.

■ THE PRETEST   Using the 10 pairs of words below, say each pair in turn. Direct the learner to say "Yes" if the pair rhymes and to say "No" if the pair does not rhyme. If the learner does not understand the concept of rhyming, modify the directions to say "sounds the same at the end." Criterion for mastery is 80 percent.

house/boy	rug/hug	apple/donkey	desk/chair	book/look
store/more	grass/glass	chick/church	flower/tower	quiet/quick

■ DIRECTING THE LEARNER'S ATTENTION   The purpose of this task is to teach the learner the concept of different as it relates to the ending sounds of words. Next to identifying the beginning sounds, the most helpful cue to the learner seeking to identify unknown words is the ending sound. Typically, he will focus on the initial sound as his primary cue and then turn to the final sound as a secondary cue when needed. Therefore, he must be helped to isolate and identify the phonetic elements at the ends of words as well as at the beginning. At this beginning level, you must provide the learner with the concept of different and teach him how to determine what makes one word different from another at the end. When teaching this skill, you must be certain that the learner attends to your oral directions and to the ending sounds of each pair of words.

> **Key objective** for developing skill in noting differences in the ending sounds of words and in identifying specific ending sounds.

■ TEACHING ACTIVITIES / *The model activity*   Say a single word and have the learner repeat the word. Then say the ending sound of the word and ask the learner to repeat this. *Note:* In repeating ending sounds of rhyming words such as *rug* and *hug*, the sound to be said is *ug*. However, in repeating the ending consonant sound in words such as *fish*, you should employ the say-it-slow,-say-it-fast technique described in the storehouse of activities for IIB 2. For example, you can say, "Listen carefully as I say this word slowly. Fi——sh. Now I'll say it fast. Fish." In using this latter technique, always put the word back together fast so the learner gets in the habit of viewing the word as a whole and not as isolated sounds. Provide a second word, repeating the above process. Then say the first word, its ending sound, the second word, its ending sound, and ask the learner to repeat these. Then say, "Is the ending sound in the first word the same as the ending sound in the second word?"

/ *Suggestions for reteaching and/or practice*

1   Recite lines from familiar poems, leaving out the rhyming word in the second line of the couplet. Directions to the learner are, "What word goes here? What other word does it sound like? In what way does it sound like it?" Then you may say, "Can you think of another word whose ending sounds like these two words?"

2 You can play the game, "I am going to Africa." You say, "I am going to Africa, I'm going to take a ring, and I will sing. Who can go to Africa with me?" The learner must respond with something he is going to take to Africa which also ends with the *ing* rhyme. For example, if you are working with ending rhymes, he might say he is going to take a *swing*. If you are working with the ending *ng* sound, he might say he is going to take a *song*.

3 You say, "Let's play a game with words." Choose a rhyming pattern and say two words, elongating the first sound, as in "b——at, s——at, c——." In the third instance the learner completes the word. This activity can also be modified for use with ending consonant sounds as well as with rhymes.

4 Pronounce a word for the learner. He listens and then provides another word that ends with the same sound.

5 Direct the learner to listen to the ending sounds of the three words you are about to say to him, telling him that you want him to tell you which words end with the same sound. Then provide him with three words such as *hat, sit,* and *fad*.

6 Pronounce pairs of words. Direct the learner to say "Yes" if both words end with the same sound and to say "No" if they do not.

7 Direct the learner to point to and name things in the classroom or in collected pictures that end with the same sound as his name (or with the same sound as in ——).

8 Construct a shallow box divided into four squares. Place a key picture in each of the top two squares. Provide the learner with a group of pictures, directing him to sort the pictures and place them in the square beneath the picture with the same ending sound.

9 If he has difficulty in distinguishing the ending sounds, provide the learner with a mirror and help him to note how he forms the sounds at the end of words. Encourage him to use physical clues, such as the position of his tongue, to help him distinguish one ending sound from another.

10 All the techniques, activities, and games described for teaching beginning sounds (see II B 2) can be modified and used to help teach ending sounds.

■ THE POSTTEST The procedure and criterion for mastery are the same as for the pretest.

pipe/table	book/sit	play/stay	jump/bump	fly/sky
black/stack	pencil/pen	thank/thumb	floor/flew	fishhook/bookend

■ THE PERFORMANCE OBJECTIVE   Given a spoken stimulus word beginning with either the *m* or *d* sound and a group of three other words one of which begins with the *m* or *d* sound, the learner pairs the two words beginning with the same sound.

■ THE PRETEST   Using the word sets listed below, say to the learner, "Here are three words. Listen carefully." (Say the three words.) "Which one sounds like (say the stimulus word) at the beginning?" (Repeat the three words.) Criterion for mastery is 5 out of 6 correct.

elephant / pencil / monkey   Which one sounds like *mouse* at the beginning?
                                Repeat first three words.
milk / coat / bicycle   Which one sounds like *mouse* at the beginning?
                                Repeat first three words.
dinosaur / tree / baby   Which one sounds like *dog* at the beginning?
                                Repeat first three words.
never / music / needle   Which one sounds like *mouse* at the beginning?
                                Repeat first three words.
dive / plane / sky   Which one sounds like *dog* at the beginning?
                                Repeat first three words.
baby / balloon / dump truck   Which one sounds like *dog* at the beginning?
                                Repeat first three words.

Do your learners like you? If not, check your reinforcement system (see Chapter 3).

■ DIRECTING THE LEARNER'S ATTENTION   The purpose of this task is to cue the learner to the importance of listening to the beginning sounds of words and to help him distinguish the *m* and the *d* sounds from other consonant sounds. As such, the task is similar to that described in IIB 2, and you should select your teaching activity from among the storehouse of teaching techniques described there. When teaching this skill, you must be certain that the learner attends to the oral directions and to the beginning sounds of the words in each spoken sequence.

■ THE POSTTEST   Procedure and criterion for mastery are the same as the pretest.

can / sidewalk / did   Which one sounds like *dog* at the beginning?
                                Repeat the first three words.
book / mine / cloud   Which one sounds like *mouse* at the beginning?
                                Repeat the first three words.

dark / bird / shoot	Which one sounds like *dog* at the beginning? Repeat the first three words.
sign / doctor / ball	Which one sounds like *dog* at the beginning? Repeat the first three words.
moon / go / car	Which one sounds like *mouse* at the beginning? Repeat the first three words.
mother / school / night	Which one sounds like *mouse* at the beginning? Repeat the first three words.

IIB 5 KEY OBJECTIVE

■ THE PERFORMANCE OBJECTIVE Given spoken words beginning with *m* or *d* sounds, the learner identifies the beginning letter as *m* or *d*.

■ THE PRETEST Give the learner two cards, one with the letter *m* printed on it and the other with the letter *d* printed on it. Say the following words, directing the learner to point to the letter that begins the word. Criterion for mastery is 80 percent, with no letter sound being missed more than once.

menthol	deadeye	den	dial	match
mast	mammoth	design	may	duffel

■ DIRECTING THE LEARNER'S ATTENTION The purpose of this task is to help the learner establish a sound-symbol connection between the letters *m* and *d* and words that begin with the *m* and *d* sounds. This is a particularly crucial task for the reader to learn, since his ability to analyze or sound out the word *man* will depend to a large extent on his ability to connect the correct sound with the letter *m*, while his ability to sound out the word *dog* will depend largely on his ability to connect the correct sound with the letter *d*. This task requires both visual and auditory attention on the part of the learner, since he must *listen* to the sound produced as he *looks* at the visual form of the letter. Therefore, when teaching this skill you must be certain that the learner attends to the sound at the beginning of each spoken word while simultaneously looking at the card containing the correct letter.

Key objective for developing skill in establishing connections between alphabet letters and the sounds they produce.

■ TEACHING ACTIVITIES / *The model activity* Gather together a series of objects or pictures the names of which begin with the letter to be taught.

Put these in a sack and direct the learner to select at random an object or a picture from the sack. Direct him to name the object, pair it with the letter card on his desk, and say the name of the object while looking at both the object and the letter card. Ask him, "What letter does ———— begin with?" He responds by saying, "———— begins with the letter —." Then say, "Can you think of another word that begins with this letter?" When he responds correctly, have the learner take both the object and the letter card to a specified place where he repeats the name of the object while looking at both the object and the letter card.

To illustrate, if you are working with the letter *m*, the sack would have objects or pictures of objects such as *money*, *mice*, and *men*, and each learner would have on his desk a card with the letter *m* printed on it. If he draws some money from the sack, he puts that to the right of the letter *m* on his desk and says "Money" while looking at both the money and the letter *m*. When you ask him what letter *money* begins with, he responds by saying, "*Money* begins with the letter *m*." When asked for another word beginning with that letter, he might respond with "Monkey."

This process can then be reversed by having the learner pick the letter card out of the sack and directing him to match it with an object or picture whose name begins with that sound.

/ *Suggestions for reteaching and/or practice*

1 Give the learner a card with the letter to be learned on it and pictures of objects the names of which begin with that sound. Direct him to place the letter card to the left of each object, to get his mouth ready to make the sound while looking at the card, and to name the object in one sweep of sound. For example, if the letter to be learned is *m* and the object is *money*, the learner places the letter *m* to the left of the money, looks at the letter card, and says, "M——money."

2 Make a shutter device out of tagboard so that you can control the opening of the shutter. Insert a card that has the letter to be learned at the left and, on the right, a picture of an object having a name that begins with the sound of that letter. Open the shutter to reveal first the letter and then the picture. Direct the learner to form the letter sound with his mouth and to blend that sound into the picure name as it is exposed.

3 Use the same device as described in No. 2, but this time insert a picture first, then the letter, then the picture again. Direct the learner to say the picture name, then the letter sound heard at the beginning of the picture name, and finally to blend that sound into the picture name as it is exposed the second time.

4 Use flash cards containing the letters to be learned. Flash a letter to the learner and direct him to respond with a word in his vocabulary that begins with that letter sound. Encourage the learner to "get his mouth ready" to say the sound as he sees the letter. This will provide him with a lead-in to the whole word.

5 To help the learner connect the letter and the sound, display pictures of common objects, such as *dogs, money,* etc., with the letter the object begins with printed to the left of the picture. Encourage the learner to use these pictures when trying to remember the sound that a particular letter produces.

6 Make a box and label it with a large printed form of the letter you are teaching. Place in the box pictures and objects the names of which begin with the letter to be learned. Direct the learner to reach into the box, draw a picture or object, name it, and tell with what letter the name of the object begins. Make sure he looks at the letter on the box while saying the name of the object.

7 For learners who need review on a number of letters and their corresponding sounds, you may modify the activity described in No. 6 by placing several letters on the outside of the box and by placing objects that begin with all these letters in the box. The learner then draws an object, names it, and points to the letter on the box with which the name of the object begins.

8 Give each learner a group of pictures, some of which begin with the letter to be worked on and some of which do not. Hold up a letter card and direct the learner to hold up any picture he has that begins with the sound associated with that letter.

9 Using a flannelboard or a pocket chart, place a letter card to the left and a row of three pictures to the right. Two of the pictures should begin with the sound associated with the letter at the left and one should not. Direct the learner to pick out the two pictures that begin with the sound associated with the letter at the left.

10 Make a bulletin board or a large chart showing the letters to be learned. Beside each letter have a flap under which is a picture of an object the name of which begins with the sound associated with that letter. The learner can use this device to remind himself of the letter sound. When he cannot remember the sound of *m*, for example, he can go to the bulletin board, look under the flap next to *m* and say to himself, "Oh, the sound of *m* is what we hear at the beginning of *money*" (or whatever is pictured under the flap).

11 Make a tagboard chart with the letters to be learned listed down one side and pictures beginning with the sounds of these letters listed down the other. Attach pieces of string to the letters and direct the learner to connect the string for each letter to an object the name of which begins with the sound of that letter.

12 Provide the learner with a number of letters. Play a game with him in which you say, "I see a letter whose sound we hear at the beginning of the word *money*. What letter do I see?" The learner responds by holding up the proper letter card, looking at it, and saying, "*Money* begins with the letter *m*."

13 Make a set of picture cards for each letter sound being learned. Teach the learner to play a card game in which several cards are dealt to each player. The learner tries to pair picture cards beginning with the same letter sound. Each player takes turns asking his opponents, "Do you have a picture card beginning with the letter *m*?" If one does, he gives the picture card to the learner requesting it and then has the opportunity to draw a card from the learner's hand in return. The learner having the most pairs at the end wins.

14 Give the learners a group of letter cards. Each learner takes turns saying, "I have a letter. *Money* starts with the sound of my letter. What letter do I have?" The learner who responds correctly is the next one to select a letter.

15 Play a game of dramatization with learners in which you hold up a letter card and ask them to act out something that begins with the sound of that letter. The rest of the learners must try to guess what begins with the letter sound that the actor is dramatizing.

■ THE POSTTEST   Procedure and criterion for mastery remain the same as for the pretest.

deadly	machine	delay	march	dusty
magnet	maple	demand	meter	deputy

IIB **6**

■ THE PERFORMANCE OBJECTIVE   Given a spoken stimulus word beginning with either the *l* or hard *c* sound and a group of three other words one of which begins with the *l* or hard *c* sound, the learner pairs the two words beginning with the same sound.

■ THE PRETEST   Using the word sets below, say to the learner, "Here are three words. Listen carefully." (Say the three words.) "Which one sounds like (say the stimulus word) at the beginning?" (Then repeat the first three words.) Criterion for mastery is 5 out of 6 correct.

dog / pipe / list	Which one sounds like *lip* at the beginning? Then repeat first three words.
last / toe / feel	Which one sounds like *lip* at the beginning? Then repeat first three words.
tall / bell / cake	Which one sounds like *can* at the beginning? Then repeat first three words.
hate / list / purr	Which one sounds like *lip* at the beginning? Then repeat first three words.

kite / book / hat	Which one sounds like *can* at the beginning? Then repeat first three words.
pen / flower / cup	Which one sounds like *can* at the beginning? Then repeat first three words.

■ DIRECTING THE LEARNER'S ATTENTION The purpose of this task is to cue the learner to the importance of listening to the beginning sounds of words and to help him distinguish the *l* and hard *c* sounds from other consonant sounds. This task is similar to that described in IIB 2, and you should select your teaching activity from among the storehouse of techniques described there. When teaching this skill, you must be certain that the learner attends to the oral directions and to the beginning sounds of the words in each spoken sequence.

■ THE POSTTEST Procedure and criterion for mastery are the same as for the pretest.

bowl / table / like	Which one sounds like *lip* at the beginning? Then repeat the first three words.
loop / pick / fall	Which one sounds like *lip* at the beginning? Then repeat the first three words.
fell / leaf / come	Which one sounds like *can* at the beginning? Then repeat the first three words.
far / lend / bush	Which one sounds like *lip* at the beginning? Then repeat the first three words.
car / dope / sell	Which one sounds like *can* at the beginning? Then repeat the first three words.
pat / sleep / cap	Which one sounds like *can* at the beginning? Then repeat the first three words.

IIB 7

■ THE PERFORMANCE OBJECTIVE Given spoken words beginning with *l* or hard *c* sounds, the learner identifies the beginning letters as *l* or *c*.

■ THE PRETEST Give the learner two cards, one with the letter *l* printed on it and the other with the letter *c* printed on it. Say the following words, directing the learner to point to the letter that begins the word. Criterion for mastery is 80 percent.

loop	lucky	catch	loose	cannon
coupon	custom	lamp	locket	cover

Have you reread Appendix H to see if you are meeting the learning conditions necessary for successful skill instruction?

■ DIRECTING THE LEARNER'S ATTENTION   The purpose of this task is to help the learner establish a sound-symbol connection between the letters *l* and *c* and words that begin with the *l* and hard *c* sounds. This task is similar to that described in IIB 5, and you should select your teaching activity from among the storehouse of techniques described there. When teaching this skill, you must be certain that the learner attends to the sound at the beginning of each spoken word while simultaneously looking at the card containing that letter.

■ THE POSTTEST   Procedure and criterion for mastery remain the same as in pretest.

last	loaf	cabbage	lady	costume
carton	cardinal	locust	lower	carve

IIB 8

■ THE PERFORMANCE OBJECTIVE   Given a spoken stimulus word that begins with either the *s* or *h* sound and a group of three other words one of which begins with the *s* or *h* sound, the learner pairs the two words beginning with the same sound.

■ THE PRETEST   Using the words listed below, say to the learner, "Here are three words. Listen carefully." (Say the three words.) "Which one sounds like (say the stimulus word) at the beginning?" (Then repeat the first three words.) Criterion for mastery is 5 out of 6 correct.

cow / luck / soon	Which one sounds like *sew* at the beginning? Then repeat the first three words.
sit / roll / fall	Which one sounds like *sew* at the beginning? Then repeat the first three words.
ball / pit / has	Which one sounds like *his* at the beginning? Then repeat the first three words.
sock / bike / leg	Which one sounds like *sew* at the beginning? Then repeat the first three words.
hit / glass / roof	Which one sounds like *his* at the beginning? Then repeat the first three words.
paper / tall / hunt	Which one sounds like *his* at the beginning? Then repeat the first three words.

■ DIRECTING THE LEARNER'S ATTENTION   The purpose of this task is to cue the learner to the importance of listening to the beginning sounds of words and to help him distinguish the sounds of *s* and *h* from other consonant sounds. This task is similar to that described in IIB 2, and you should select your teaching activity from among the storehouse of techniques described there. When teaching this skill, you must be certain that the learner attends to the oral directions and to the beginning sounds of the words in each spoken sequence.

■ THE POSTTEST Procedure and criterion for mastery remain the same as for the pretest.

cash / loop / sip	Which one sounds like *sew* at the beginning? Then repeat the first three words.
suck / rice / fish	Which one sounds like *sew* at the beginning? Then repeat the first three words.
bill / past / hurt	Which one sounds like *his* at the beginning? Then repeat the first three words.
sort / bill / lake	Which one sounds like *sew* at the beginning? Then repeat the first three words.
horse / glue / row	Which one sounds like *his* at the beginning? Then repeat the first three words.
past / teach / hand	Which one sounds like *his* at the beginning? Then repeat the first three words.

IIB 9

■ THE PERFORMANCE OBJECTIVE Given spoken words beginning with *s* or *h* sounds, the learner identifies the beginning letter as being either *s* or *h*.

■ THE PRETEST Give the learner two cards, one having the letter *s* printed on it and the other having the letter *h* printed on it. Say the following words, directing the learner to point to the letter that begins the word. Criterion for mastery is 80 percent.

| silly | soap | set | hick | sunny |
| hide | house | single | happy | hippy |

■ DIRECTING THE LEARNER'S ATTENTION The purpose of the task is to help the learner establish a sound-symbol connection between the letters *s* and *h* and words that begin with the sounds of *s* and *h*. This task is similar to that described in IIB 5, and you should select your teaching activity from among the storehouse of techniques described there. When teaching this skill, you must be certain that the learner attends to the sound at the beginning of each spoken word while simultaneously looking at the card containing that letter.

■ THE POSTTEST Procedure and criterion for mastery remain the same as in the pretest.

| high | settle | hobby | soup | hill |
| same | supper | hard | hurry | saddle |

■ THE PERFORMANCE OBJECTIVE Given a spoken incomplete sentence, the learner adds words necessary to make a complete and grammatically sensible sentence unit.

■ THE PRETEST Read aloud the following sentence fragments (or others that you feel would be appropriate for your particular group), directing the learner to "Finish what I want to say."

Criterion for mastery is the addition of any words that are grammatically accurate and that produce a complete sentence. Four out of 5 sentences must meet this criterion.

At the grocery store, my mother bought . . . .

Most brothers and sisters . . . .

Sometimes the weather is . . . .

Will you . . . ?

If . . . ?

■ DIRECTING THE LEARNER'S ATTENTION The purpose of this task is to help the learner develop the ability to use context and to anticipate meaning. When teaching this skill, you must be certain that the learner attends to the directions and to the meaning of the words provided.

■ TEACHING ACTIVITIES / *The model activity* This type of learning can be done in a game situation. A typical example is: "Let's play a game before we go to recess. Let's see if you can guess what I have in my head. I'm going to say some words. You listen carefully because when I stop, I want you to see if you can finish what I want to say." You then produce the beginning of a sentence as described in the pretest and stop before completing it. The learner is encouraged to produce as many endings as he can.

/ Suggestions for reteaching and/or practice

1 This learning activity presupposes a sophisticated oral language base. If the learner has persistent difficulty with this task, you can create model structures and then repeat part of the structure for the learner, asking him to finish it. For example, you can say, "We put the game into the cupboard." Then say, "We put the . . ." and ask the learner to complete what was just said. This is a memory task, but it can be transferred into a context task by encouraging the learner to create alternate solutions to the model structure. For example, the learner could be led to say, "We put the game on the table," etc.

2 Any oral activity such as "Show and Tell" will support this learning task and will provide the teacher with the opportunity to develop a sense of context.

3 As learners become sophisticated in this skill, they can be asked to produce sentences in which each supplies one word. For example, you can say, "I," next learner says, "go," the next learner says, "to," and so on until a thought is completed.

■ THE POSTTEST   Procedure and criterion for mastery are the same as for the pretest.

I live on . . . .   It was raining and I . . . .

Do you like . . . ?   I like to go to . . . .

The bird is . . . .

IIB ▇

■ THE PERFORMANCE OBJECTIVE   Given a spoken sentence in which one word is missing, the learner supplies a word in the missing spot to make a complete and sensible sentence unit.

■ THE PRETEST   Read aloud the following sentences one at a time, saying the word *blank* where the omitted word should go. Following each sentence, say, "What word should go in the place where I said "Blank" to make the sentence say what I want it to say?" Criterion for mastery is the addition of any word that makes sense and that is grammatically accurate. Four out of 5 of the sentences must meet this criterion.

I wore my bathing suit when I went ——.

When the dog saw the man, he started to ——.

It started to rain, and I got all ——.

The boy and the —— were jumping rope.

Out on the ——, we played with the ball.

■ DIRECTING THE LEARNER'S ATTENTION   The purpose of this task is to help the learner develop the ability to use context to anticipate a single unknown word. When teaching this skill, you must be certain that the learner attends to the directions and grasps the sense of the sentence.

■ TEACHING ACTIVITIES / *The model activity*   Use the model provided for IIB 10, but modify the activity to fit a situation in which only one word, rather than a group of words, is missing.

/ *Suggestions for reteaching and/or practice*

1 Develop some paragraphs about topics familiar to the learner. Leave out the last word in each paragraph. Read the paragraph orally, directing the learner to supply the last word. A typical paragraph might be one like the following:

My Daddy was making me a desk in the cellar. Suddenly, I heard him shout. "Ouch," he said, "I hit my thumb with my ———."

2 When you read stories or poems to your class, examine the material ahead of time, looking for places where, if you stopped reading, the learners might be able to supply the next word. Mark these spots, and occasionally try this device as you read to the class.

3 Encourage your learners to make up their own oral sentences in which a word is left out. They can then try these with each other.

4 Try a variation of a chain story with your learners. The first learner starts an oral sentence, but leaves the last word or phrase out. The next learner supplies that word or phrase. Then the next learner must start a new sentence that continues from the first, leaving off the last word or phrase. This procedure is followed until the story is completed.

5 The idea of a chain story as described in No. 4 can be adapted for use with familiar, often-told stories, such as "Goldilocks and the Three Bears." This technique is particularly effective with learners who initially seem unable to generate their own sentences independently.

6 If the learner has persistent difficulties with the task, he should be redirected to IIB 10 and provided with more experience at that level before being required to perform on this objective.

■ THE POSTTEST Procedure and criterion for mastery remain the same as for the pretest.

My ears were cold so I put on my ———.

They got into a fight and started to ——— each other.

The bright sun made me feel very ———.

At the park we played on the swings and made castles in the ———.

During the ——— I had a bad dream.

KEY OBJECTIVE IIB **12**

■ THE PERFORMANCE OBJECTIVE Given an oral sentence with one word missing and cued for the missing word with a card having printed on it the first letter of that word (*m, d, l, c, s, h*), the learner says a word that fits the context and begins with that letter sound.

■ THE PRETEST Make cards with the above letters printed on them. Say, "I am going to read you a sentence with one word missing. You look at the card and say a word that begins with the letter on the card and that finishes what I want to say." Use the following sentences. Display the letter card only when you come to the blank. Criterion for mastery is 10 out of 12, with no letter being missed more than once. *Caution:* If, in your judgment, the learner's experience does not match the context of any or all of these sentences, construct alternate sentences appropriate to his background. This caution applies to all context tasks that follow.

I like to spend m——.

I gave a bone to the d——.

The hat looks pretty on the l——.

A c—— likes to drink milk.

The s—— was shining brightly.

The man was painting the h——.

I have m—— toys.

I like to d—— when I swim.

I l—— at the funny joke.

Can you c—— me?

The mattress is s——.

H—— me find my pencil. It is lost.

■ DIRECTING THE LEARNER'S ATTENTION   The purpose of this task is to help the learner use his knowledge of context sense and letter–sound correspondence to identify unknown words. In prior objectives, the learner has been taught what is meant by the beginning of a spoken word, has learned to differentiate certain sounds at the beginning of words, has associated these sounds with certain letters, and has learned to anticipate the appearance of certain words in a sentence because of the context effect. In this objective, the learner is helped to use all these skills in combination as a means for quickly identifying unknown words. To teach this effectively, you must provide the learner with a sentence that is clear and full of clues regarding its topic, and you must provide him with the beginning letter of the word missing from the sentence. (This letter must always be one for which he has a sound association.) When teaching this skill, you must be certain that the learner attends to the directions, to the sense of the sentence, and to the letter provided and its sound value.

Key objective for developing skill in using both context sense and letter-sound correspondence to identify unknown words.

■ TEACHING ACTIVITIES / *The model activity*   Since the learner has previously completed objectives on both context and sound-symbol correspondence, his difficulty with this task may be related to a misunderstanding of the process itself. One activity that may clear up this difficulty is the following. Give the learner a letter card and have him supply a word beginning with that letter and a sentence in which he uses this word. Then have him say the sentence, omitting the word, and you supply the missing word. In other words, the pretest model simply has been reversed, with the learner in the teacher's role.

/ Suggestions for reteaching and/or practice

1 Learner difficulty in mastering this task is usually associated with an inadequate mastery of the prerequisite skills associated with context and sound–symbol connection of the letters being used. At the first sign of learner difficulty, you should check his proficiency in using context generally and his mastery of the letters and sounds being used, redirecting him as needed to the storehouse activities described in the objectives where these were originally taught.

2 Read a paragraph to the learner. Tell him that you will stop reading every once in awhile and hold up a letter card. Direct him to keep the paragraph in mind, to look at the letter on the card, to think of the sound associated with that letter, and to say a word that both begins with that letter sound and that fits the sense of the paragraph.

3 Play games with the learner that require him to use both context and sound–symbol connections as a part of his participation. For example, direct the learner to listen to a sentence such as, "I went to the store and bought a mouse, a ———, a ———, and a ———." Hold up a letter card to indicate the beginning sound of each unknown word. The learner expands the sentence by adding words that begin with the sound associated with the letter you show.

4 Group your learners in pairs. Give each pair a supply of letter cards. Let each take a turn in making up a sentence in which one word is left out. The learner must hold up the beginning letter of the missing word at the appropriate spot in the sentence. His opponent uses the sense of the sentence and the sound–symbol connection of the letter card to guess what word goes in the space. If he correctly identifies the missing word, it is his turn to make up a sentence.

5 Give learners riddles in which the context supplies only a minimum outline of what the missing word is. For example, you could provide the sentence, "The swimmer dived into the ———." Elicit learner response, encouraging a variety of answers, such as *water, pool, lake,* and *river.* Then place a letter card, such as the letter *w,* at the left of the blank space and say, "Now what word must go in the blank space?"

■ THE POSTTEST   Procedure and criterion for mastery remain the same as on the pretest.

The sun comes out in daytime but the m—— comes out at night.

When you cross the street, you m—— look both days.

The teacher said, "Shut the d——."

What do you d—— on a rainy day?

It is dark. Turn on the l——.

I l—— candy.

Don't eat c—— before dinner.

Will you c—— to my party?

Put your shoes and s—— under the bed.

Wash your hand with s—— and water.

He put the h—— on his head.

I h—— a new bicycle.

IIIA

WHAT THE LEARNER LOOKS AT

IIIA **1**

■ THE PERFORMANCE OBJECTIVE   Given three letters that are exactly alike and one that is somewhat similar, the learner marks the one that is different.

■ THE PRETEST   Direct the learners to indicate (mark or point to as appropriate) which letter in each of the following sets is different. Criterion for mastery is 80 percent.

SET I	q	q	g	q		SET VI	o	o	o	c
SET II	o	a	a	a		SET VII	p	q	p	p
SET III	m	n	m	n		SET VIII	l	l	h	l
SET IV	v	v	v	u		SET IX	w	w	w	v
SET V	b	d	b	b		SET X	i	i	j	i

■ DIRECTING THE LEARNER'S ATTENTION   The purpose of this task is to teach the learner to note the fine differences in letters. This task is similar to that described in IA 1, and you should select your teaching activity from among the storehouse of techniques described there. When teaching this skill, you must be certain that the learner attends to the oral directions and to the visual form of the letters in each set.

■ THE POSTTEST   Same directions and criterion for mastery as on the pretest.

SET I	l	l	i	l		SET VI	t	l	t	t
SET II	o	o	o	c		SET VII	e	e	e	a
SET III	y	y	g	y		SET VIII	q	p	q	q
SET IV	d	b	d	d		SET IX	n	m	n	n
SET V	u	u	u	v		SET X	w	w	m	w

IIIA **2**

■ THE PERFORMANCE OBJECTIVE   Given a few seconds to examine a letter that is easily confused with other letters, the learner reproduces the letter from memory, to the satisfaction of the teacher.

■ THE PRETEST   Prepare 10 flash cards, each card having one of the following letters printed on it.

g   a   m   v   b   o   p   h   w   i

Flash each for the count of three. Then direct the learner to reproduce it. Criterion for mastery is teacher judgment.

■ DIRECTING THE LEARNER'S ATTENTION   The purpose of this task is to develop the learner's visual memory for easily confused letters. This task is similar to that described in IA 2, and you should select your teaching activity from among the storehouse of techniques described there. Remember to be certain that the learner attends to the letter to be remembered for as long as it is shown.

■ THE POSTTEST   The procedure and the criterion for mastery is the same as for the pretest. Use the following sequence of letters:

q   o   n   u   d   c   p   l   v   j

IIIA 3

■ THE PERFORMANCE OBJECTIVE   Given three words that are exactly alike and one word that is somewhat similar, the learner marks the word that is different.

■ THE PRETEST   Direct the learner to indicate (mark or point to as appropriate) which word in each of the following sets is different. Criterion for mastery is 80 percent.

SET I	dog / dog / cat / dog	SET VI	look / book / look / look
SET II	girl / boy / girl / girl	SET VII	like / lake / lake / lake
SET III	to / to / to / on	SET VIII	box / dox / box / box
SET IV	ten / ten / net / ten	SET IX	chair / chair / chair / char
SET V	fox / box / box / box	SET X	saw / was / was / was

■ DIRECTING THE LEARNER'S ATTENTION   The purpose of this task is to teach the learner to note the fine differences in words. This task is similar to that described in IA 1, and you should select your teaching activity from among the storehouse of techniques described there. When teaching this skill, you must be certain that the learner attends to your oral directions and to the key visual discriminator found in each word in each set.

■ THE POSTTEST   Procedure and criterion for mastery are the same as for the pretest.

SET I	desk / desk / desk / chair	SET VI	fish / wish / fish / fish
SET II	bird / song / bird / bird	SET VII	bake / bike / bike / bike
SET III	in / in / in / on	SET VIII	dog / bog / dog / dog
SET IV	ban / ban / nab / ban	SET IX	ship / ship / ship / shin
SET V	mop / top / top / top	SET X	on / no / on / on

IIIA 4

■ THE PERFORMANCE OBJECTIVE   Given a few seconds to examine a word that is easily confused with other words, the learner reproduces the word from memory to the satisfaction of the teacher.

■ THE PRETEST   Prepare 10 flash cards, each card having one of the following words printed on it. Flash each for the count of three. Then direct the learner to reproduce it. Criterion for mastery is teacher judgment.

dog   cat   boy   to   ten   fox   look   like   box   saw

■ DIRECTING THE LEARNER'S ATTENTION   The purpose of the task is to develop the learner's visual memory for easily confused word forms. This task is similar to that described in IA 2, and you should select your teaching activity from among the storehouse of techniques described there. When teaching this skill, you must be certain that the learner attends to your oral directions and to the visual form of the word for as long as it is shown.

■ THE POSTTEST   Procedure and criterion for mastery are the same as on the pretest. Use the following sequence of words.

girl   on   net   box   book   lake   chair   was   fox   to

IIIA 5

■ THE PERFORMANCE OBJECTIVE   Given a few seconds to examine a word, the learner picks out another word with the same initial consonant from among a group of four words.

■ THE PRETEST   Prepare flash cards, each having printed on it one of the words listed at the left in the following sequence. Give the learner a duplicated list that has printed on it the five sets of four words each shown at the right below. Flash each card for the count of three and direct the learner to mark the word in the set which has the same first letter. Criterion for mastery is 80 percent.

SET I	love	take / come / look / boy
SET II	kite	kiss / card / board / pipe
SET III	hit	paper / cat / hole / done
SET IV	men	now / make / near / win
SET V	dig	big / pig / did / gig

■ DIRECTING THE LEARNER'S ATTENTION   The purpose of this task is to cue the learner to the importance of visually noting and remembering the first letter in words. When teaching this skill, you must be certain that the learner attends to the oral directions, to the first letter of the flashed word, and to the first letters of the response words.

Are you reading and applying those sections in each objective titled, "Directing the Learner's Attention"?

■ TEACHING ACTIVITIES / *The model activity*   A learner who has difficulty with this task should be cued to vocalizing the first letter of the flash word. For example, if the flashed word is *love*, the learner should be told to say "*l*" and to use this as his cue when he looks at the response words.

/ *Suggestions for reteaching and/or practice*

If the learner has persistent difficulty with this task, the problem lies either with a misunderstanding regarding the concept of first and last or with a visual memory difficulty. Therefore, learners having problems with this task should be redirected to IB 5 and IB 7 to check on the first and last concept and to IIIA 2 and IIIA 4 to check on the visual memory skills.

■ THE POSTTEST   Procedure and criterion for mastery remain the same as in the pretest.

SET I	like	task / cool / love / bang
SET II	kitchen	keep / cord / bottle / pasture
SET III	house	part / candy / harder / donkey
SET IV	mine	never / mask / next / window
SET V	doll	ball / tall / down / fall

IIIA **6** KEY OBJECTIVE

■ THE PERFORMANCE OBJECTIVE   Given a fraction of a second to examine each of 10 flash cards having printed on them words he selected as wanting to learn to read, the learner pronounces each word within one second.

■ THE PRETEST   This pretest presupposes another activity—one in which you elicit from the learner the 10 words he would like to learn to read. Once he selects the words, you print each on separate flash cards. Then flash each word to the learner, giving him only a second or less to examine the word. Criterion for mastery is 100 percent. *Note:* You should keep track of the words missed on the pretest because it is only the missed words that need to be taught.

■ DIRECTING THE LEARNER'S ATTENTION   The purpose of this task is to teach the learner to recognize and pronounce words of his choice instantly when they are printed on cards. Though he has been taught previously to recognize instantly the words *yes, no,* and his name, this is the first of a series of objectives in which the learner will be taught instantly to recognize multiple words.

The task of recognizing words instantly is a crucial one for the learner for several reasons. First, our job is to develop readers who read fluently, not readers who must analyze and sound out each word in turn. Fluent readers are readers who can instantly recognize words. Second, since many of the words we read in the English language do not lend themselves to sounding out because they do not follow the common phonetic principles of the language. The only efficient way to teach such words is to help the learner recognize each at sight. Finally, to master the complete phonetic system of English is a long and laborious process, and if we were to wait until the learner mastered this system, it would take too long before we let him read independently. By teaching him to read certain words instantly, we are allowing him to read independently many materials at a stage when he would otherwise be unable to do so.

The learning of words at sight is a visual task, and you must provide the learner with the skill of looking at a word, noting its distinguishing visual characteristics, and forming a visual memory of the word. The previously taught objectives relating to visual discrimination and visual memory are crucial prerequisites to this task, and learners who experience difficulty here should be redirected to those earlier objectives.

In teaching this skill, you must be certain that the learner attends to the visual form of the word and to its distinguishing characteristics. At this stage, the primary characteristics will be the beginning and ending letters.

Key objective for developing skill in recognizing words instantly.

■ TEACHING ACTIVITIES / *The model activity* For every two words the learner needs to learn, follow this procedure. First, make him familiar with the words by telling him what they are, by getting him to say the words, and by having him use them in sentences. Second, when it is obvious that he is familiar with the words and can use them in his oral language, show him the printed form of the words, saying, "Here's the word that says ———." "And here is the word that says ———." Third, connect the visual form of the word with the word name by saying, "Now, look at the word and say its name. Now look at this word and say its name. Who can look at this word and say its name?" Fourth, give the learner a chance to respond by asking questions such as "Who can hold up the word card that says ———?" Or you can start a sentence and have the learner point to the card that has printed on it the word which completes the sentence. Don't forget the importance of first and last letters as memory aids.

/ Suggestions for reteaching and/or practice

1 Difficult words can be put on flash cards. Direct the learner to examine each word carefully and to note characteristics of the word, such as initial and final letters, length, shape, and double letters, that will help him to remember its form. Then the word is flashed to him repeatedly.

2 Words that are unusually difficult can be taught through the sense of touch. Print a large form of the word on paper, in sand, or on some rough material such as sandpaper, saying the word as you print it. Direct the learner to trace your copy, also saying the word as he traces. Repeat this several times, then direct the learner to write the word independently, again saying it as he writes.

3 Write the words to be learned at sight on the chalkboard. One learner is sent out into the hall and another goes to the board and points to one of the words. The rest of the class pronounces the word to be certain that all the learners know it. Then the first learner is brought back into the room and he tries to guess which word has been pointed to. He points to one word and says, "Is it ———?" He continues in this way until he identifies the word.

4 Make up racing games in which learners progress in the race by pronouncing at sight the words to be learned. For example, construct an auto-racing course, dividing the track into squares of equal size. Give each learner a toy racing car, and provide yourself with a pack of cards on which are printed the words you want the class to learn. Flash one word to each learner in turn. If he pronounces it instantly, he moves his racing car one square closer to the finish line. If he is unable to pronounce the word, his car does not move. The first learner to get his car to the finish line wins.

5 Help learners construct self-help references for the words they find difficult. For instance, each learner can be provided with a 3- by 5-inch file box and a supply of file cards. He then writes each word he has difficulty in learning on the file card together with a picture or other aid to help him remember the word. The learner refers to his file frequently to study the words and to remind himself of what the word is if he is unable to identify it when he meets it in his reading.

6 A class dictionary can be made in which the new words to be taught are printed in alphabetical order in a large notebook. The learners use old magazines to find pictures illustrating the words. The learners are then encouraged to use this dictionary to look up a word whenever they are reading.

7 Words that are particularly difficult for the learner can be printed using color codes or some other device. This will direct the learner's attention to the part of the word that he needs to note most carefully in order to distinguish it from other similar words. For example, the words *where* and *there* may be printed on cards with the *wh* and *th* printed in red and the *ere* printed in black.

8 Make a habit of sending short personal notes to your learner. For example, when he comes in the room before school in the morning, he may find on his desk a note from you saying, "Can you help me at my desk?" or "How do you feel?" or even something as simple as "I like you." In leaving these notes, you should make sure that they use words that the learner needs to practice, but that no words are used that the learner has never been exposed to. This is a highly motivating device for encouraging a learner to master sight words.

9 Construct ladder games in which a paper ladder leads to a place where a reward of some kind is waiting. For example, the ladder can be leading to the upper branches of a paper apple tree with many paper apples on it. Each rung of the ladder has a sight word attached to it. The learner must pronounce the word on each rung of the ladder instantly. If he successfully reaches the top of the ladder, he receives a reward such as a real apple or a check on his progress chart.

10 A multitude of games for building sight words can be devised based on the idea of a trip. This trip may be a reconstruction of the adventures of some famous story character such as Peter Rabbit, a trip that the learners are actually going to go on, or a trip that is completely imaginary, such as a trip to the moon or a trip to a distant city. In any case, a gameboard is constructed upon which is drawn the path to be followed in reaching the destination, the hazards to be overcome along the way, and so on. Each learner progresses on his trip by correctly pronouncing the words flashed to him when his turn comes up. The first learner to complete the trip wins the game.

11 A fishing game can be played in which learners are given a pole constructed of a stick and a string with a magnet tied to the end. Paper fish with the words to be learned printed on them are placed in a box or something else that will serve as a pond. Attach a paper clip to each fish. Learners drop their line into the pond until the magnet attracts the paper clip on a fish. They pull the fish out and are permitted to keep it if they can correctly pronounce the word printed on its side. The learner who catches the most fish wins.

12 Make nine packs of 10 cards each. The nine packs represent the nine holes of a golf course, and the words printed on the cards are the words to be learned at sight. The cards are shuffled, and the player puts the pack for the first hole face down on his desk. He turns each card over in turn, pronounces it, and goes on. Every time he is unable to pronounce a word correctly, a mark is placed on the scorecard, and the number he gets wrong on the first hole (first pack of cards) is his score for that hole. He continues in this manner through the nine packs of word cards, trying to get as small a score as possible. You should encourage him to keep a chart record of his score on this course so that he can note his progress in "mastering the course." New courses offering new challenges can be constructed as new words need to be learned.

13 Put the words to be learned on cards, placing a numerical value in the upper right-hand corner of each card in accordance with its degree of difficulty in being remembered. For example, *dinosaur* is a fairly easy word for learners to identify and would only be given a value of 1, but *the* is very difficult for young learners to recognize and would be given a value of 3. Learners take turns drawing the cards, reading the words, and noting their scores. If they pronounce the word correctly, their score is the numerical value noted on the corner of the card. The learner with the most points at the end wins.

14 Play a treasure hunt game in which several packets of 10 or more words each are hidden around the classroom. Give the learner the first packet and direct him to read each word. He goes through the words as quickly as he can, and the last card will tell him where the next packet is hidden. He goes to that packet and repeats the process. The final packet will direct him to a spot in the classroom where he will receive a prize for having completed the game.

15 Another variation of television's "Concentration" game can be played. Place the words to be learned on cards and put them face down on the table. In picking up the cards, the learner must remember where there are two cards exactly alike and try to pick up matching pairs. As the player turns over each card, he must pronounce the word on the card. If he succeeds in picking up a word that matches the first word, he gets another turn. The learner with the most pairs at the end wins.

■ THE POSTTEST Procedure and criterion for mastery remain the same as for the pretest.

IIIA 7

■ THE PERFORMANCE OBJECTIVE Given a fraction of a second to examine flash cards having the following words printed on them, the learner pronounces each word within one second.

I   and   the   a   to   was   in   it   of   my   he

■ THE PRETEST   Print each of the above words on flash cards. Flash each card to the learner, giving him less than one second to examine each word, and have him pronounce the word aloud. Criterion for mastery is 100 percent.

■ DIRECTING THE LEARNER'S ATTENTION   The purpose of this task is to teach the learner to recognize instantly the words listed in the objective when they are printed on cards. This task is similar to that described in IIIA 6, and you should select your teaching activity from among the storehouse of techniques described there. When teaching this skill, you must be certain that the learner attends to the visual form of the word and to its distinguishing characteristics.

■ THE POSTTEST   The procedure and criterion for mastery remain the same as for the pretest.

IIIA 8

■ THE PERFORMANCE OBJECTIVE   Given cards with words he has learned to pronounce at sight printed on them, the learner, when directed, points to the first letter and then to the last letter in each of these words.

■ THE PRETEST   Provide the learner with cards on which are printed words he recognizes at sight. The learner reads each word and when directed points to the first and last letter in each of these words as he names them. The criterion for mastery is 100 percent.

■ DIRECTING THE LEARNER'S ATTENTION   The purpose of this task is to re-inforce the learner's understanding of the importance of the first and the last letters in words and to reinforce the concept of left-to-right progression in words. This task is similar to that described in IIA 8, and you should select your teaching activity from among the storehouse of techniques there. When teaching this skill, you must be certain that the learner attends to your oral directions, to the visual form of the word, and to the first and last letters in each word.

■ THE POSTTEST   Procedure and criterion for mastery remain the same as for the pretest.

IIIA 9

■ THE PERFORMANCE OBJECTIVE   Given sentence frames spoken by the teacher and words he recognizes printed on individual cards, the learner points to the card containing the word that completes the sentence frame.

■ THE PRETEST   Provide the learner with cards, each of which has printed on it a word he recognizes instantly. Then construct sentence frames, each sentence having a blank space that can be filled by one of the words the learner knows. For example, if one of the learner's self-selected words is *elephant*, a sentence such as the following can be constructed: "I went to the zoo and I saw an ———." Say each sentence to the learner, ask him to listen to it carefully, and direct him to point to the card that has printed on it the word "that finishes what I want to say." Criterion for mastery is 100 percent.

■ DIRECTING THE LEARNER'S ATTENTION   The purpose of the task is to teach the learner to use the words he recognizes at sight in a sentence context. When teaching this skill, you must be certain that the learner attends to the directions of the teacher, to the spoken sentence, and to the form of the words on the cards.

Does the environment of your room invite an interest in reading (see Chapter 7)?

■ TEACHING ACTIVITIES / *The model activity*   Give the learner the cards on which are printed the words he recognizes instantly. Direct him to point to and read one word. Have him make up a sentence of his own using the word. Then direct him to say a sentence skipping the word he chose and pointing to the card that names the omitted word. Then you point to a word card, say a sentence with that word omitted, and have the learner point to the card that names the omitted word. Finally, repeat the procedure outlined in the pretest above.

/ *Suggestions for reteaching and/or practice*

Learners who have persistent difficulty with this task should be redirected to IIB 10, IIB 11, and IIB 12 for review in the ability to use context in oral language.

■ THE POSTTEST   Procedures and criterion for mastery remain the same as for the pretest.

KEY OBJECTIVE IIIA 10

■ THE PERFORMANCE OBJECTIVE   Given words he instantly recognizes, the learner creates and reads a single-sentence story using these words.

■ THE PRETEST Provide the learner with cards, on each of which is printed a word that he recognizes instantly. Say to the learner, "Today, we are going to do something that is very hard. We are going to send messages. Look at the cards you have in front of you. Each card has a word on it that you know. Can you send me a message using the words you have there? If you want to send a message using a word you don't have on a card, tell me, and I will make a card for you having that word on it." Criterion for mastery is the combination of any number of words that is grammatically accurate and that makes sense. When the learner has formed his sentence, you should reinforce the value of his effort by reading it aloud.

■ DIRECTING THE LEARNER'S ATTENTION The purpose of this task is to teach the learner to produce and read messages using the individual words he knows. This is an important skill because it accurately reflects the actual role of language and gives the learner an opportunity to use each crucial facet of the communication act simultaneously. The message to be written is a product of the learner's own thinking. He is first encouraged to express it orally, and then to match it in written form by arranging his word cards to form the message. This, in turn, is then read and understood by you and by his peers. This task, then, provides the learner with a tangible concept of what the reading–writing act is really all about.

You should encourage your learner to create a message even if he has learned to read only one word in that message. Your concern is not to teach all the unknown "new" words in the story, but to have the learner put to use in the total communication act a word he may have previously read only in isolation.

In teaching this skill, you must be certain that the learner attends to your oral directions, to the idea or message he wishes to convey, to the individual words, and to the order in which the words are placed in the sentence.

Key objective for developing skill in creating and reading sentences and stories.

■ TEACHING ACTIVITIES / *The model activity* Have a set of word cards on which are printed the same words that the learner has on his. Scramble the cards and say, "Let's see if I can send *you* a message this time. Let's see. What message do I want to send to you? I know. I'll tell you where I was yesterday. Do you know where I was? Yes, I was on my boat. Let's see. What words will I need to send you that message?" At this point, you and the learner together look for the needed words, fit them together in the proper order, and read the sentence back. This process is repeated, with the learner encouraged to take an ever-greater role, until he finally thinks of a message *he* wants to send, and *you* help *him*. Your role gradually becomes less and less, until the learner is able to do the task alone.

/ Suggestions for reteaching and/or practice

1 Difficulty with this task may be due to the learner's inability to come up with a message he wants to send. He can be aided in selecting a message if you talk with him, leading him to tell about himself and some things that have happened to him, saying, "That sounds like an interesting message. Why don't you see if you can put *that* into words?"

2 Persistent difficulty with this task would indicate a need to provide the learner with intensive experiences in using oral language as a basis for communication. Use situations such as "Show-and-Tell," dramatization, storytelling, games, and message carrying to provide the learner with opportunities to communicate orally.

3 If you feel the learner is inhibited in his ability to perform this task because of a hesitancy to ask you to supply unknown words, direct him to arrange his word cards in the correct order, leaving a blank space where the unknown word should go. Then, when you read the message, read all the words he has supplied, having the learner say the word that should go in the blank space. Such an activity will strengthen his use of oral context and will help him with this task.

4 Make use of "experience charts" on which common experiences of the class are recorded on large chart paper using a sequence of steps such as the following: The learners first participate in an interesting and significant experience and discuss it among themselves and with you. Then you help them plan a title, the general content, and the exact sentences for the chart. The learners dictate the sentences to you, and you print them on the chart. Be careful to use either words that the learners have been taught to recognize or that you have adequately identified for them. You then read the chart to the learners, and they each take turns in reading it alone.

5 If an experience chart has been constructed, make individual word cards for each word that appears on the chart. Mix these up and give them to the learner, directing him to identify the words, sort them, and arrange the word cards to tell the same story as is told on the experience chart. He may use the large chart as a model from which to work.

6 An activity similar to that described in No. 5 is one in which the learners are provided with sentence strips rather than with individual words. The sentences are arranged to duplicate the story told on the experience chart. This is sometimes a helpful device for a learner who seems to be stymied by the large number of word cards he must sort through in order to reconstruct the chart. The sentence strips provide the learner with a transition step that he can go through before having to use the word cards.

■ THE POSTTEST Procedure and criterion for mastery remain the same as in the pretest.

IIIB

■ THE PERFORMANCE OBJECTIVE   Given a spoken stimulus word beginning with the *t*, *b*, or *p* sounds and a group of three other words one of which begins with the *t*, *b*, or *p* sound, the learner pairs two words beginning with the same sound.

■ THE PRETEST   Using the word sets listed below, say to the learner, "Here are three words. Listen carefully." (Say the words.) "Which one sounds like (say the stimulus word) at the beginning?" (Repeat the three original words.) Criterion for mastery is 5 out of 6 correct.

dog / house / tooth	Which one sounds like *top* at the beginning? Repeat the first three words.
bike / rock / frog	Which one sounds like *boy* at the beginning? Repeat the first three words.
dance / fall / took	Which one sounds like *top* at the beginning? Repeat the first three words.
push / run / rush	Which one sounds like *pat* at the beginning? Repeat the first three words.
stand / band / like	Which one sounds like *boy* at the beginning? Repeat the first three words.
art / list / part	Which one sounds like *pat* at the beginning? Repeat the first three words.

■ DIRECTING THE LEARNER'S ATTENTION   The purpose of this task is to cue the learner to the importance of listening to the beginning sounds of words and to help him distinguish the *t*, *b*, and *p* sounds from other consonant sounds. This task is similar to that described in IIB 2, and you should select your teaching activity from among the storehouse of techniques described there. When teaching this skill, you must be certain that the learner attends to the oral directions and to the beginning sound in each spoken word.

■ THE POSTTEST   The procedure and criterion for mastery are the same as for the pretest.

rest / pass / last	Which one sounds like *pat* at the beginning? Repeat the first three words.
box / fox / likes	Which one sounds like *boy* at the beginning? Repeat the first three words.
ran / fan / pan	Which one sounds like *pat* at the beginning? Repeat the first three words.
able / table / fall	Which one sounds like *top* at the beginning? Repeat the first three words.
best / rest / first	Which one sounds like *boy* at the beginning? Repeat the first three words.
fell / blue / tell	Which one sounds like *top* at the beginning? Repeat the first three words.

IIIB 2

■ THE PERFORMANCE OBJECTIVE   Given spoken words beginning with the *t*, *b*, or *p* sounds, the learner identifies the beginning letters as *t*, *b*, or *p*.

■ THE PRETEST   Give the learner three cards, one with the letter *t* printed on it, another with the letter *b*, and a third with the letter *p*. Say the following words, directing the learner to point to the letter that begins the word just spoken. Criterion for mastery is 80 percent, with no letter sound being missed more than once.

bench	tuba	task	tower	bubble
powder	table	busy	pencil	bunch

■ DIRECTING THE LEARNER'S ATTENTION   The purpose of this task is to help the learner establish a sound–symbol connection between the letters *t*, *b*, and *p* and words that begin with the *t*, *b*, and *p* sounds. This task is similar to that described in IIB 5, and you should select your teaching activity from among the storehouse of techniques described there. When teaching this skill, you must be certain that the learner attends to the sound at the beginning of each spoken word while simultaneously looking at the correct letter.

■ THE POSTTEST   The procedure and criterion for mastery remain the same as for the pretest.

teeth	banana	beetle	buggy	taxi
bush	pig	pastor	buzz	teach

IIIB 3

■ THE PERFORMANCE OBJECTIVE   Given a spoken stimulus word beginning with the *w*, *r*, or *f* sounds and a group of three other words one of which begins with the *w*, *r*, or *f* sound, the learner pairs the two words beginning with the same sound.

■ THE PRETEST   Using the word sets listed below, say to the learner, "Here are three words. Listen carefully." (Say the words.) "Which one sounds like (say the stimulus word) at the beginning?" (Repeat the three original words.) Criterion for mastery is 5 out of 6 correct.

test / man / wish	Which one sounds like *win* at the beginning? Repeat the first three words.
fall / tall / note	Which one sounds like *fan* at the beginning? Repeat the first three words.
nest / rest / box	Which one sounds like *run* at the beginning? Repeat the first three words.
task / fast / look	Which one sounds like *fan* at the beginning? Repeat the first three words.
fell / talk / well	Which one sounds like *win* at the beginning? Repeat the first three words.
stone / reap / top	Which one sounds like *run* at the beginning? Repeat the first three words.

What are you doing for the learner who doesn't seem to catch on? Have you checked Appendix I to pinpoint what you might do to get him started?

■ DIRECTING THE LEARNER'S ATTENTION   The purpose of this task is to cue the learner to the importance of listening to the beginning sounds of words and to help him distinguish the *w*, *r*, and *f* sounds from other consonant sounds. This task is similar to that described in IIB 2, and you should select your teaching activity from among the storehouse of techniques described there. When teaching this skill, you must be certain that the learner attends to the oral directions and to the beginning sound in each spoken word.

■ THE POSTTEST   The procedure and criterion for mastery are the same as for the pretest.

real / true / big	Which word sounds like *run* at the beginning? Repeat the first three words.
go / fate / wait	Which word sounds like *win* at the beginning? Repeat the first three words.
wish / fish / stop	Which word sounds like *fan* at the beginning? Repeat the first three words.
up / rope / hope	Which word sounds like *run* at the beginning? Repeat the first three words.
fact / down / ran	Which word sounds like *fan* at the beginning? Repeat the first three words.
fence / out / went	Which word sounds like *win* at the beginning? Repeat the first three words.

IIIB 4

■ THE PERFORMANCE OBJECTIVE   Given spoken words beginning with the *w*, *r*, or *f* sounds, the learner identifies the beginning letters as *w*, *r*, or *f*.

■ THE PRETEST   Give the learner three cards, one with the letter *w* printed on it, another with the letter *r*, and a third with the letter *f*. Say the following words, directing the learner to point to the letter which begins the word just spoken. Criterion for mastery is 80 percent, with no letter sound being missed more than once.

wash	rush	fool	rascal
fire	fasten	window	windy

■ DIRECTING THE LEARNER'S ATTENTION   The purpose of this task is to help the learner establish a sound–symbol connection between the letters *w*, *r*, and *f* and words that begin with the *w*, *r*, and *f* sounds. This task is similar to that described in IIB 5, and you should select your teaching activity from among the storehouse of techniques described there. When teaching this skill, you must be certain that the learner attends to the sound at the beginning of each spoken word while simultaneously looking at the correct letter.

■ THE POSTTEST   Procedure and criterion for mastery remain the same as for the pretest.

ready	razor	fix	farmer	fence
wash	wider	weapon	rocket	water

IIIB **5**

■ THE PERFORMANCE OBJECTIVE   Given a spoken stimulus word beginning with the *k*, *j*, *n*, or hard *g* sound and a group of three other words, one of which begins with the *k*, *j*, *n*, or hard *g* sound, the learner pairs the two words beginning with the same sound.

■ THE PRETEST   Using the word sets listed below, say to the learner, "Here are three words. Listen carefully." (Say the three words.) "Which one sounds like (say stimulus word) at the beginning?" (Repeat the original three words.) Criterion for mastery is 7 out of 8 correct.

fate / sun / gate	Which one sounds like *good* at the beginning? Repeat the first three words.
kiss / look / miss	Which one sounds like *kite* at the beginning? Repeat the first three words.
toy / jack / ask	Which one sounds like *joy* at the beginning? Repeat the first three words.
keel / desk / floor	Which one sounds like *kite* at the beginning? Repeat the first three words.
bet / fall / net	Which one sounds like *no* at the beginning? Repeat the first three words.
golf / tape / bag	Which one sounds like *good* at the beginning? Repeat the first three words.
food / bed / juice	Which one sounds like *joy* at the beginning? Repeat the first three words.
night / day / grass	Which one sounds like *no* at the beginning? Repeat the first three words.

■ DIRECTING THE LEARNER'S ATTENTION   The purpose of this task is to cue the learner to the importance of listening to the beginning sounds of words and to help him distinguish the *k*, *j*, *n*, and hard *g* sounds from other consonant sounds. This task is similar to that described in IIB 2, and you should select your teaching activity from among the storehouse of techniques described there. When teaching this skill, you must be certain that the learner attends to the oral directions and to the beginning sound in each spoken word.

■ THE POSTTEST   The procedure and the criterion for mastery are the same as for the pretest.

never / soon / fear	Which one sounds like *no* at the beginning? Repeat the first three words.
bird / case / jockey	Which one sounds like *joy* at the beginning? Repeat the first three words.
gas / comic / house	Which one sounds like *good* at the beginning? Repeat the first three words.

pouch / clip / night	Which one sounds like *no* at the beginning? Repeat the first three words.
kangaroo / bat / flower	Which one sounds like *kite* at the beginning? Repeat the first three words.
folder / junk / bunk	Which one sounds like *joy* at the beginning? Repeat the first three words.
king / many / best	Which one sounds like *kite* at the beginning? Repeat the first three words.
down / hold / give	Which one sounds like *good* at the beginning? Repeat the first three words.

IIIB 6

■ THE PERFORMANCE OBJECTIVE   Given spoken words beginning with the *k*, *j*, *n*, or hard *g* sounds, the learner identifies the beginning letters as *k*, *j*, *n*, or *g*.

■ THE PRETEST   Give the learner four cards, one with the letter *g* printed on it, another with *k*, another with *j*, and the last with *n*. Say the following words, directing the learner to point to the letter that begins the word just spoken. Criterion for mastery is 10 out of 12 correct, with no letter sound being missed more than once.

| get | goose | kite | near | jackrabbit | navy |
| king | jar | gone | keep | jerk | neat |

■ DIRECTING THE LEARNER'S ATTENTION   The purpose of this task is to help the learner establish a sound-symbol connection between the letters *k*, *j*, *n*, and *g* and words that begin with the *k*, *j*, *n*, and hard *g* sounds. This task is similar to that described in IIB 5, and you should select your teaching activity from among the storehouse of techniques described there. When teaching this skill, you must be certain that the learner attends to the sound at the beginning of each spoken word while simultaneously looking at the correct letter.

■ THE POSTTEST   The procedure and the criterion for mastery are the same as for the pretest.

| nest | jar | ketch | gobble | judge | kill |
| neighbor | june bug | none | kiss | gossip | guess |

IIIB 7

■ THE PERFORMANCE OBJECTIVE   Given an oral sentence with one word missing and cued for the missing word with a card having printed on it the first letter of the missing word (*t*, *b*, *p*, *w*, *r*, *f*, *g*, *k*, *j*, and *n*), the learner says a word beginning with the letter that fits the context of the sentence.

■ THE PRETEST Make cards with the above letters printed on them. Say, "I am going to say a sentence with one word missing. You look at the card and say a word that begins with the letter on the card and which finishes what I want to say." Use the following sentences. Criterion for mastery is 80 percent, with no letter being missed more than once. *The letter card should not be exposed until the blank is reached.*

After the number nine comes the number t____.

When I play hard, I get t____.

The girl and b____ were playing ball.

I rode my b____ to school.

I wrote my name with a p____.

I will p____ the wagon.

I'm sick and don't feel very w____.

I hope we w____ the game.

In the game I r____ very fast.

I put the r____ on my finger.

When playing, I tripped and f____.

I lost the ball. Can you f____ it?

The car stopped. It was out of g____.

On Halloween I saw a g____.

I flew my k____ today.

I saw the k____ and the queen.

I will run and j____ over the fence.

I broke the glass j____.

The sun doesn't shine at n____.

She had a necklace around her n____.

■ DIRECTING THE LEARNER'S ATTENTION The purpose of this task is to help the learner use his knowledge of context sense and letter–sound correspondence to identify unknown words. This task is similar to that described in IIB 12, and you should select your teaching activity from among the storehouse of activities described there. When teaching this skill you must be certain that the learner attends to the directions, to the sense of the sentence, and to the sound value of the letter provided.

■ THE POSTTEST The procedure and the criterion for mastery are the same as for the pretest.

The bike was n____ to the house.

I want Ann to sit n____ to me.

For breakfast I had some orange j____.

I will play with the ball and the j____.

My grandmother k____ me on the cheek.

I found it. Can I k____ it?

I looked for my friend, but he was g____.

I am g____ to the store.

He can run very f____.

The f____ was swimming in the pond.

He tied the package with a r____.

In the fall I r____ the leaves.

I threw the paper in the w____ basket.

I w____ I was very rich.

I cooked the meat in a frying p_____.   I want to go to the birthday p_____.

Sam is my b_____ friend.   I cut my finger so I put a b_____ on it

The car had a flat t_____.   Is it t_____ to go to school?

IIIB **8**

■ THE PERFORMANCE OBJECTIVE   Given a stimulus word ending with an *m*, *d*, *l*, or voiceless *s* (*miss*) sound and a group of three other words one of which ends with an *m*, *d*, *l*, or voiceless *s* sound, the learner pairs the two words *ending* with the same sound.

■ THE PRETEST   Using the word sets listed below, say to the learner, "Here are three words. Listen carefully." (Say the three words). "Which one sounds like (say the stimulus word) at the end?" (Repeat the three original words.) Criterion for mastery is 7 out of 8 correct.

Sam / ran / are	Which word sounds like *same* at the end? Repeat the first three words.
had / went / rain	Which word sounds like *mind* at the end? Repeat the first three words.
chair / hid / soon	Which word sounds like *mind* at the end? Repeat the first three words.
book / floor / ball	Which word sounds like *hill* at the end? Repeat the first three words.
picture / lamps / knob	Which word sounds like *miss* at the end? Repeat the first three words.
steal / rat / waste	Which word sounds like *hill* at the end? Repeat the first three words.
limb / book / flower	Which word sounds like *same* at the end? Repeat the first three words.
top / recess / belt	Which word sounds like *miss* at the end? Repeat the first three words.

■ DIRECTING THE LEARNER'S ATTENTION   The purpose of this task is to cue the learner to the importance of listening to the final sounds in words and to help him distinguish the final *n*, *d*, *l*, and voiceless *s* sounds from other final consonant sounds. This task is similar to that described in IIB 3, and you should select your teaching activity from among the storehouse of techniques described there. When teaching this skill, you must be certain that the learner attends to your oral directions and to the ending sounds in each sequence of words.

■ THE POSTTEST   The procedure and criterion for mastery remain the same.

not / if / seem	Which word sounds like *same* at the end? Repeat the first three words.
key / said / any	Which word sounds like *mind* at the end? Repeat the first three words.
all / painted / book	Which word sounds like *mind* at the end? Repeat the first three words.
begin / word / maul	Which word sounds like *hill* at the end? Repeat the first three words.
football / to / have	Which word sounds like *hill* at the end? Repeat the first three words.
sew / paint / walrus	Which word sounds like *miss* at the end? Repeat the first three words.
bomb / after / pen	Which word sounds like *same* at the end? Repeat the first three words.
like / difference / it	Which word sounds like *miss* at the end? Repeat the first three words.

IIIB 9

■ THE PERFORMANCE OBJECTIVE Given spoken words ending with *m, d, l,* or voiceless *s* sounds, the learner identifies the ending letters as *m, d, l,* or *s.*

■ THE PRETEST Give the learner four cards, one with the letter *m* printed on it, another with *d,* another with *p,* and the last with *s.* Say the following words, directing the learner to point to the letter that ends the word just spoken. Criterion for mastery is 10 out of 12 correct, with no letter sound being missed more than once.

came	repeal	assume	dad	walks	cream
hippopotamus	shall	desks	red	skill	watered

■ DIRECTING THE LEARNER'S ATTENTION The purpose of this task is to help the learner establish a sound–symbol connection between the letters *m, d, l,* and *s* and words that end with the *m, d, l,* and voiceless *s* sounds. This task is similar to that described in IIB 5, except that the focus of the learner's attention is on the ending rather than the beginning sounds. You should select your teaching activity from among the storehouse of techniques described in IIB 5. When teaching this skill, you must be certain that the learner attends to the sound at the end of each spoken word and simultaneously looks at the correct letter.

■ THE POSTTEST The procedure and the criterion for mastery are the same as for the pretest.

rhinoceros	this	flame	pull	mad	child
find	chase	him	fell	random	bell

IVA

WHAT THE LEARNER
LOOKS AT

IVA 1

■ THE PERFORMANCE OBJECTIVE   Given a fraction of a second to examine a flash card having printed on it either the words *here, fast, to, me, at,* or *come,* the learner pronounces each word within one second.

■ THE PRETEST   Print each of the above words on flash cards. Flash each card to the learner, giving him less than one second to examine each word before he pronounces it. Criterion for mastery is 100 percent.

■ DIRECTING THE LEARNER'S ATTENTION   The purpose of this task is to teach the learner to recognize instantly the words listed in the objective when they are printed on cards. This task is similar to that described in IIIA 6, and you should select your teaching activity from among the storehouse of techniques described there. When teaching this skill, you must be certain that the learner attends to the visual form of the word and to its distinguishing characteristics.

■ THE POSTTEST   The procedure and the criterion for mastery are the same as for the pretest.

IVA 2

■ THE PERFORMANCE OBJECTIVE   Given a sentence frame spoken by the teacher and words he recognizes at sight printed on individual cards, the learner points to the word card that completes the sentence frame.

■ THE PRETEST   Provide the learner with cards, each of which has printed on it a word that he instantly recognizes (be sure to include those from IVA 1). Next, construct sentence frames on the order of the example shown for the pretest in IIIA 9. Say each sentence to the learner, ask him to listen carefully, and direct him to point to the word card "that finishes what I want to say." Criterion for mastery is 100 percent.

■ DIRECTING THE LEARNER'S ATTENTION   The purpose of the task is to teach the learner to use the words he recognizes at sight in a correct sentence context. When teaching this skill, you must be certain that he attends to the directions, to the spoken sentence, and to the form of the words on the cards.

Do you deserve *your learner's attention?*

■ TEACHING ACTIVITIES / *The model activity*   Follow the same procedure as outlined in IIIA 9, modifying it for use with the new sight words.

/ *Suggestions for reteaching and/or practice*

1   Learners having persistent difficulty with this task should be redirected to IIB 10, IIB 11, and IIB 12 for additional instruction in using context in oral language.
2   If the learner's difficulty lies in his inability to recognize at sight the words on the cards, these words should be retaught using the suggestions in IIIA 6.

■ THE POSTTEST   Procedures and criterion for mastery remain the same as for the pretest.

IVA ▣3

■ THE PERFORMANCE OBJECTIVE   Given a fraction of a second to examine flash cards with the word*s see, help, home,* and *work* printed on them, the learner pronounces each word within one second.

■ THE PRETEST   Print each of the above words on flash cards. Flash each card to the learner, giving him less than one second to examine each word before pronouncing it. Criterion for mastery is 100 percent.

■ DIRECTING THE LEARNER'S ATTENTION   The purpose of this task is to teach the learner to recognize instantly the words listed in the objective when they are printed on cards. This task is similar to that described in IIIA 6, and you should select your teaching activity from among the storehouse of techniques described there. When teaching this skill, you must be certain that the learner attends to the visual form of the word and to its distinguishing characteristics.

■ THE POSTTEST   The procedure and the criterion for mastery are the same as for the pretest.

IVA 4

■ THE PERFORMANCE OBJECTIVE   Given a sentence frame spoken by the teacher and the words *see, help, home*, and *work* printed on individual cards, the learner points to the card with a word printed on it that completes the sentence frame.

■ THE PRETEST   Provide the learner with cards having printed on them the words *see, help, home*, and *work* (as well as any other known sight words that you may wish to add). Next, construct sentence frames on the order of the example shown for the pretest in IIIA 9. Say each sentence to the learner, ask him to listen carefully, and direct him to point to the word card "that finishes what I want to say." Criterion for mastery is 100 percent.

■ DIRECTING THE LEARNER'S ATTENTION   The purpose of this task is to teach the learner to use the words he recognizes at sight in a correct sentence context. When teaching this skill, you must be certain that he attends to the directions, to the spoken sentence, and to the form of the words on the cards.

■ TEACHING ACTIVITIES / *The model activity*   Follow the same procedure as outlined in IIIA 9, modifying it for use with the new sight words.

/ *Suggestions for reteaching and/or practice*

Follow the suggestions made in IVA 2.

■ THE POSTTEST   The procedure and criterion for mastery remain the same as for the pretest.

IVA 5

■ THE PERFORMANCE OBJECTIVE   Given five known words in which the first letter is printed in lower case, the learner matches each word to the same word with the first letter printed in upper case.

■ THE PRETEST   Prepare cards on which are written previously taught sight words with the first letter printed in lower case. Then prepare a duplicate set on which are written the same words with the first letter printed in upper case. Direct the learner to pronounce each word printed all in lower case. The learner then looks through his second group of cards, finds the same word with the first letter printed in upper case, and reads that word.

■ DIRECTING THE LEARNER'S ATTENTION   The purpose of the task is to teach the learner to recognize known sight words when the first letter is printed in either lower or upper case. When teaching this skill, you must be certain that the learner attends to your oral directions, to the form of the whole word as it is printed with the initial letter in lower case, and to the form of the whole word as it is printed with the initial letter in upper case.

Are you using dramatics, choral speaking, artwork, music activities, and other creative projects to support your reading program?

■ TEACHING ACTIVITIES / *The model activity*   Choose a known word and print it, with a lower-case letter in the initial position, on the blackboard. Direct the learner to read it. Following the learner's correct identification of the word, print it again, but this time use the upper-case form of the first letter. Point to the first letter of the word printed in the lower-case form and ask the learner to give the letter name. Then point to the first letter of the word printed in upper case and ask him to give the letter name. Then say, "Can you read both words now?" Lead him to see that alternate forms of manuscript writing do not change the pronunciation of the word.

/ *Suggestions for reteaching and/or practice*

If the learner experiences persistent difficulty in performing this task, it is probably because he has not yet learned to associate the upper-case with the lower-case form of the letters. To correct this, redirect him to IIA 7 and select an activity for reteaching this skill from among the storehouse of techniques provided there.

■ THE POSTTEST   The procedure and criterion for mastery remain the same as for the pretest.

IVA 6

■ THE PERFORMANCE OBJECTIVE   Given a page of writing and directed to point to the first word and last word in a line of print and to the first word and last word on a page, the learner instantly does so.

■ THE PRETEST   Open a book to a page that has a solid block of writing. *Caution:* Do not use title pages, glossaries, or tables of contents. Direct the learner to look at the page and point to the first word on the page or on a specified line. Give similar directions for the last word of a line or page. The learner must respond immediately with 100 percent accuracy.

■ DIRECTING THE LEARNER'S ATTENTION   The purpose of this task is to help the learner to approach the reading of a printed page from top to bottom and from left to right. This task is similar to that described in IIA 8, and you should select your teaching activity from among the storehouse of techniques described there. When teaching this skill, you must be certain that the learner attends to your oral directions and to the print on the page, as opposed to distractions such as pictures, margins, and page numbers.

■ THE POSTTEST   The procedure and criterion for mastery remain the same as for the pretest.

IVA 7

■ THE PERFORMANCE OBJECTIVE   Given a fraction of a second to examine flash cards with the words *down* and *up* printed on them, the learner pronounces each word within one second.

■ THE PRETEST   Print each of these words on flash cards. Flash each card to the learner, giving him less than one second to examine each word before he pronounces it. Criterion for mastery is 100 percent.

■ DIRECTING THE LEARNER'S ATTENTION   The purpose of this task is to teach the learner to recognize instantly the words listed in the objective when they are printed on cards. This task is similar to that described in IIIA 6, and you should select your teaching activity from among the storehouse of techniques described there. When teaching this skill, you must be certain that the learner attends to the visual form of the word and to its distinguishing characteristics.

■ THE POSTTEST   The procedure and criterion for mastery remain the same as for the pretest.

IVA 8

■ THE PERFORMANCE OBJECTIVE   Given a fraction of a second to examine flash cards with the color words *white, black, red, blue, green,* and *yellow* printed on them, the learner pronounces each word within one second.

■ THE PRETEST   Print each of the above words on flash cards. Flash each card to the learner, giving him less than one second to examine each word before he pronounces it. Criterion for mastery is 100 percent.

■ DIRECTING THE LEARNER'S ATTENTION   The purpose of this task is to teach the learner to recognize instantly the words listed in the objective when they are printed on cards. This task is similar to that described in IIIA 6, and you should select your teaching activity from among the storehouse of techniques described there. When teaching this skill, you must be certain that the learner attends to the visual form of the word and to its distinguishing characteristics.

■ THE POSTTEST   The procedure and criterion for mastery remain the same as for the pretest.

IVA 9

■ THE PERFORMANCE OBJECTIVE   Given a fraction of a second to examine flash cards with the number words *one* to *ten* printed on them, the learner pronounces each word within one second.

■ THE PRETEST   Print each of the above words on flash cards. Flash each card to the learner, giving him less than one second to examine each word before he pronounces it. Criterion for mastery is 100 percent.

■ DIRECTING THE LEARNER'S ATTENTION   The purpose of this task is to teach the learner to recognize instantly the words listed in the objective when they are printed on cards. This task is similar to that described in IIIA 6, and you should select your teaching activity from among the storehouse of techniques described there. When teaching this skill, you must be certain that the learner attends to the visual form of the word and to its distinguishing characteristics.

■ THE POSTTEST   The procedure and criterion for mastery remain the same as for the pretest.

IVA 10

■ THE PERFORMANCE OBJECTIVE   Given words he recognizes instantly, the learner creates and reads multiple-sentence stories using these words.

■ THE PRETEST   Provide the learner with cards, each of which has printed on it a word that he recognizes instantly. Follow the specific directions regarding instructions provided in IIIA 10. Criterion for mastery is the formation of more than one sentence using any combination of words that are grammatically accurate and that make sense. When the learner has formed his sentences, have him read them back to you.

■ DIRECTING THE LEARNER'S ATTENTION   The purpose of this task is to teach the learner to produce messages using words he knows and to read these sentences. This task is similar to that described in IIIA 10, and you should select your teaching activity from among the storehouse of techniques described there. When teaching this skill, you must be certain that the learner attends to the oral directions, to the idea or message he wishes to convey, to the individual words, and to the order in which the words are placed in the sentences.

■ THE POSTTEST   The procedure and criterion for mastery remain the same as for the pretest.

IVB **1**

■ THE PERFORMANCE OBJECTIVE   Given a spoken stimulus word beginning with the *sh* or voiceless *th* sound and a group of three other words one of which begins with the *sh* or voiceless *th* sound, the learner pairs the two words beginning with the same sound.

■ THE PRETEST   Using the word sets listed below, say to the learner, "Here are three words. Listen carefully." (Say the words.) "Which one sounds like (say the stimulus word) at the beginning? (Repeat the three original words.) Criterion for mastery is 5 out of 6 correct.

paint / leaf / shoe	Which one sounds like *ship* at the beginning? Repeat the first three words.
trip / shell / black	Which one sounds like *ship* at the beginning? Repeat the first three words.
first / thank / page	Which one sounds like *thick* at the beginning? Repeat the first three words.
shine / chip / train	Which one sounds like *ship* at the beginning? Repeat the first three words.
thirsty / when / who	Which one sounds like *thick* at the beginning? Repeat the first three words.
car / thud / street	Which one sounds like *thick* at the beginning? Repeat the first three words.

■ DIRECTING THE LEARNER'S ATTENTION   The purpose of this task is to cue the learner to the importance of listening to the beginning sounds of words and to help him distinguish the *sh* and voiceless *th* sounds from other consonant sounds. This task is similar to that described in IIB 2, and you should select your teaching activity from among the storehouse of techniques described there. When teaching this skill, you must be certain that the learner attends to the oral directions and to the beginning sounds in each spoken sequence of words.

■ THE POSTTEST   The procedure and criterion for mastery remain the same as for the pretest.

think / block / fall	Which one sounds like *thick* at the beginning? Repeat the first three words.
bed / storm / thumb	Which one sounds like *thick* at the beginning? Repeat the first three words.
throw / shot / blue	Which one sounds like *ship* at the beginning? Repeat the first three words.
show / snow / flow	Which one sounds like *ship* at the beginning? Repeat the first three words.
third / green / tall	Which one sounds like *thick* at the beginning? Repeat the first three words.
clip / trial / shop	Which one sounds like *ship* at the beginning? Repeat the first three words.

IVB 2

■ THE PERFORMANCE OBJECTIVE   Given spoken words beginning with the *sh* or voiceless *th* sounds, the learner identifies the beginning letters as *sh* or *th*.

■ THE PRETEST   Give the learner two cards, one with the digraph *sh* and the other with the digraph *th* printed on it. Say the following words, directing the learner to point to the letters that begin the word just spoken. Criterion for mastery is 80 percent, with no letter sound missed more than once.

thigh	shove	think	shack	shout
thought	shirt	thirty	short	thimble

■ DIRECTING THE LEARNER'S ATTENTION   The purpose of this task is to establish a sound–symbol connection between the digraphs *sh* and *th* and words that begin with the *sh* and voiceless *th* sounds. This task is similar to that described in IIB 5, and you should select your teaching activity from among the storehouse of techniques described there. When teaching this skill, you must be certain that the learner attends to the sound at the beginning of each spoken word and simultaneously looks at the correct letter.

■ THE POSTTEST   The procedure and criterion for mastery remain the same as for the pretest.

thorn	shower	theater	shock	thaw
shy	shut	shift	thin	thump

IVB 3

■ THE PERFORMANCE OBJECTIVE   Given an oral sentence with one word missing and cued for the missing word with a card having the *sh* or *th* digraph printed on it, the learner says a word beginning with the digraph that fits the context of the sentence.

■ THE PRETEST   Make cards with the above digraphs printed on them. Say, "I am going to say a sentence with one word missing. You look at the card and say a word that begins with the letters on the card and that finishes what I want to say." Use the following sentences. Criterion for mastery is 80 percent, with no letter being missed more than once. *Caution*: The letter card should not be exposed except at the blank.

The little girl learned to tie her sh——.

It was hot. I took off my sh——.

We went across the ocean on a sh——.

There was no water fountain, and I was th——.

The boy didn't eat much, and he was very th——.

I am tall, but he is sh——.

I was second in line, and she was th——.

He has a gun. He might sh—— it.

I want to th—— you for the present.

On our hand we have four fingers and a th——.

■ DIRECTING THE LEARNER'S ATTENTION   The purpose of this task is to help the learner use his knowledge of context sense and letter–sound correspondence to identify unknown words. This task is similar to that described in IIB 12, and you should select your teaching activity from among the storehouse of techniques described there. When teaching this skill, you must be certain that the learner attends to your directions, to the sense of the sentence, and to the letter provided and its sound value.

■ THE POSTTEST   The procedure and criterion for mastery remain the same as for the pretest.

That little girl is very bashful and sh——.

You have twenty pieces of candy, but I have th——.

The paper is thin, but the door is th——.

When you want to know how hot it is, you look at the th——.

Please don't sh——. You are making too much noise.

Sometimes I can't do anyth—— right.

Don't fall into those bushes or you will get a th—— in your finger.

I know where it is. I'll sh—— you·

When you come in the house, be sure that you sh—— the door.

I dug a big hole with my sh——.

CHAPTER FIVE / IF THE LEARNER KNOWS SOME WORDS BUT DOES NOT READ FLUENTLY

Skill Objectives for Teaching Word Recognition

This chapter provides intensive study of the techniques a learner must master in order to identify words. It builds upon the sequence of skills in Chapter 4, developing more sophisticated and refined techniques of recognition and analysis. If you work with learners of any age who lack fluency in reading, start them with the objectives contained in this chapter.

SKILLS TAUGHT IN THIS CHAPTER

Like Chapter 4, this chapter is divided into two major categories consistent with the recognition and analysis aspects of word recognition. The first, "Sight Words," is concerned with teaching learners to recognize and use selected words instantly. The second, "Word Analysis," is concerned with teaching learners to analyze words on the basis of phonetic, structural, and contextual elements.

Included in this chapter are objectives for instantly recognizing words at sight, for discriminating among easily confused words, for using known words in writing and reading, for connecting phonetic sounds to their letters, for recognizing basic vowel phonograms, for learning the principle of letter substitution, for using phonetic generalizations, and for recognizing prefixes, suffixes, compounds, and simple syllabication units. This chapter focuses on providing a large stock of words that are recognized instantly, on developing a problem-solving approach to breaking the English spelling code, and on analyzing words in terms of common word structures. Learners who master the skills of this chapter will be able to:

1 Recognize 300 high-utility words at sight.
2 Distinguish between 34 easily confused words.
3 Create and read sentences and stories using the words known at sight.

4 Differentiate among sounds heard at the beginning of words and match these with their corresponding letters.

5 Differentiate among sounds heard at the ends of words and match these with their corresponding letters.

6 Identify basic short and long vowel phonograms and use the principle of substitution to identify unknown words.

7 Use context and understanding of the sound-symbol relationship of initial letters to identify unknown words.

8 Pronounce words illustrating the major long-vowel generalizations.

9 Pronounce words containing deviant vowel patterns such as the diphthong and the schwa.

10 Analyze and pronounce words illustrating the most common patterns of syllabication.

11 Pronounce words containing common silent letter combinations.

12 Pronounce words containing common structural beginnings and endings.

13 Analyze and pronounce compound words.

14 Analyze and pronounce contractions.

SOURCE OF THE WORDS TAUGHT

Deciding which words and which analysis techniques a learner must possess to achieve functional literacy can be a controversial issue. Authors use techniques ranging from their own particular views to the use of some kind of analysis based on word frequency. This book relies upon the latter technique.

The authors used lists of words that appear most frequently in beginning reading: Dolch's list of 220 words,[1] Fry's list of 300 words,[2] and Stone's revision of the Dale list of 769 useful words.[3] Using these, the authors proceeded in the following manner.

First, the words appearing on all three lists were considered to be the most utilitarian. These are taught as sight words in Chapter 4 or early in this chapter.

Second, each word on all three lists was analyzed in terms of its phonetic and structural elements. For example, all the words illustrating the *at* phonogram were listed together, all the compound words are listed together, and so on.

Third, each of these lists was inspected to determine which phonetic and structural elements occur most frequently. These elements were considered to be the most utilitarian and are, consequently, taught in

[1] E. W. Dolch, *Teaching Primary Reading*, Champaign, Illinois, Garrard Press, 1941.
[2] Edward Fry, "Developing a Word List for Remedial Reading," *Elementary English* (November 1957), 456–458.
[3] Clarence R. Stone, "Measuring Difficulty of Primary Reading Material: A Constructive Criticism of Spache's Measure," *Elementary School Journal* (October 1956), 36–41.

Chapter 4 or early in this chapter. The elements that appear less frequently are taught later in this chapter. Elements appearing so infrequently as to be nonutilitarian as a skill of functional literacy are not taught at all.

Fourth, words that do not utilize the phonetic or structural elements identified above and that do not appear on all three lists were considered to be irregular and are taught as sight words. Also taught as sight words are those regularly spelled words used as key words for generalizing to one of the phonetic or structural generalizations taught in this chapter. For example, the word *cat* is taught as a sight word and can be used as a known element in teaching the *at* phonogram in Objective IB 7 of this chapter.

When a learner has mastered what Chapters 4 and 5 teach, he will be able to recognize or successfully analyze more than 900 words.

USING THIS CHAPTER

The numbering system used in this chapter is similar to that used in Chapter 4. For example, Objective IA 2 in this chapter refers to the second objective in Section A, "Sight Words," of the first cluster, and Objective VIIB 3 refers to the third objective in Section B, "Word Analysis," of the seventh cluster. The Key Objective system remains the same as in Chapter 4.

The specific skills to be taught if the learner knows some words but does not read fluently begin on the next page. Use the placement test in Appendix E to determine each learner's approximate skill level. Refer to Chapter 1 for an overall description of the strategy employed in using the objectives, to Chapter 2 for specific guidelines in using this book, and to Chapter 3 for techniques of instruction and management.

IA **1**

■ THE PERFORMANCE OBJECTIVE   Given a flash presentation of each of the following words, the learner pronounces each word within one second. The words to test are:

saw	after	who	on	then	cat	an
mother	get	boy	some	we	get	be
girl	is	go	you	did	sit	they
look	not	good	jump	father	hot	for
on	she	like	little	make	but	were

■ THE PRETEST   Print each of the above words on flash cards. Then flash each word to the learner, giving him only a second or less to examine the word. Criterion for mastery is 100 percent. *Note*: The teacher should keep track of the words missed on the pretest because it is only the missed words that need to be taught. A missed word is any word on which the learner hesitates or makes *any* confusing response.

■ DIRECTING THE LEARNER'S ATTENTION   The purpose of this task is to teach the learner to recognize instantly the words listed in the objective when they are printed on cards. This task is similar to that described in IIIA 6 of the previous chapter, and you should select your teaching activity from among the storehouse of techniques described there. When teaching this skill, you must be certain that the learner attends to the visual form of the word and to its distinguishing characteristics.

■ THE POSTTEST   The procedure and criterion for mastery remain the same as for the pretest.

IA **2** KEY OBJECTIVE

■ THE PERFORMANCE OBJECTIVE   Given a flash presentation of each of the frequently confused words *on–no*, *was–saw*, and *the–then*, the learner pronounces each word within one second.

■ THE PRETEST   The procedure and criterion for mastery are the same as for the pretest of the previous objective.

■ DIRECTING THE LEARNER'S ATTENTION   The purpose of this task is to teach the learner to recognize instantly each of the above easily confused words when they are presented on cards. Although this objective is very similar to the objectives designed to teach sight words generally, the focus here is deliberately being placed on the word demons that readers frequently confuse and that teachers find most difficult to teach.

To teach learners to recognize these word demons, you must decide which visual discriminator can act as a cue to a word. For example, the learner must focus on the letter *n* in order to separate *then* from *the*. Hence, you must direct the learner to this cue—his attention must be focused on the visual discriminator that acts as the cue for contrasting the easily confused words.

> **Key objective** for developing skill in instantly recognizing easily confused words.

■ TEACHING ACTIVITIES / *The model activity*   It is assumed that you have already tried to teach these words as a part of Objective IA 1 and that the procedure outlined under the model activity has been followed. If it has not, start with that procedure because the following suggestions are needed only if, after a period of initial instruction, the learner still confuses these words.

To teach two easily confused words, you must first identify the discriminator that distinguishes one from the other. Then you must direct the learner's attention to this discriminator. For example, for the words *the* and *then*, you can write *the* on the board and direct the learner to read it. When he does, direct him to watch what you do. Next add an *n* to the word *the* to make *then*. Say, "What word do we have now? How did I make the word *the* into the word *then?*" Direct the learner to describe how he can tell *the* and *then* apart, emphasizing the importance of looking at the whole word to see if an *n* has been added. Make sure that he verbalizes the visual differences between the two words so that you are sure he is focusing on the discriminator. Then give him practice in responding to flash presentation of the two words to be certain that his response becomes habitual.

/ Suggestions for reteaching and/or practice

1   It is to be anticipated that the teaching of any two easily confused words will necessitate much repetition. Hence, one alternate activity should certainly include much drill in recognizing these words when they are placed on cards and flashed to the learner.

2 Words that are particularly difficult can be taught by using the sense of touch as described in the storehouse of activities in IIIA 6 in Chapter 4.
3 It is often helpful to put the easily confused words in sentences, where all the words are easily recognized by the learner except the two words being taught. Such exercises should be planned on a blitz principle, in which many sentences offering multiple opportunities for using the easily confused words should be used. For example, to provide practice in recognizing *the* and *then*, sentences such as the following could be used:

> *Then the* boy and *then* the girl were good.

4 Color coding can also be used to help the learner distinguish between easily confused words. For example, the letter *n* in *then* can be given a color different from the other letters to help the learner focus on the discriminator.
5 Words of similar length and shape can be written on the chalkboard in a row, with all the words alike except the one that is to be distinguished from the others, as in:

> then   then   the   then   then

The learner is directed to draw a circle around each word that says *then*, or the word that says *the*.
6 Present the pair of easily confused words to the learner together. Ask him to examine the two words, to tell how they are different, and to tell you how he is going to remember which word is which.
7 Many of the activities described in the storehouse of activities listed in IIIA 6 in Chapter 4 can be adapted for use in teaching learners to distinguish between easily confused words.

■ THE POSTTEST   The procedure and criterion for mastery remain the same as for the pretest.

IA 3

■ THE PERFORMANCE OBJECTIVE   Given words he recognizes at sight, the learner creates and reads stories using these words.

■ THE PRETEST   Provide the learner with cards, each of which has printed on it a word that he recognizes instantly. Say to him, "Today, we are going to do something that is very hard. We are going to write our own stories. Look at the cards you have in front of you. Each card has a word on it that you know. Can you tell me a little story using the words you have here? If you want to make a story using a word you don't have on a card, tell me and I will make a card with that word on it." Direct the learner to "write" his story by placing the word cards in the proper order so that you can read them. Criterion for mastery is the combination of any number of words that are grammatically accurate and that make sense. When the learner has formed his story, have him read it back to you, encouraging him to make any changes in word order or word choice that he desires. The story can be of any length.

■ DIRECTING THE LEARNER'S ATTENTION   The purpose of this task is to teach the learner to produce and read messages using the individual words he knows. This task is similar to that described in IIIA 10 of the previous chapter, and you should select your teaching activity from among the storehouse of techniques described there. When teaching this skill, you must be certain that the learner attends to the oral directions, to the idea or message he wishes to convey, to the individual words, and to the order in which the words are placed in the sentence.

■ THE POSTTEST   The procedure and criterion for mastery remain the same as for the pretest.

WORD ANALYSIS

IB **1**

■ THE PERFORMANCE OBJECTIVE   Given a spoken stimulus word beginning with the *q*, *v*, *y*, or *z* sound and a group of three other words one of which begins with the *q*, *v*, *y*, and *z* sound, the learner pairs the two words beginning with the same sound.

■ THE PRETEST   Using the word sets listed below, say to the learner, "Here are three words. Listen carefully." (Say the words.) "Which one sounds like (say the stimulus word) at the beginning?" (Repeat the three original words.) Criterion for mastery is 6 out of 7 correct.

basket / veil / fall	Which one sounds like *vote* at the beginning? Repeat the first three words.
cane / top / quack	Which one sounds like *queen* at the beginning? Repeat the first three words.
zip / lip / size	Which one sounds like *zoo* at the beginning? Repeat the first three words.
quiet / cap / king	Which one sounds like *queen* at the beginning? Repeat the first three words.
joke / fell / yell	Which one sounds like *yes* at the beginning? Repeat the first three words.
vain / fool / win	Which one sounds like *vote* at the beginning? Repeat the first three words.
hole / yak / when	Which one sounds like *yes* at the beginning? Repeat the first three words.

■ DIRECTING THE LEARNER'S ATTENTION   The purpose of this task is to cue the learner to the importance of listening to the beginning sounds of words and to help him distinguish the *q*, *v*, *y*, and *z* sounds from other consonant sounds. This task is similar to that described in IIB 2 of the previous chapter, and you should select your teaching activity from among the storehouse of techniques described there. When teaching this skill, you must be certain that the learner attends to the oral directions and to the beginning sounds of the words in each spoken sequence.

■ THE POSTTEST   The procedure and criterion for mastery are the same as for the pretest. Use the words provided in the following list:

get / zombie / juice	Which one sounds like *zoo* at the beginning? Repeat the first three words.
hide / yarn / whip	Which one sounds like *yes* at the beginning? Repeat the first three words.
vat / note / whip	Which one sounds like *vote* at the beginning? Repeat the first three words.
tub / fake / yellow	Which one sounds like *yes* at the beginning? Repeat the first three words.
quite / seen / case	Which one sounds like *queen* at the beginning? Repeat the first three words.
zone / lie / sip	Which one sounds like *zoo* at the beginning? Repeat the first three words.
cap / tale / quick	Which one sounds like *queen* at the beginning? Repeat the first three words.
bike / vice / fox	Which one sounds like *vote* at the beginning? Repeat the first three words.

IB 2

■ THE PERFORMANCE OBJECTIVE   Given a spoken word beginning with the *q*, *v*, *y*, or *z* sound, the learner identifies the beginning letter as *q*, *v*, *y*, or *z*.

■ THE PRETEST   Give the learner four cards, one with the letter *q* printed on it, one with the letter *v*, one with the letter *y*, and the last with the letter *z*. Say the following words, directing the learner to point to the letter that begins the word. Criterion for mastery is 80 percent, with no letter sound being missed more than once.

quite	voice	vest	zone	yard	zoom
yankee	zipper	quiet	vast	quake	young

■ DIRECTING THE LEARNER'S ATTENTION   The purpose of this task is to help the learner establish a sound–symbol connection between the letters *q*, *v*, *y*, and *z* and words that begin with the sounds of *q*, *v*, *y*, and *z*. This task is similar to that described in IIB 5 of the previous chapter, and you should select your teaching activity from among the storehouse of techniques described there. When teaching this skill, you must be certain that the learner attends to the sound at the beginning of each spoken word while simultaneously looking at the correct letter.

■ THE POSTTEST   The procedure and criterion for mastery remain the same as for the pretest. Use the words provided below.

van	question	you	yoke	quad	zebra
zero	yet	quarter	valve	zither	vase

IB 3

■ THE PERFORMANCE OBJECTIVE Given an oral sentence with one word missing and cued for the missing word with a card having printed on it the first letter of that word (q, v, y, or z), the learner says a word beginning with the letter that fits the context for the sentence.

■ THE PRETEST Make cards with the above letters printed on them. Say, "I am going to say a sentence with one word missing. You look at the card and say a word that begins with the letter on the card and that finishes what I want to say." Use the following sentences. Criterion for mastery is 10 out of 12 correct, with no letter sound being missed more than once.

I like the animals in the z——.

I didn't understand, so I asked a q——.

When the teacher asked me if I wanted any candy, I said, "Y——."

I don't want to go to bed because I'm not tired y——.

The king and the princess were looking for the q——.

The animal with the stripes is called a z——.

In the election I v—— for Sally.

I fell against the table and knocked over my mother's new v——.

The z—— broke on my jacket.

I'm too tired to play anymore. I'm going to q——.

I am going to play in my back y——.

Mary has a beautiful singing v——.

Do you scream, do you threaten, or do you manage? Do you need to reread Chapter 3?

■ DIRECTING THE LEARNER'S ATTENTION The purpose of this task is to help the learner use his knowledge of context sense and letter–sound correspondence to identify unknown words. This task is similar to that described in IIB 12 of the previous chapter, and you should select your teaching activity from among the storehouse of activities described there. When teaching this skill, you must be certain that the learner attends to the directions, to the sense of the sentence, and to the letter provided and its sound value.

■ THE POSTTEST The procedure and criterion for mastery remain the same as for the pretest.

I want to be healthy, so I take my v____ every morning.

She wants to go with me, but I want to go with y____.

It is too noisy in here. We must be q____.

From the top of the mountain we went down into the v____.

It was very cold. On the thermometer it was below z____.

Her dress was blue; but mine was y____.

You are too slow. You must do the work more q____.

My airplane z____ through the air.

I play a guitar, but he plays a v____.

I can't go yet. I'm not q____ done.

I am very old, but you are y____.

I saw a lion in the z____.

IB 4

■ THE PERFORMANCE OBJECTIVE   Given a spoken stimulus word beginning with the *ch*, *wh*, or voiced *th* sound and a group of three other words one of which begins with the *ch*, *wh*, or voiced *th* sound, the learner pairs the two words beginning with the same sound.

■ THE PRETEST   Follow the same pattern described in IB 1 of this chapter. Use the following word sets. Criterion for mastery is 5 out of 6 correct.

church / curb / look
Which one sounds like *chug* at the beginning?
Repeat the first three words.

where / this / then
Which one sounds like *whip* at the beginning?
Repeat the first three words.

tip / those / whose
Which one sounds like *this* at the beginning?
Repeat the first three words.

wind / shoe / when
Which one sounds like *whip* at the beginning?
Repeat the first three words.

third / them / miss
Which one sounds like *this* at the beginning?
Repeat the first three words.

ship / chop / catch
Which one sounds like *chug* at the beginning?
Repeat the first three words.

■ DIRECTING THE LEARNER'S ATTENTION   The purpose of this task is to cue the learner to the importance of listening to the beginning sounds of words and to help him distinguish the *ch*, *wh*, and voiced *th* sounds from other consonant sounds. This task is similar to that described in IIB 4 of the previous chapter, and you should select your teaching activity from among the storehouse of techniques described there. When teaching this skill, you must be certain that the learner attends to the oral directions and to the beginning sounds in each word of the spoken sequence.

■ THE POSTTEST   The procedure and criterion for mastery remain the same as for the pretest.

then / when / ten	Which word sounds like *this* at the beginning? Repeat the first three words.
show / charm / cat	Which word sounds like *chug* at the beginning? Repeat the first three words.
win / shop / why	Which word sounds like *whip* at the beginning? Repeat the first three words.
tin / these / think	Which word sounds like *this* at the beginning? Repeat the first three words.
what / won / then	Which word sounds like *whip* at the beginning? Repeat the first three words.
chore / core / shine	Which word sounds like *chug* at the beginning? Repeat the first three words.

IB 5

■ THE PERFORMANCE OBJECTIVE   Given spoken words beginning with the *ch*, *wh*, or voiced *th* sound, the learner identifies the beginning letters as *ch*, *wh*, or *th*.

■ THE PRETEST   Follow the same procedure as described for IB 2 of this chapter. Use the words listed below. Criterion for mastery is 80 percent, with no letter sound being missed more than once.

church	those	chop	this	chose
where	when	why	them	

■ DIRECTING THE LEARNER'S ATTENTION   The purpose of this task is to help the learner establish a sound–symbol connection between the digraphs *ch*, *wh*, and *th* and words that begin with the sounds of *ch*, *wh*, and the voiced *th*. This task is similar to that described in IIB 5 of the previous chapter, and you should select your teaching activity from among the storehouse of techniques described there. When teaching this skill, you must be certain that the learner attends to the sound at the beginning of each spoken word and simultaneously looks at the correct letters.

■ THE POSTTEST   The procedure and criterion for mastery remain the same as for the pretest. Use the following words.

them	chirp	charge	child	these
whirl	which	wheat	that	

■ THE PERFORMANCE OBJECTIVE   Given an oral sentence with one word missing and cued for the missing word with a card having printed on it the digraph with which the word begins (*ch*, *wh*, or *th*), the learner says a word beginning with the digraph that fits the context of the sentence.

■ THE PRETEST   Follow the same procedure described for the pretest in IB 3 of this chapter. Use the sentences listed below. Criterion for mastery is 8 out of 9 correct.

On Sunday we go to ch——.

It isn't here. It is over th——.

I can't find it. Wh—— is it?

I don't want to go with you. I want to go with th——.

I found my desk, but I can't find my ch——.

Mice like to eat ch——.

The front wh—— on my bicycle broke when I fell off.

They aren't going with anybody. They're going all by th——.

The old man had long white wh—— on his face.

■ DIRECTING THE LEARNER'S ATTENTION   The purpose of this task is to help the learner use his knowledge of context sense and letter–sound correspondence to identify unknown words. This task is similar to that described in IIB 12 of the previous chapter, and you should select your teaching activity from among the storehouse of techniques described there. When teaching this skill, you must be certain that the learner attends to the directions, to the sense of the sentence, and to the letter provided and its sound value.

■ THE POSTTEST   The procedure and criterion for mastery remain the same as for the pretest. Use the following sentences.

My coat was yellow, but yours is wh——.

They aren't here. They are over th——.

My big brother can't sing, but he can wh—— through his teeth.

The teacher was writing on the blackboard with ch——.

When she came in from outdoors, her face was red, and she had rosy ch——.

I don't want this one. I want th—— one.

The man wanted the horse to run faster, so he wh—— him.

They are nice people. I like th——.

I got my pants all wet in the snow, and I will have to ch—— them.

IB 7 KEY OBJECTIVE

■ THE PERFORMANCE OBJECTIVE　Given known words composed of the vowel–consonant phonograms *at, et, it, ot, ut,* the learner replaces the first consonant in each known word with another consonant or digraph and pronounces the new word.

■ THE PRETEST　Use the lists of words provided below. The first word in each list has been taught previously as a sight word. Read the first word in the list and ask the learner to read the remaining words in each list. Criterion for mastery is 25 out of 29 correct with no initial consonant or digraph being missed more than once.

cat	*get*	*sit*	*hot*	*but*
fat	met	fit	got	cut
hat	set	hit	lot	nut
pat	wet	bit	shot	shut
sat	let	kit	pot	rut
that	bet	wit		
rat	whet			
bat	net			
chat	pet			

■ DIRECTING THE LEARNER'S ATTENTION　The purpose of this task is to help the learner recognize the regular short-vowel spelling pattern used in English and to give him experience in using this pattern to analyze and identify unknown words. This is a crucial analyzing skill for the learner, because it provides him with a problem-solving technique to use when trying to determine the pronunciation of an unknown word. For example, if he is unable to pronounce the word *bat,* but he already knows the word *cat,* he can say to himself, "I know that *c-a-t* spells *cat,* and I know the sound that *b* makes at the beginning of words, so if I replace the *c* in *cat* with a *b,* the unknown word must be —— *bat.*" As his experience with the spelling patterns of English increases and his sophistication in using this substitution skill grows, he can use variations of this problem-solving technique in substituting ending sounds, in substituting both beginning and ending sounds, and in substituting medial vowels.

To teach a learner to use this problem-solving technique, you must provide him with a known word (such as *cat* above) that illustrates the spelling pattern, with a letter for which he has established a letter–sound correspondence, with the technique of examining words for similarity in both visual form and sound, and with practice in substituting one letter for another in such words. In teaching this skill, then, you must be certain that the learner attends to the directions, to the pronunciation of the key word, to the initial letter of succeeding words, and to the sound value of each initial letter.

> **Key objective** for developing skill in using common spelling patterns as a means for analyzing unknown words.

■ TEACHING ACTIVITIES / *The model activity* Use a known sight word that illustrates the spelling pattern being taught. Print this on the chalkboard, asking the learner to read it. Then ask the question, "Let's see how many new words we can find that are relatives of this word." Print an unknown word that illustrates the same spelling pattern directly under the known word, making sure that the similar letters in both words are directly under each other.

Example: cat
bat

Say "See, this new word is related to our old word because it has the same letters at the end (or at the beginning or in the middle, as the case may be), but it is different at the beginning (or in the middle or at the end)." Direct the learner to say the sound that is the same in both words. Then tell him to "get his mouth ready" to say the letter sound that is different in the new word, to say that sound, and to quickly blend it with the sound that is the same in both words. Repeat this process with other words illustrating the same spelling pattern.

/ *Suggestions for reteaching and/or practice*

1 Print only the common parts of the word family on the chalkboard. For example, if you are working with *cat* and *bat*, print only the *at*. Ask the learner to pronounce this sound unit. Then ask, "What would I do to make this into *cat*?" Direct the learner to the initial consonant *c*, and then challenge him to "see how many other new words we can make out of this same word part." *Note*: Because you will be asking the learner to supply a letter in response to an auditory cue here, it is really a spelling task rather than a reading task. You are urged, therefore, to reverse the process as quickly as possible to conform with the reading act, requiring the learner to supply a letter sound in response to a visual cue—that is, asking the learner to look at the letters *b-a-t* and say "bat."

2 Persistent difficulty in remembering the sounds of any particular consonant letter or digraph would indicate that the learner should be redirected to the objective where that sound–symbol connection was originally encountered and retaught the skill. The storehouse of rhyming activities described in IIB 3 of the previous chapter might also be helpful in aiding learners having difficulty with this task.

3 A useful device to help learners master this task is the word wheel. You can construct word wheels by cutting two circles, one slightly larger than the other, from tagboard. On the larger wheel, print words in which the initial element is missing, starting each about the same distance from the center and progressing toward the outer edge like the spokes of a wheel. On the smaller circle, cut a slot of the size and position to expose only one word ending at a time, printing the consonant letter, blend, or digraph to be used to the left of the slot. Fasten the two circles together with a paper fastener. As you rotate the lower circle, the letters on the upper circle will make a new word as they are combined with each ending on the lower circle. This same principle can be reversed so that the ending remains constant and the beginning changes.

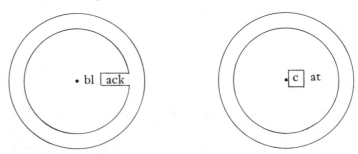

4 A similar device is the slip card, in which the spelling pattern being worked on is written on a wide piece of tagboard and the letters to be substituted are written on narrower cards and attached to the larger piece in a manner that allows one letter at a time to be shown with the spelling pattern.

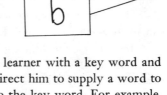

5 Use activities in which you provide the learner with a key word and a sentence in which one word is missing. Direct him to supply a word to fill the blank. This word must be related to the key word. For example, give him the key word *cat* and the sentence, "I hit the ball with the ————." He must supply the word *bat*.

6 Play games with the learner in which you start with a common spelling pattern written on the board. He substitutes another letter for either the initial or the final letter, and pronounces the new word. The next learner must change it again and pronounce the new word. The pattern of words may look something like this:

> *cat* is changed to *bat*
> *bat* is changed to *bag*
> *bag* is changed to *bad*
> *bad* is changed to *had*
> *had* is changed to *has*

7 Have one learner write on the chalkboard a word illustrating a common spelling pattern. He must then pronounce the word and make up a sentence using that word. The next learner goes to the chalkboard, changes either the initial or final consonant in the word, pronounces the new word, and uses it in a new sentence. At first you may want to accept any sentence the learner produces. As he becomes more skillful, however, you can modify the activity by having him produce successive sentences that are related to each other and that tell a story. For example, the sentences may proceed in this manner:

> The *cat* is in the house.
> He is sleeping near the *bat*.
> A man put the cat in a *bag*.
> He must be a *bad* man.

8 Make word cards using words incorporating the common spelling patterns you have been working on. Include also a number of cards that have the word "changeover" written on them. Deal each learner five cards. One learner starts by laying down any word card and naming it. The next player must play a card that is related to that word. If he cannot play, he draws from the deck until he either has a word he can play or has drawn three cards. If he has the changeover card, he can play that and name a new word to be played on it. The first person out of cards wins the game.

9 Play a variation of "Crazy Eights" by making a deck of 40 cards that have printed on them words containing the spelling patterns you have been working on. Make six cards with the numeral *8* on them. Each learner gets four cards, with the rest of the cards placed in the center of the table. The first learner lays down a card and pronounces the word on it. The next player must play a card from his hand that contains the same word element or an *8* card. If he has neither a word card that fits nor an *8* card, he must draw a card from the deck. The learner who gets rid of all his cards first is the winner.

10 A variation of bingo can be played in which the common spelling patterns you have been working on are printed in the squares of the game card. The learner has a number of consonant letters, blends, and digraphs in his possession. The leader holds up a letter card, and the learner sees if he has the letter in his pile. If he does, he tries to combine it with one of the spelling patterns on his game card. When he has formed all the words in a row, he may call "bingo." If he then can pronounce each word he has formed in the row, he wins the game.

11 To help a learner see the relationships in a group of words using the same common spelling patterns, help him build a structure similar to the following:

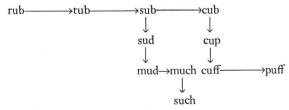

During the building of this structure you should be certain that the learner sees the similarities and differences between each word and the related word from which it is generated. Be sure you use only phonetic elements for which the learner has established a letter–sound correspondence.

■ THE POSTTEST The pretest can be used also for the posttest. Procedure and criterion for mastery remain the same.

IB 8

■ THE PERFORMANCE OBJECTIVE Given words he pronounced in previous objectives, the learner replaces the final consonant with another consonant or digraph and pronounces the new word.

■ THE PRETEST Use the lists of words provided below. The first word in each list has been taught previously as a sight word or as one of the words analyzed in the previous objective. Read the first word in the list and ask the learner to read the remaining words. Criterion for mastery is 30 out of 33 correct.

cat	*hat*	*bat*	*rat*	*chat*	*met*	*bet*
cap	had	bad	rash	chap	men	bed
can	has	bag			mesh	beg
		bath	*fit*	*sit*		
bit	*fit*		fix	sip	*hot*	*lot*
big	fish	*hit*	fib		hop	lob
bid		his	fin			
bib	*rut*	hid				
	rub					
but		*got*				
bus	*set*	God				
bug	sex	gosh				
buzz						
bun						

Are you reading poems and stories to your learners every day?

■ DIRECTING THE LEARNER'S ATTENTION The purpose of this task is to help the learner substitute new endings in known words as a means of identifying new words. This task is similar to the one described in IB 7 of this chapter, and you should select your teaching activity from among the storehouse of techniques described there. When teaching this skill, you must be certain that the learner attends to the directions, to the pronunciation of the key words, to the final letter of succeeding words, and to the sound the final letter produces.

■ THE POSTTEST The pretest can be used also for the posttest. Procedure and criterion for mastery remain the same.

IB 9

■ THE PERFORMANCE OBJECTIVE Given the key words introduced in the previous two objectives or identified during the course of this objective, the learner changes either the beginning or the ending of the words and pronounces the new words.

■ THE PRETEST Use the lists of words provided below. The first word in each list has been taught previously or is a word the learner has pronounced previously in this objective. Read the first word in each list and ask the learner to read the remaining words. Criterion for mastery is 40 out of 45 correct.

cap	*can*	*cab*	*had*	*bad*	*men*	*bed*
sap	ran	fab	lad	mad	hen	fed
tap	than	gas			mess	led
	man		*fix*	*fin*		red
big		*fish*	six	kin	*sip*	
dip	*wit*	dish			tip	*hop*
pig	with		*sub*	*lob*		shop
	wish	*cub*	sud	bob	*beg*	pop
bun		cup	mud	box	leg	top
fun	*rub*	cuff	much	fox		
run	cub	puff	such			
sun	tub					
shun						
shush						
rush						

■ DIRECTING THE LEARNER'S ATTENTION The purpose of this task is to help the learner use his knowledge of common spelling patterns, beginning sounds, and ending sounds to identify unknown words. It is similar to the task described in IB 7 of this chapter, and you should select your teaching activity from among the storehouse of techniques described there. When teaching this skill, you must be certain that the learner attends to the directions, to the pronunciation of the key word, to the similarity between the key word and the word to be pronounced, to the letter(s) in the new word that differs from the key word, and to the sound value of that letter or letters.

■ THE POSTTEST The pretest can be used also for the posttest. The procedure and criterion for mastery remain the same.

IB 10

■ THE PERFORMANCE OBJECTIVE Given a spoken stimulus word ending with the *ck* sound and a group of three other words one of which ends with the *ck* sound, the learner pairs the two words that end with the *ck* sound.

■ THE PRETEST Using the word sets listed below, say to the learner, "Here are three words. Listen carefully." (Say the three words.) "Which one sounds like (say the stimulus word) at the end?" (Repeat the three original words.) Criterion for mastery is 4 out of 5 correct.

land / band / back	Which word sounds like *neck* at the end? Repeat the first three words.
sick / sit / Ned	Which word sounds like *neck* at the end? Repeat the first three words.
love / luck / tube	Which word sounds like *neck* at the end? Repeat the first three words.
lot / shot / rock	Which word sounds like *neck* at the end? Repeat the first three words.
nut / miss / stick	Which word sounds like *neck* at the end? Repeat the first three words.

■ DIRECTING THE LEARNER'S ATTENTION The purpose of this task is to help the learner distinguish between the ending sound of *ck* and other ending sounds. This task is similar to that described in IIB 3 in Chapter 4, and you should select your teaching activity from among the storehouse of techniques described there. When teaching this skill, you must be certain that the learner attends to the directions and to the final sound in each of the words in the spoken sequence.

■ THE POSTTEST The procedure and criterion for mastery remain the same as for the pretest.

pill / pit / pick	Which word sounds like *neck* at the end? Repeat the first three words.
sack / sill / sash	Which word sounds like *neck* at the end? Repeat the first three words.

dove / duck / nest

Which word sounds like *neck* at the end?
Repeat the first three words.

lot / net / lock

Which word sounds like *neck* at the end?
Repeat the first three words.

check / net / check

Which word sounds like *neck* at the end?
Repeat the first three words.

IB **11**

■ THE PERFORMANCE OBJECTIVE   Given a spoken word, the learner points to the letters *ck* if the word ends in the *ck* sound.

■ THE PRETEST   Give the learner a card with the letters *ck* printed on it. Say the following words, directing the learner to point to the *ck* card each time a word is spoken that ends with that sound. Criterion for mastery is 8 out of 10 correct.

bat	pick	rock	much	back
luck	chest	cast	duck	neck

■ DIRECTING THE LEARNER'S ATTENTION   The purpose of this task is to help the learner establish a sound–symbol connection between the letters *ck* and words that end with the *ck* sound. This task is similar to that described in IIB 5 in Chapter 4, except that the focus here is on ending sounds rather than on beginning sounds. You should select your teaching activity from among the storehouse of techniques described in IIB 5. When teaching this skill, you must be certain that the learner attends to the sound at the end of each spoken word and simultaneously looks at the letters *ck*.

■ THE POSTTEST   The procedure and criterion for mastery remain the same as for the pretest.

sack	flab	bet	pack	shell
lock	sick	buck	back	camp

IB **12**

■ THE PERFORMANCE OBJECTIVE   Given words he pronounced in previous objectives, the learner replaces the final consonant in these words with *ck* and pronounces the new word.

■ THE PRETEST   Use the lists of words provided below. The first word in each list has been taught previously as a sight word or as one of the words analyzed in previous objectives. Read the first word in the list and ask the learner to read the remaining words. Criterion for mastery is 20 out of 25 correct.

bat	*bet*	*sit*	*lot*	*but*
back	beck	sick	lock	buck
rack	neck	kick	shock	luck
hack	check	chick	hock	muck
shack		pick	rock	shuck
pack		hick	mock	chuck
sack				duck

■ DIRECTING THE LEARNER'S ATTENTION   The purpose of this task is to help the learner use the principle of consonant substitution as a means of identifying words ending with the *ck* letters. This task is similar to that described in IB 7 of this chapter, and you should select your teaching activity from among the storehouse of techniques described there. When teaching this skill, you must be certain that the learner attends to the directions, to the pronunciation of the key word, to the similarities and differences in succeeding words in the list, and to the sound produced by the *ck*.

■ THE POSTTEST   The pretest can also be used for the posttest. The procedure and criterion for mastery remain the same.

IB 13 KEY OBJECTIVE

■ THE PERFORMANCE OBJECTIVE   Given a word he has analyzed previously or has learned to recognize at sight, the learner adds the structural ending *ed*, *ing*, or *s* and pronounces the new word.

■ THE PRETEST   Use the following lists of words. Read the first word in each list and ask the learner to read the remaining words. Criterion for mastery is 30 correct out of 32, with no structural ending being missed more than once.

like	*kick*	*fish*	*go*	*boy*	*sit*
liked	kicked	fishing	going	boys	sits
fished	picked	backing	locking	hats	wets
backed	locked	packing	shocking	cats	fits
racked	rocked	kicking	rocking	rats	cuts
packed	ducked	picking	ducking	bats	rubs
				nuts	its

■ DIRECTING THE LEARNER'S ATTENTION   The purpose of this task is to help the learner pronounce new words that are composed of a known root and the *ed, ing,* or *s* endings. This skill is one of a number of skills in which the learner identifies unknown words by looking at word parts or word structures. For example, he identifies the parts in prefixed words such as *un-happy,* in suffixed words such as *back-ing,* and in compound words such as *snow-man.* (*Caution*: Note that this skill is not the same as syllabication, which divides words into parts on the basis of *sound units* rather than on the basis of *meaning units* as is done here.) Analyzing by structure is another problem-solving technique the learner can use when he meets a word he does not know at sight. For example, if he is unable to pronounce the word *backing* but already knows the word *back* and the sound produced by the *ing* ending, he can say to himself, "I know that *b-a-c-k* is pronounced *back* and I know the sound *ing* makes at the ends of words, so *back* and *ing* must say —— *backing.*" This is a particularly important skill because it allows for rapid identification of the unknown word.

To use this skill well, the learner must understand how to examine unknown words for known word parts, he must be able to recognize the root word at sight or be able to sound it out using the phonetic elements he has been taught, he must know the sound value associated with the prefix, suffix, or parts of the compound, and he must be able to blend the pronunciation of the two parts together. When teaching the skill, then, you must be certain that the learner attends to the root word or words and to the prefix or suffix and its sound value.

Key objective for developing skill in analyzing words in terms of word parts or structure.

■ TEACHING ACTIVITIES / *The model activity*   When teaching prefixed and suffixed words, choose one root word, print it on the chalkboard, and ask the learner to say the word and use it in a sentence. Next, print the word with the structural ending added, pronounce it for the learner, have him pronounce it, and ask him to use it in a sentence. Then have the learner explain the difference in meaning between the root word and the same word with the structural ending added. Next, direct the learner to inspect the root word and the root word with the ending as they are printed on the board, having him isolate the letters that make up the ending. Finally, have him pronounce separately first the root word, then the ending, and finally the root word and the ending together. Repeat the same process using other root words with the same structural ending.

When teaching compound words, select a relatively easy one, such as *into,* for illustration. Pronounce the word, write it on the chalkboard, and use the word in a sentence. Then say, "This word is made by putting together two words that you already know. Watch me and see if you can tell me what these two words are." Then cover up *to* by placing your hand over it, saying, "What word is at the beginning of this word?" Then cover up *in* and say, "What word is at the end?" Direct the learner to tell the two words that form the compound and to pronounce them together. Help the learner go through the same process with another compound. For each word analyzed in this manner, be sure to indicate that the meaning of the compound is a combination of the meaning of the two words that make it up. *Caution*: Do not teach the learner to "look for the little word in the big word" because this process is not helpful in analyzing words that are not compounds. For example, it is of little help to look for the little word *at* in *boat* or the little word *fat* in *father*.

/ Suggestions for reteaching and/or practice

1 If the learner has difficulty with this task because he is unable to remember the root word, you should redirect him to the objective in which the word was originally taught and provide him with additional instruction in recognizing this word.

2 If the learner has difficulty with this task because he has not associated a sound value with any particular prefix or suffix, you should select appropriate teaching techniques from IIB 5 in Chapter 4 and adapt these for use in developing a sound–symbol connection between the unknown prefix or suffix and its sound value.

3 The word wheel and word slip techniques can be adapted for use in teaching the addition of structural elements to known words. A description of the construction and use of word wheels and word slips is contained in the storehouse of suggestions provided in IB 7 of this chapter.

4 Context activities can be used to develop this skill. Provide the learner with sentences in which one word is missing, giving him a choice of a root word or a root and its structural ending to fill the space. For example, a sample sentence might be: "The two ——— (boy, boys) went to the store." The learner chooses the correct word to fill the blank, pronounces it, and tells why that word is the correct one. *Caution*: The successful use of this technique presupposes that the learner already knows orally the correct form of the word. Certain dialects will not contain many of these inflected and derived forms. Teach these as oral responses prior to the activity described above.

5 If the learner has difficulty with this task because he is unable to differentiate the sounds of the structural elements, you should adapt and use the say-it-slow,-say-it-fast technique described in the storehouse of teaching suggestions provided in IIB 2 in Chapter 4.

6 It is sometimes helpful to reverse the process described in the model teaching activity. That is, ask the learner to *create* words having prefixes or suffixes, or words that are compound. In such a case, you should print the known words and word parts on separate cards, scramble them up, and have the learner choose one. Then he must choose another word card that will go with the word, making it either a prefixed word, a suffixed word, or a compound word. Be sure that you have the learner pronounce the word he has created.

7 Structural elements can be taught by marking the word parts in some distinctive way. For example, the words forming a compound can be printed in two different colors, or the separate words can be circled or have a line drawn between them. The learner then pronounces the new word as a whole.

8 Make a chart or a worksheet in which root words or initial parts of compounds are listed on the left side and suffixes or the second part of the compound are listed on the right side. Attach strings to the words in the left-hand column and direct the learner to connect the string with the suffix or other part of the compound in the right-hand column so as to make a new word.

9 Make up crossword puzzles in which only compound words and/or prefixed and suffixed words can be used as answers.

10 Play a card game in which each player is dealt cards having root words written on them. Another deck, containing only prefixes and/or suffixes is placed in the center of the table. The learners take turns drawing cards from the deck and trying to match the drawn card with one of the root words to form a new word. If a learner can do so, he lays the two cards down together and pronounces the new word. If he draws a card he cannot use, he puts it back on the bottom of the pile. The first player to get rid of all his cards is the winner.

11 Give context experiences in which the learner must complete a series of sentences using the same root word in each. For example, you can provide him with the root word *play* and tell him to use it together with suffixes to complete these sentences (see *Caution* in Activity 4):

He is a baseball ———.   Yesterday he ——— football.

He is ——— in the game.   When he ———, he is happy.

■ THE POSTTEST   The pretest can be used for the posttest. The procedure and criterion for mastery remain the same.

IIA **1**

■ THE PERFORMANCE OBJECTIVE   Given a flash presentation of each of the following words, the learner pronounces each word within one second. The words to test are:

out	new	been	too	want	shall	laugh	water
him	said	her	baby	went	pull	ball	woman
us	this	much	something	where	if	gone	word
or	what	them	from	door	long	pretty	write
have	all	about	house	dog	other	surprise	

■ THE PRETEST   Print each of the above words on flash cards. Then flash each word to the learner, giving him only a second or less to examine the word. Criterion for mastery is 100 percent. *Note*: You should keep track of the words missed on the pretest because only these words need to be taught.

■ DIRECTING THE LEARNER'S ATTENTION   The purpose of this task is to teach the learner to recognize instantly the words listed in the objective when they are printed on cards. This task is similar to that described in IIIA 6 in Chapter 4, and you should select your teaching activity from among the storehouse of techniques described there. When teaching this skill, you must be certain that the learner attends to the visual form of the word and to its distinguishing characteristics.

■ THE POSTTEST   The procedure and criterion for mastery remain the same as for the pretest.

IIA **2**

■ THE PERFORMANCE OBJECTIVE   Given a flash presentation of each of the frequently confused words *it–if* and *they–then–the–them*, the learner pronounces each word within one second.

■ THE PRETEST   The procedure and criterion for mastery are the same as for the pretest in the previous objective.

■ DIRECTING THE LEARNER'S ATTENTION   The purpose of this task is to teach the learner to recognize each of the above easily confused words when they are printed on cards. This task is similar to that described in IA 2 of this chapter, and you should select your teaching activity from among the storehouse of techniques described there. When teaching this skill, you must be certain that the learner attends to the visual discriminator that acts as the cue for contrasting these easily confused words.

■ THE POSTTEST   The procedure and criterion for mastery remain the same as for the pretest.

IIA 3

■ THE PERFORMANCE OBJECTIVE   Given words he recognizes at sight, the learner creates and reads stories using these words.

■ THE PRETEST   Provide the learner with cards each of which has printed on it a word he recognizes instantly. Say to the learner, "Today we are going to write our own stories. Look at the cards you have in front of you. Each card has a word on it that you know. Can you tell me a little story using the words you have here? If you want to use a word you don't have on a card, tell me and I will make a card having that word on it." Direct the learner to "write" his story by placing the word cards in the proper order so that you can read them. Criterion for mastery is the combination of any number of words that are grammatically accurate and that make sense. When the learner has formed his story, have him read it back to you, encouraging him to make any changes he desires. The story can be of any length, but a single sentence indicates adequate achievement.

■ DIRECTING THE LEARNER'S ATTENTION   The purpose of this task is to teach the learner to produce and read messages using the individual words he knows. This task is similar to that described in IIIA 10 in Chapter 4, and you should select your teaching activity from among the storehouse of techniques described there. When teaching this skill, you must be certain that the learner attends to the oral directions, to the idea or message he wishes to convey, to the individual words, and to the order in which the words are placed in the sentences.

■ THE POSTTEST   The procedure and criterion for mastery remain the same as for the pretest.

IIB ∎

■ THE PERFORMANCE OBJECTIVE Given a spoken stimulus word beginning with the sound produced by the consonant blend *br*, *cr*, *dr*, *fr*, *gr*, *tr*, or *pr*, and a group of three other words one of which begins with the sound of *br*, *cr*, *dr*, *fr*, *gr*, *tr*, or *pr*, the learner pairs the two words beginning with the same sound.

■ THE PRETEST Using the word sets listed below, say to the learner, "Here are three words. Listen carefully." (Say the words.) "Which one sounds like (say the stimulus word) at the beginning?" (Repeat the three original words.) Criterion for mastery is 13 out of 14 correct.

dress / pray / think	Which one sounds like *press* at the beginning? Repeat the first three words.
bread / drink / shirt	Which one sounds like *bring* at the beginning? Repeat the first three words.
cap / come / cross	Which one sounds like *crash* at the beginning? Repeat the first three words.
doll / drink / think	Which one sounds like *drop* at the beginning? Repeat the first three words.
from / for / thumb	Which one sounds like *friend* at the beginning? Repeat the first three words.
three / gas / grape	Which one sounds like *grow* at the beginning? Repeat the first three words.
true / tee / tiger	Which one sounds like *tree* at the beginning? Repeat the first three words.
glue / grass / gone	Which one sounds like *grow* at the beginning? Repeat the first three words.
pin / pest / prize	Which one sounds like *press* at the beginning? Repeat the first three words.
top / truck / luck	Which one sounds like *tree* at the beginning? Repeat the first three words.
crop / cow / kite	Which one sounds like *crash* at the beginning? Repeat the first three words.
bake / brave / blue	Which one sounds like *bring* at the beginning? Repeat the first three words.

drum / dive / hive	Which one sounds like *drop* at the beginning? Repeat the first three words.
fish / fine / free	Which one sounds like *friend* at the beginning? Repeat the first three words.

■ DIRECTING THE LEARNER'S ATTENTION   The purpose of this task is to cue the learner to the importance of listening to the beginning sounds of words and to help him distinguish the combination *r* blend from other consonant sounds. This task is similar to that described in IIB 2 in Chapter 4, and you should select your teaching activity from among the storehouse of techniques described there. When teaching this skill, you must be certain that the learner attends to the oral directions and to the beginning sounds of the words in each spoken sequence.

■ THE POSTTEST   The procedure and criterion for mastery are the same as for the pretest.

freeze / fight / fly	Which one sounds like *friend* at the beginning? Repeat the first three words.
drill / dish / dip	Which one sounds like *drop* at the beginning? Repeat the first three words.
bat / bread / black	Which one sounds like *bring* at the beginning? Repeat the first three words.
creep / keep / cash	Which one sounds like *crash* at the beginning? Repeat the first three words.
tail / train / twist	Which one sounds like *tree* at the beginning? Repeat the first three words.
pine / prune / pail	Which one sounds like *press* at the beginning? Repeat the first three words.
glass / get / great	Which one sounds like *grow* at the beginning? Repeat the first three words.
trade / tale / free	Which one sounds like *tree* at the beginning? Repeat the first three words.
thank / gave / grease	Which one sounds like *grow* at the beginning? Repeat the first three words.
fry / try / fly	Which one sounds like *friend* at the beginning? Repeat the first three words.
desk / dream / mop	Which one sounds like *drop* at the beginning? Repeat the first three words.
call / clash / creep	Which one sounds like *crash* at the beginning? Repeat the first three words.
bright / bless / big	Which one sounds like *bring* at the beginning? Repeat the first three words.
drug / price / pen	Which one sounds like *press* at the beginning? Repeat the first three words.

IIB 2

■ THE PERFORMANCE OBJECTIVE   Given spoken words beginning with the *br*, *cr*, *dr*, *fr*, *gr*, *tr*, or *pr* sounds, the learner identifies the beginning letters in each word.

■ THE PRETEST   Give the learner seven cards, with one of the blends being tested (*br*, *cr*, *dr*, *fr*, *gr*, *tr*, and *pr*) printed on each card. Say the following words, directing the learner to point to the card with the letters that begin the word. Criterion for mastery is 13 out of 14 correct.

| pretty | grade | tractor | braid | cradle | dragon | fresh |
| prove | ground | frog | brain | trick | crowd | drug |

■ DIRECTING THE LEARNER'S ATTENTION   The purpose of this task is to help the learner establish a sound–symbol connection between the letters *br*, *cr*, *dr*, *fr*, *gr*, *tr*, and *pr* and words that begin with the sounds produced by these blends. This task is similar to that described in IIB 5 in Chapter 4, and you should select your teaching activity from among the storehouse of techniques described there. When teaching this skill, you must be certain that the learner attends to the sound at the beginning of each spoken word and simultaneously looks at the correct letter combination.

■ THE POSTTEST   The procedure and criterion for mastery remain the same as for the pretest. Use the following words.

| brake | crack | grab | trap | draw | free | prince |
| print | drive | front | gray | trigger | cream | brat |

IIB 3

■ THE PERFORMANCE OBJECTIVE   Given an oral sentence with one word missing and cued for the missing word with a card having printed on it the blend with which the word begins (*br*, *cr*, *dr*, *fr*, *gr*, *tr*, *pr*), the learner says a word beginning with the letter blend that fits the context of the sentence.

■ THE PRETEST   Make cards with the above letter blends on them. Say, "I am going to say a sentence with one word missing. You look at the card and say a word that begins with the letters on the card and that finishes what I want to say." Use the following sentences. Criterion for mastery is 12 out of 14, with no letter blend being missed more than once.

We go to church to pr——.   I like to put milk and fr—— on my cereal.

The person who is in charge of the school is called a pr——.

I like to dr—— pictures.

We didn't have to pay any money because it was fr——.

In our back yard the gr—— is green.

At Halloween we play a lot of tr——.

I would like to play the dr—— in the band.

I like to watch the tr—— go down the tracks.

I'm going to be a baseball player when I gr—— up.

The baby was sleeping in her cr——.

I like to eat jelly on my br——.

There were lots and lots of people in the cr——.

In order to get over the river we had to build a br——.

Are you captivating your learners, or are they just captive?

■ DIRECTING THE LEARNER'S ATTENTION   The purpose of this task is to help the learner use his knowledge of context sense and letter–sound correspondence of the combination *r* blends to identify unknown words. This task is similar to that described in IIB 12 in Chapter 4, and you should select your teaching activity from among the storehouse of activities described there. When teaching this skill, you must be certain that the learner attends to the directions, to the sense of the sentence, and to the letter combination provided and its sound value.

■ THE POSTTEST   The procedure and criterion for mastery remain the same as for the pretest. Use the following sentences.

The sun was so br—— that it hurt my eyes.

The lines he drew are not straight. They are cr——.

I have a sister who is in the third gr—— in school.

The farmer was sitting on his big tr——.

I was thirsty, so I got a dr——.

My mother put the ice cream in the fr—— so it wouldn't melt.

It was my birthday, so I got a pr——.

It was so cold that I nearly fr—— my toes off.

The little girl wore a new dr——.

I won a pr—— because I was first in the race.

The cat ran up into the big tr——.

The shirt was brown and gr——.

The house was made out of wood and br——.

Always look both ways before you cr—— the busy street.

IIB 4

■ THE PERFORMANCE OBJECTIVE　Given a word he has learned previously, the learner substitutes the blends *br*, *cr*, *dr*, *fr*, *gr*, *tr*, and *pr* in the initial position and pronounces the new word.

■ THE PRETEST　Use the lists of words provided below. The first word in each list has been previously taught as a sight word or as a word analyzed in previous objectives. Read the first word in the list and ask the learner to read the remaining words. Criterion for mastery is 15 out of 19 correct, with no blend being missed more than once.

cap	*fed*	*sip*	*top*	*tub*	*cab*	*cat*
trap	tred	drip	drop	drub	drab	brat
	Fred	grip	prop		crab	
buck		trip	crop		grab	
truck	*rush*					
	crush	*bib*	*mess*			
		crib	press			
			dress			

■ DIRECTING THE LEARNER'S ATTENTION　The purpose of this task is to help the learner recognize the regular spelling patterns used in English and to help him transfer his knowledge of initial consonant blends and spelling patterns to the identification of unknown words. This task is similar to that described in IB 7 of this chapter, and you should select your teaching activity from among the storehouse of techniques described there. When teaching this skill, you must be certain that the learner attends to the directions, to the pronunciation of the key word, to the initial blends of the succeeding words, and to the sound value of the blend.

■ THE POSTTEST　The pretest can be used also for the posttest. The procedure and criterion for mastery remain the same.

IIB 5

■ THE PERFORMANCE OBJECTIVE　Given a word learned in a previous objective, the learner changes either the beginning or the ending of the word and pronounces the new word.

■ THE PRETEST　Use the following lists of words. The first word in each list has been taught previously. Read the first word in the list and ask the learner to read the remaining words in each list. Criterion for mastery is 7 out of 8 correct.

Fred	*trip*	*crop*	*ran*
fresh	trick	crock	ranch
	brick	frock	branch
		frog	

■ DIRECTING THE LEARNER'S ATTENTION   The purpose of this task is to help the learner use his knowledge of common spelling patterns, beginning sounds, and ending sounds to identify unknown words. This task is similar to that described in IB 7 of this chapter, and you should select your teaching activity from among the storehouse of techniques described there. When teaching this skill, you must be certain that the learner attends to the directions, to the pronunciation of the key word, to the similarity between the key word and the word to be pronounced, to the letter(s) in the new word that differs, and to the sound value of that letter or letters.

■ THE POSTTEST   The pretest can be used also for the posttest. The procedure and criterion for mastery remain the same.

IIB 6

■ THE PERFORMANCE OBJECTIVE   Given a spoken stimulus word beginning with the sound produced by the consonant blend *bl, cl, fl, pl, gl,* or *sl* and a group of three other words one of which begins with the sound of *bl, cl, fl, pl, gl,* or *sl,* the learner pairs the two words that begin with the same sound.

■ THE PRETEST   Using the word sets listed below, say to the learner, "Here are three words. Listen carefully." (Say the words.) "Which one sounds like (say the stimulus word) at the beginning?" (Repeat the three original words.) Criterion for mastery is 11 out of 12 correct.

sheep / keep / slab	Which one sounds like *sleep* at the beginning? Repeat the first three words.
grab / glee / me	Which one sounds like *glad* at the beginning? Repeat the first three words.
click / quick / cry	Which one sounds like *cliff* at the beginning? Repeat the first three words.
pray / plank / pan	Which one sounds like *plow* at the beginning? Repeat the first three words.
my / friend / fluff	Which one sounds like *fly* at the beginning? Repeat the first three words.

sack / brown / blink

Which one sounds like *black* at the beginning?
Repeat the first three words.

glum / grow / got

Which one sounds like *glad* at the beginning?
Repeat the first three words.

prize / plump / hunt

Which one sounds like *plow* at the beginning?
Repeat the first three words.

sweep / sweet / slant

Which one sounds like *sleep* at the beginning?
Repeat the first three words.

flint / from / try

Which one sounds like *fly* at the beginning?
Repeat the first three words.

crime / clad / kiss

Which one sounds like *cliff* at the beginning?
Repeat the first three words.

bloom / broom / boom

Which one sounds like *black* at the beginning?
Repeat the first three words.

■ DIRECTING THE LEARNER'S ATTENTION   The purpose of this task is to cue the learner to the importance of listening to the beginning sounds of words and to help him distinguish the combination *l* blends from other consonant sounds. This task is similar to that described in IIB 2 in Chapter 4, and you should select your teaching activity from among the storehouse of techniques described there. When teaching this skill, you must be certain that the learner attends to the oral directions and to the beginning sound of the words in each spoken sequence.

What have you planned for today that is really exciting and different?

■ THE POSTTEST   The procedure and criterion for mastery remain the same as for the pretest. Use the word sets listed below.

blond / brown / back

Which one sounds like *black* at the beginning?
Repeat the first three words.

crowd / cloth / cold

Which one sounds like *cliff* at the beginning?
Repeat the first three words.

flour / from / fry

Which one sounds like *fly* at the beginning?
Repeat the first three words.

stump / creep / slump

Which one sounds like *sleep* at the beginning?
Repeat the first three words.

pride / plume / flower

Which one sounds like *plow* at the beginning?
Repeat the first three words.

gleam / grow / got

Which one sounds like *glad* at the beginning?
Repeat the first three words.

bright / buy / bleach

Which one sounds like *black* at the beginning?
Repeat the first three words.

fresh / find / fleet	Which one sounds like *fly* at the beginning? Repeat the first three words.
prove / plod / poor	Which one sounds like *plow* at the beginning? Repeat the first three words.
clerk / cross / come	Which one sounds like *cliff* at the beginning? Repeat the first three words.
grace / glance / mad	Which one sounds like *glad* at the beginning? Repeat the first three words.
shot / sweet / slum	Which one sounds like *sleep* at the beginning? Repeat the first three words.

IIB 7

■ THE PERFORMANCE OBJECTIVE   Given spoken words beginning with the *bl*, *cl*, *fl*, *pl*, *gl*, and *sl* sounds, the learner identifies the beginning letters in each word.

■ THE PRETEST   Give the learner six cards with one of the blends being tested (*bl*, *cl*, *fl*, *pl*, *gl*, and *sl*) printed on each card. Say the following words, directing the learner to point to the card with the letters that begin the word. Criterion for mastery is 11 out of 12 correct.

blare	pluck	slot	flannel	glow	clear
claim	slash	blend	gland	plunge	flush

■ DIRECTING THE LEARNER'S ATTENTION   The purpose of this task is to help the learner establish a sound–symbol connection between the letter blends *bl*, *cl*, *fl*, *pl*, *gl*, and *sl* and words that begin with the sounds produced by these blends. This task is similar to that described in IIB 5 in Chapter 4, and you should select your teaching activity from among the storehouse of techniques described there. When teaching this skill, you must be certain that the learner attends to the sound at the beginning of each spoken word while simultaneously looking at the correct letter combination.

■ THE POSTTEST   The procedure and criterion for mastery remain the same as in the pretest. Use the following words.

slate	clever	slacks	glow	glare	clam
plenty	blank	flesh	flop	plastic	blab

IIB 8

■ THE PERFORMANCE OBJECTIVE   Given an oral sentence with one word missing and cued for the missing word by a card having printed on it the blend with which the word begins (*bl*, *cl*, *fl*, *pl*, *gl*, or *sl*), the learner says a word beginning with that letter blend which fits the context of the sentence.

■ THE PRETEST   Make cards with the above letter blends printed on them. Say, "I am going to say a sentence with one word missing. You look at the card I hold up and say a word that begins with the letters on the card and that finishes what I want to say." Use the following sentences. Criterion for mastery is 10 out of 12, with no letter blend being missed more than once.

I cut my finger, and it started to bl——.

The preacher said, "God bl—— you."

After the movie we all cl—— our hands.

We take a bath so that we will be cl——.

One of the first things we do each day in school is stand and salute the fl——.

We went close to the vase so that we could smell the pretty fl——.

I drank my milk out of a gl——.

It was cold outside, so I put on my gl——.

After school we went outside to pl——.

My mother put my food on my pl——.

Because he was mad, he sl—— the door as he left the room.

I slid down the hill on my sl——.

■ DIRECTING THE LEARNER'S ATTENTION   The purpose of this task is to help the learner use context and letter–sound correspondence of the combination *l* blends to identify unknown words. This task is similar to that described in IIB 12 in Chapter 4, and you should select your teaching activity from among the storehouse of activities described there. When teaching this skill, you must be certain that the learner attends to the directions, to the sense of the sentence, and to the letter combination provided and its sound value.

■ THE POSTTEST   The procedure and criterion for mastery remain the same as for the pretest. Use the following sentences.

The baby sat on the floor and played with his bl——.

I dropped my pencil on the fl——.

To find out what time it is, the man looked at the cl——.

The big bird picked up the little animal in his cl——.

I wish I could fl—— like a bird.

The wind was so strong it made my hat bl—— off.

I am so tired I could sl—— all day.

I am real gl—— to see that you are all better.

I like all kinds of fruit, including pears, peaches, and pl——.

The teacher said, "Two pl—— two equals four."

The vase fell and broke, but we used gl—— to put it back together.

Be careful that you don't sl—— on the ice!

IIB 9

■ THE PERFORMANCE OBJECTIVE Given a word he has learned previously, the learner substitutes the blends *bl, cl, fl, pl, gl,* or *sl* in the initial position and pronounces the new word.

■ THE PRETEST Use the lists of words provided below. The first word in each list has been taught previously as a sight word or as a word analyzed in previous objectives. Read the first word in the list and ask the learner to read the remaining words. Criterion for mastery is 20 out of 25 correct, with no blend being missed more than once.

cap	*bed*	*tip*	*hop*	*rub*	*mad*	*neck*	*bib*
clap	fled	clip	flop	club	glad	fleck	glib
slap	sled	flip	plop				
		slip	slop	*mess*	*back*		
rock	*luck*			bless	black		
block	pluck	*shush*	*fat*				
clock	cluck	flush	flat				
flock		blush	flag				

■ DIRECTING THE LEARNER'S ATTENTION The purpose of this task is to help the learner recognize the regular spelling patterns used in English and to transfer his knowledge of initial consonant blends and spelling patterns to the identification of unknown words. This task is similar to that described in IB 7 of this chapter, and you should select your teaching activity from among the storehouse of techniques described there. When teaching this skill, you must be certain that the learner attends to the directions, to the pronunciation of the key word, to the initial blends of the succeeding words, and to the sound value of each letter blend.

■ THE POSTTEST The pretest can also be used as the posttest. The procedure and criterion for mastery remain the same.

IIB 10

■ THE PERFORMANCE OBJECTIVE Given a spoken stimulus word ending with the *ng* sound and a group of three other words one of which ends with the *ng* sound, the learner pairs the two words that end with the *ng* sound.

■ THE PRETEST   Using the words listed below, say to the learner, "Here are three words. Listen carefully." (Say the three words.) "Which one sounds like (say the stimulus word) at the end?" (Repeat the three original words.) Criterion for mastery is 4 out of 5 correct.

land / back / sling	Which one sounds like *sang* at the end? Repeat the first three word.
bang / bag / block	Which one sounds like *sang* at the end? Repeat the first three words.
big / bring / help	Which one sounds like *sang* at the end? Repeat the first three words.
finger / tick / fling	Which one sounds like *sang* at the end? Repeat the first three words.

■ DIRECTING THE LEARNER'S ATTENTION   The purpose of the task is to help the learner distinguish the ending *ng* sound from other ending sounds. This task is similar to that described in IIB 3 in Chapter 4, and you should select your teaching activity from among the storehouse of techniques described there. When teaching this skill, you must be certain that the learner attends to the oral directions and to the final sound of the words in each spoken sequence.

■ THE POSTTEST   The procedure and criterion for mastery remain the same as for the pretest. Use the following word sets.

flake / sand / fang	Which one sounds like *sang* at the end? Repeat the first three words.
task / bring / sack	Which one sounds like *sang* at the end? Repeat the first three words.
wing / wig / wise	Which one sounds like *sang* at the end? Repeat the first three words.
tag / tang / tan	Which one sounds like *sang* at the end? Repeat the first three words.
swig / swim / swing	Which one sounds like *sang* at the end? Repeat the first three words.

IIB 11

■ THE PERFORMANCE OBJECTIVE   When given a spoken word, the learner points to the letters *ng* if the word ends in the *ng* sound.

■ THE PRETEST   Give the learner a card having the letters *ng* printed on it. Say the following words, directing the learner to point to the *ng* card each time a word is spoken that ends with the sound. Criterion for mastery is 100 percent.

tag   bang   pick   thing   sing

■ DIRECTING THE LEARNER'S ATTENTION   The purpose of this task is to help the learner establish a sound–symbol connection between the letters *ng* and words that end with the *ng* sound. This task is similar to that described in IIB 5 in Chapter 4 except that the focus here is on ending sounds rather than on beginning sounds. You should select your teaching activity from among the storehouse of techniques described in IIB 5. When teaching this skill, you must be certain that the learner attends to the sound at the end of each spoken word and simultaneously looks at the letters *ng*.

■ THE POSTTEST   Procedure and criterion for mastery remain the same. Use the following words.

sting   flag   fig   strong   tongue

IIB 12

■ THE PERFORMANCE OBJECTIVE   Given a word he pronounced in previous objectives, the learner replaces the final consonant in the word with the letters *ng*, then substitutes an initial sound he knows and pronounces each new word.

■ THE PRETEST   Use the lists of words provided below. The first word in each list has been taught previously as a sight word or as one of the words analyzed in previous objectives. Read the first word in the list and ask the learner to read the remaining words. Criterion for mastery is 5 out of 6 correct.

bag	*sit*
bang	sing
sang	wing
fang	thing

■ DIRECTING THE LEARNER'S ATTENTION   The purpose of the task is to help the learner use the principle of consonant substitution as a means of identifying words ending with the letters *ng*. This task is similar to that described in IB 7 of this chapter, and you should select your teaching activity from among the storehouse of techniques described there. When teaching this skill, you must be certain that the learner attends to the directions, to the pronunciation of the key word, to the similarities and differences in succeeding words in the list, and to the sound produced by the *ng* combination.

■ THE POSTTEST The pretest can also be used as the posttest. The procedure and criterion for mastery remain the same.

IIB 13

■ THE PERFORMANCE OBJECTIVE Given compound words composed of two known words, the learner pronounces the compound words.

■ THE PRETEST Print the following words on cards. Present each card to the learner one at a time, encouraging him to analyze and pronounce each word. Criterion for mastery is 100 percent. The words are:

another	anyone	anything	without	into

■ DIRECTING THE LEARNER'S ATTENTION The purpose of this task is to help the learner identify unknown compound words by isolating and identifying the known words that form the compound. This task is similar to that described in IB 13 of this chapter, and you should select your teaching activity from among the storehouse of techniques described there. When teaching this skill, you must be certain that the learner attends to the directions and to the two known words which form the compound.

■ THE POSTTEST The pretest can also be used for the posttest. The procedure and criterion for mastery remain the same.

IIIA

SIGHT WORDS

■ THE PERFORMANCE OBJECTIVE Given a flash presentation of each of the following words, the learner pronounces each word within one second. The words to test are:

before	push	day	will	talk	tell	horse
please	any	our	are	today	children	orange
old	by	with	busy	as	walk	keep
there	how	bigger	just	off	wash	table
again	song	do	apple	child	first	which
his	very	know	when	take	full	guess
chair	am	put				

■ THE PRETEST Print each of the above words on flash cards. Then flash each word to the learner, giving him only a second or less to examine the word. Criterion for mastery is 100 percent. *Note:* Keep track of the words missed on the pretest because only these words need to be taught.

■ DIRECTING THE LEARNER'S ATTENTION The purpose of this task is to teach the learner to recognize instantly the words listed in the objective when they are printed on cards. This task is similar to that described in IIIA6 in Chapter 4, and you should select your teaching activity from among the storehouse of techniques described there. When teaching this skill, you must be certain that the learner attends to the visual form of the word and to its distinguishing characteristics.

■ THE POSTTEST The procedure and criterion for mastery on the posttest remain the same as for the pretest.

■ THE PERFORMANCE OBJECTIVE Given a flash presentation of the frequently confused words *then–when* and *here–were*, the learner pronounces each word within one second.

■ THE PRETEST   The procedure and criterion for mastery are the same as for the pretest of the previous objective.

■ DIRECTING THE LEARNER'S ATTENTION   The purpose of this task is to teach the learner to recognize each of the above easily confused words when they are printed on cards. This task is similar to that described in IA 2 of this chapter, and you should select your teaching activity from among the storehouse of techniques described there. When teaching this skill, you must be certain that the learner attends to the visual discriminator that acts as the cue for distinguishing the easily confused words.

■ THE POSTTEST   The procedure and criterion for mastery remain the same as for the pretest.

IIIA ❸

■ THE PERFORMANCE OBJECTIVE   Given words he recognizes at sight, the learner creates and reads stories using these words.

■ THE PRETEST   Provide the learner with cards, on each of which is printed a word that he recognizes instantly. Say to the learner, "Today we are going to write stories as we have done several times before. Look at the cards you have in front of you. Each card has a word on it that you know. Can you tell me a little story using the words you have here? If you want to make a story using a word you don't have on a card, tell me and I will make a card having that word on it." Direct the learner to "write" his story by placing the word cards in the proper order so that you can read them. Criterion for mastery is the combination of any number of words that are grammatically accurate and that make sense. When the learner has formed his story, have him read it back to you, encouraging him to make any changes he desires in word choice or word order. The story can be of any length.

Does your reading instruction end with the skill groups or do you find ways to help your learners apply these skills each hour of the day?

■ DIRECTING THE LEARNER'S ATTENTION   The purpose of the task is to teach the learner to produce and read messages using the individual words he knows. This task is similar to that described in IIIA 10 in Chapter 4, and you should select your teaching activity from among the storehouse of techniques described there. When teaching this skill, you must be certain that the learner attends to the oral directions, to the idea or message he wishes to convey, to the individual words, and to the order in which these words are placed in the sentences.

■ THE POSTTEST The procedure and criterion for mastery remain the same as for the pretest.

IIIB

■ THE PERFORMANCE OBJECTIVE   Given a known word composed of the vowel-consonant phonograms *en*, *in*, or *an*, the learner replaces the initial consonant in each word with another consonant, digraph, or blend that he knows and pronounces the new word.

■ THE PRETEST   Use the lists of words provided below. The first word in each list has been taught previously as a sight word or is a word analyzed in a previous objective. Read the first word in the list and ask the learner to pronounce the remaining words. Criterion for mastery is 15 out of 17 correct, with no initial consonant, digraph, or blend being missed more than once.

ten	*in*	*can*
men	tin	fan
then	fin	tan
when	sin	than
	thin	plan
	shin	bran
	chin	clan
	grin	
	win	

■ DIRECTING THE LEARNER'S ATTENTION   The purpose of this task is to help the learner recognize the regular spelling patterns used in English and to transfer this knowledge and his knowledge of initial sounds to the analysis of unknown words. This task is similar to that described in IB 7 of this chapter and you should select your teaching activity from among the storehouse of techniques described there. When teaching this skill, you must be certain that the learner attends to the directions, to the pronunciation of the key word, to the initial letter(s) of the succeeding words, and to the sound the initial letter(s) produces.

■ THE POSTTEST   The pretest can also be used for the posttest. The procedure and criterion for mastery remain the same.

■ THE PERFORMANCE OBJECTIVE Given a spoken stimulus word beginning with the sound produced by the consonant blend *sk, sw, sm, sn, sp,* or *st* and a group of three other words one of which begins with the sound of *sk, sw, sm, sn, sp,* or *st,* the learner pairs the two words beginning with the same sound.

■ THE PRETEST Using the words listed below, say to the learner, "Here are three words. Listen carefully." (Say the words.) "Which one sounds like (say the stimulus word) at the beginning?" (Repeat the three original words.) Criterion for mastery is 11 out of 12 correct.

slip / skim / sin	Which one sounds like *sky* at the beginning? Repeat the first three words.
swan / sun / skip	Which one sounds like *swing* at the beginning? Repeat the first three words.
some / fall / smack	Which one sounds like *small* at the beginning? Repeat the first three words.
swap / sneak / smart	Which one sounds like *snake* at the beginning? Repeat the first three words.
space / save / soon	Which one sounds like *spoon* at the beginning? Repeat the first three words.
slap / staff / snow	Which one sounds like *stick* at the beginning? Repeat the first three words.
smooth / some / snob	Which one sounds like *small* at the beginning? Repeat the first three words.
sell / sew / swell	Which one sounds like *swing* at the beginning? Repeat the first three words.
soon / skit / fly	Which one sounds like *sky* at the beginning? Repeat the first three words.
sun / bake / snort	Which one sounds like *snake* at the beginning? Repeat the first three words.
stock / block / sick	Which one sounds like *stick* at the beginning? Repeat the first three words.
socks / spot / some	Which one sounds like *spoon* at the beginning? Repeat the first three words.

■ DIRECTING THE LEARNER'S ATTENTION The purpose of this task is to cue the learner to the importance of listening to the beginning sounds of words and to help him distinguish the combination *s* blend sounds from other beginning consonant sounds. As such, the task is similar to that described in IIB 2 in Chapter 4, and you should select your teaching activity from among the storehouse of techniques described there. When teaching this skill, you must be certain that the learner attends to the oral directions and to the beginning sounds of the words in each spoken sequence.

■ THE POSTTEST The procedure and criterion for mastery are the same as for the pretest.

skeleton / speed / sun	Which one sounds like *sky* at the beginning? Repeat the first three words.
sag / snag / stag	Which one sounds like *snake* at the beginning? Repeat the first three words.
pear / soon / spice	Which one sounds like *spoon* at the beginning? Repeat the first three words.
swamp / slip / sing	Which one sounds like *swing* at the beginning? Repeat the first three words.
sell / smash / tall	Which one sounds like *small* at the beginning? Repeat the first three words.
sand / stand / span	Which one sounds like *stick* at the beginning? Repeat the first three words.
see / clear / sneer	Which one sounds like *snake* at the beginning? Repeat the first three words.
spoil / soil / stiff	Which one sounds like *spoon* at the beginning? Repeat the first three words.
slick / stool / spool	Which one sounds like *stick* at the beginning? Repeat the first three words.
suds / fudge / smudge	Which one sounds like *small* at the beginning? Repeat the first three words.
stitch / sling / switch	Which one sounds like *swing* at the beginning? Repeat the first three words.
sketch / stretch / sweat	Which one sounds like *sky* at the beginning? Repeat the first three words.

IIIB 3

■ THE PERFORMANCE OBJECTIVE Given spoken words beginning with the *sk, sw, sm, sn, sp,* and *st* sounds, the learner identifies the beginning letters in each word.

■ THE PRETEST Give the learner six cards, with one of the blends being tested printed on each card (*sk, sw, sm, sn, sp,* or *st*). Say the following words, directing the learner to point to the letters that begin the word. Criterion for mastery is 11 out of 12 correct.

snarl	spark	stain	skid	swat	small
skull	snob	swift	spy	stuff	smother

■ DIRECTING THE LEARNER'S ATTENTION   The purpose of the task is to help the learner establish a sound–symbol connection between the letter blends *sk, sw, sm, sn, sp,* and *st* and words that begin with the sounds produced by these blends. This task is similar to that described in IIB 5 in Chapter 4, and you should select your teaching activity from among the storehouse of techniques described there. When teaching this skill, you must be certain that the learner attends to the sound at the beginning of each spoken word and simultaneously looks at the correct letter combination.

■ THE POSTTEST   The procedure and criterion for mastery remain the same as for the pretest. Use the following words.

| stake | smart | swim | spade | snail | skill |
| smoke | swap | skip | steam | speech | snap |

IIIB 4

■ THE PERFORMANCE OBJECTIVE   Given an oral sentence with one word missing and cued for the missing word with a card having printed on it the blend with which the word begins (*sk, sw, sm, sn, sp,* or *st*), the learner says a word that begins with the letters on the card and that fits the context of the sentence.

■ THE PRETEST   Make cards with the above letter blends printed on them. Say, "I am going to say a sentence with one word missing. You look at the card and say a word that begins with the letter blend on the card and that finishes what I want to say." Use the following sentences. Criterion for mastery is 10 out of 12 correct, with no letter blend being missed more than once.

When it is cold and the pond freezes, we like to go sk——.

I used the broom to sw—— the floor.

You could tell the girl was happy because she was sm——.

It was cold outside, and there was a lot of sn—— on the ground.

I knocked over the glass, and the milk sp——.

When the bell rang, I ran up the st—— and into school.

The bug was so sm—— that you could hardly see it.

When you sleep, do you sn—— and make other noises?

The candy was sticky and sw——.

Most people don't like the smell of a sk——.

I am sick, and I am going to have to st—— at home.

Baseball is my favorite sp——.

■ DIRECTING THE LEARNER'S ATTENTION   The purpose of this task is to help the learner use his context sense and letter–sound association of the combination *s* blends to identify unknown words. This task is similar to that described in IIB 12 in Chapter 4, and you should select your teaching activity from among the storehouse of activities described there. When teaching this skill, you must be certain that the learner attends to the directions, to the sense of the sentence, and to the letter combination provided and its sound value.

■ THE POSTTEST   The procedure and criterion for mastery remain the same as for the pretest. Use the following sentences.

My mother is baking cookies, and they sm—— good.

The policeman chased the man and made him st——.

The young Indian warrior threw his sp—— at the charging buffalo.

I can run faster when I have my new sn—— on.

It was so hot outside that the sw—— was dripping down my face.

In the wintertime we like to sk—— down the big hill.

I ate so much that my st—— was full.

The fly got caught in the cobweb and was eaten by the sp——.

The little girl was frightened by the sn—— she saw in the grass.

The boy got all the answers right because he is so sm——.

He loves to go to the pool to sw——.

The girl wore her new blouse and sk—— to school.

IIB 5

■ THE PERFORMANCE OBJECTIVE   Given a word learned in previous objectives, the learner changes either the beginning or the ending of the word and pronounces the new word.

■ THE PRETEST   Use the lists of words provided below. The first word in each list has been taught previously. Read the first word in the list and ask the learner to pronounce the remaining words. Criterion for mastery is 18 out of 20 correct.

bit	*in*	*sip*	*back*	*crock*	*cap*
skit	skin	skip	smack	smock	snap
	spick	sniff	smash		snack
not	spin	snip		*him*	
snot			*sun*	swim	
spot	*tan*	*top*	stun		
	span	stop	stuck		
			snuck		

■ DIRECTING THE LEARNER'S ATTENTION   The purpose of this task is to help the learner use his knowledge of common spelling patterns, beginning sounds (particularly the combination *s* blends), and ending sounds to identify unknown words. This task is similar to that described in IB 7 of this chapter, and you should select your teaching activity from among the storehouse of techniques described there. When teaching this skill, you must be certain that the learner attends to the directions, to the pronunciation of the key word, to the similarity between the key words and the word to be pronounced, to the letter(s) in the new word that is different and to the sound value of that letter or letters.

■ THE POSTTEST   The pretest can be used for the posttest. The procedure and criterion for mastery remain the same.

IIIB 6

■ THE PERFORMANCE OBJECTIVE   Given a spoken stimulus word ending with the *st* sound and a group of three other words one of which ends with the *st* sound, the learner pairs the two words that end with the *st* sound.

■ THE PRETEST   Using the word sets listed below, say to the learner, "Here are three words. Listen carefully." (Say the three words.) "Which one sounds like (say the stimulus word) at the end?" (Repeat the three original words.) Criterion for mastery is 4 out of 5 correct.

land / back / nest	Which one sounds like *lost* at the end? Repeat the first three words.
crust / crush / truck	Which one sounds like *lost* at the end? Repeat the first three words.
fall / bat / blast	Which one sounds like *lost* at the end? Repeat the first three words.
chess / close / chest	Which one sounds like *lost* at the end? Repeat the first three words.
fuss / loss / just	Which one sounds like *lost* at the end? Repeat the first three words.

Do you have a good working relationship with your librarian? Is she feeding you new books in quantity for use in your recreational reading program?

■ DIRECTING THE LEARNER'S ATTENTION   The purpose of this task is to help the learner distinguish between the ending sound of *st* and other ending sounds. This task is similar to that described in IIB 3 in Chapter 4, and you should select your teaching activity from among the storehouse of techniques described there. When teaching this skill, you must be certain that the learner attends to the oral directions and to the final sound in each spoken sequence of words.

■ THE POSTTEST   The procedure and criterion for mastery remain the same as for the pretest. Use the following word sets.

thrust / throw / truck	Which one sounds like *lost* at the end? Repeat the first three words.
fact / last / back	Which one sounds like *lost* at the end? Repeat the first three words.
crush / crest / crunch	Which one sounds like *lost* at the end? Repeat the first three words.
best / bet / let	Which one sounds like *lost* at the end? Repeat the first three words.
mud / luck / must	Which one sounds like *lost* at the end? Repeat the first three words.

IIIB 7

■ THE PERFORMANCE OBJECTIVE   Given a spoken word, the learner points to the letters *st* if the word ends in the *st* sound.

■ THE PRETEST   Give the learner a card with the letters *st* printed on it. Say the following words, directing the learner to point to the *st* card each time a word is spoken which ends with that sound. Criterion for mastery is 100 percent.

                    desk   best   fast   least   lease

■ DIRECTING THE LEARNER'S ATTENTION   The purpose of this task is to help the learner establish a sound-symbol connection between the letters *st* and words that end with the *st* sound. This task is similar to that described in IIB 5 in Chapter 4 except that the focus here is on ending rather than on beginning sounds. You should select your teaching activity from among the storehouse of techniques described in IIB 5. When teaching this skill, you must be certain that the learner attends to the sound at the end of each spoken word while simultaneously looking at the letters *st*.

■ THE POSTTEST   The procedure and criterion for mastery remain the same as for the pretest. Use the following words.

flesh   chest   cast   flask   test

IIIB 8

■ THE PERFORMANCE OBJECTIVE   Given a word he pronounced in previous objectives, the learner replaces the final consonant with the letters *st*, substitutes initial sounds he knows, and pronounces the new words.

■ THE PRETEST   Use the word lists provided below. The first word in each list has been taught previously as a sight word or as one of the words analyzed in previous objectives. Read the first word in each list and ask the learner to pronounce the remaining words. Criterion for mastery is 10 out of 11 correct.

mud	*bet*	*lad*
must	best	last
just	rest	blast
	test	
	west	
	nest	
	chest	
	crest	

■ DIRECTING THE LEARNER'S ATTENTION   The purpose of the task is to help the learner use the principle of consonant substitution as a means of identifying unknown words ending with the *st* letters. This task is similar to that described in IB 7 of this chapter, and you should select your teaching activity from among the storehouse of techniques described there. When teaching this skill, you must be certain that the learner attends to the directions, to the pronunciation of the key word, to the similarities and differences in the succeeding words in the list, and to the sound produced by the *st* letter combination.

■ THE POSTTEST   The pretest can also be used as the posttest. The procedure and criterion for mastery remain the same.

IIIB 9

■ THE PERFORMANCE OBJECTIVE   Given the contractions *I'm, can't, won't, I'll, don't, isn't, he's, it's, I've, you're, we've,* and *let's* printed on cards, the learner pronounces each contraction and identifies the two words that make up the contraction.

■ THE PRETEST Using cards that have one of the above contractions printed on them, direct the learner to look at each card in turn. Ask him to pronounce the contraction printed on each card and then to say the two words that make up the contraction. For example, for the word *I'm*, show the learner the card that has *I'm* printed on it. He responds by saying "I'm" and the two words (*I* and *am*) that make up the contraction. Criterion for mastery is 100 percent. *Note*: Keep track of the learner's errors, because only the contractions he misses on the pretest will have to be taught.

■ DIRECTING THE LEARNER'S ATTENTION The purpose of the task is to teach the learner to recognize the most common contractions when he sees them on cards and to help him understand how they are formed. The teacher must be certain that the learner attends to the directions, to the visual form of each contraction, to the placement of the apostrophe, and to the letters that are omitted in forming each contraction.

■ TEACHING ACTIVITIES / *The model activity* Illustrate the principle of contractions with *I'm*. Using cutout letters placed on the chalk tray, spell out the words *I am*. Have the learner read the two words and use them in a sentence. Then remove the letter *a* from the chalk tray and replace it with an apostrophe. Pronounce the new word for the learner, and ask him to say it after you. Ask him what the new word means and how it is formed. Then ask him once again to pronounce the word and to name the two little words from which the contraction is formed. Repeat this process with the other contractions the learner missed in the pretest.

/ *Suggestions for reteaching and/or practice*

1 Matching games sometimes help the learner to associate the contraction with the two original words. List the contractions on one side of the board and the two words that make up the contraction on the other side. The learner is helped to draw lines from each contraction to the words that form its base.

2 Give the learner word cards arranged in simple sentences. Such a sentence might be: *I am a boy*. Have the learner read the sentence and then choose from among a group of contractions the one that he could substitute for *I am*.

3 If the learner has difficulty connecting the contraction with the words it stands for, it may be helpful to create activities designed to make a connection between the two. For example, you have several word cards with the separate words on them and he has cards with the contractions on them. You hold up the words *I am*, pronouncing the words as you do so, and he searches through his cards until he finds *I'm*, which he holds up and pronounces. If this is too difficult at the outset, give him only one card and do several repetitions of this exercise with just the one contraction until he responds readily.

4 If the learner has difficulty with the words that form the contraction, it is usually an indication that he needs to learn these individual words more thoroughly by sight. Such instruction should be provided before he is given any additional help in learning the contractions.

5 Difficulty in remembering the form of any of the contractions indicates the necessity for additional help in learning the contraction itself by sight. The suggestions described in IIIA 6 in Chapter 4 can be used here and for No. 4 above.

6 Many of the suggestions provided in the storehouse of activities for IB 13 of this chapter can be adapted for use in teaching contractions.

■ THE POSTTEST   The pretest can be used for the posttest. The procedure and criterion for mastery remain the same.

IVA **1**

■ THE PERFORMANCE OBJECTIVE   Given a flash presentation of each of the following words, the learner pronounces each word within one second. The words to test are:

give	feet	well	color	bread	doll	friend	end
right	many	sure	street	milk	good-by	hurry	brother
find	their	into	does	more	could	ready	ask
would	your	may	family	away	morning	store	quiet
draw	over	upon	funny				

■ THE PRETEST   Print each of the above words on flash cards. Flash each word to the learner, giving him only a second or less to examine the word. Criterion for mastery is 100 percent. *Note*: Keep track of the words missed on the pretest, because only the missed words need to be taught.

■ DIRECTING THE LEARNER'S ATTENTION   The purpose of this task is to teach the learner to recognize instantly each of the above words when they are printed on cards. This task is similar to that described in IIIA 6 in Chapter 4, and you should select your teaching activity from among the storehouse of techniques described there. When teaching this skill, you must be certain that the learner attends to the visual form of the word and to its distinguishing characteristics.

■ THE POSTTEST   The procedure and criterion for mastery remain the same as for the pretest.

IVA **2**

■ THE PERFORMANCE OBJECTIVE   Given a flash presentation of each of the frequently confused words *his–has* and *what–that*, the learner pronounces each word within one second.

■ THE PRETEST   The procedure and criterion for mastery are the same as for the pretest of the previous objective.

■ DIRECTING THE LEARNER'S ATTENTION   The purpose of this task is to teach the learner to recognize instantly each of the above easily confused words when they are presented on cards. This task is similar to that described in IA 2 of this chapter, and you should select your teaching activity from among the storehouse of techniques described there. When teaching this skill, you must be certain that the learner attends to the visual discriminator that acts as the cue for contrasting the easily confused words.

■ THE POSTTEST   The procedure and criterion for mastery remain the same as for the pretest.

IVA 3

■ THE PERFORMANCE OBJECTIVE   Given words he recognizes at sight, the learner creates and reads stories using these words.

■ THE PRETEST   Provide the learner with cards on each of which is printed a word that he recognizes instantly. Follow the same procedure as described in the previous objectives of this nature (see IIIA 3 of this chapter), directing the learner to tell a story using the words he has. Criterion for mastery is the combination of any number of words that are grammatically accurate and that make sense. When the learner has formed his story, have him read it back to you, encouraging him to make any changes he desires in the word order or the word choice. The story can be of any length.

What skills are you teaching tomorrow for your best readers?

■ DIRECTING THE LEARNER'S ATTENTION   The purpose of this task is to help the learner use the individual words he knows to produce and read stories. This task is similar to that described in IIIA 10 in Chapter 4, and you should select your teaching activity from among the storehouse of techniques described there. When teaching this skill, you must be certain that the learner attends to the oral directions, to the idea or message he wishes to convey, to the individual words, and to the order in which the words are placed in the sentences.

■ THE POSTTEST   The procedure and criterion for mastery remain the same as for the pretest.

IVB ❶

■ THE PERFORMANCE OBJECTIVE Given known words ending with the phonograms *and, end, ight, old,* or *ind,* the learner replaces the initial consonant with another consonant, consonant blend, or digraph and pronounces the new word.

■ THE PRETEST Use the lists of words provided below. The first word in each list has been taught previously as a sight word or as a word analyzed in previous objectives. Read the first word in the list and ask the learner to pronounce the remaining words. Criterion for mastery is 28 out of 29 correct.

and	*end*	*sing*		*right*		*old*		*find*
sand	send	swing	bring	fight	flight	sold	cold	blind
bland	bend	fling	ring	tight	bright	told	hold	mind
stand	lend	thing		slight	fright	bold	gold	bind
	blend			might		fold		

■ DIRECTING THE LEARNER'S ATTENTION The purpose of this task is to help the learner recognize the regular spelling patterns used in English and to transfer this knowledge and his knowledge of initial sounds to the analysis of unknown words. This task is similar to that described in IB 7 of this chapter, and you should select your teaching activity from among the storehouse of techniques described there. When teaching this skill, you must be certain that the learner attends to the directions, to the pronunciation of the key word, to the initial letter(s) of the succeeding words, and to the sound that the initial letter(s) produces.

■ THE POSTTEST The pretest can also be used as the posttest. The procedure and criterion for mastery remain the same.

IVB ❷

■ THE PERFORMANCE OBJECTIVE Given a known word containing a double *e* in the medial postion, the learner pronounces other words containing the double *e* in this position.

■ THE PRETEST   Use the word lists provided below. The key words (*feet* and *keep*) have been learned previously as sight words. Have the learner identify the key word in each list and then ask him to pronounce the remaining words in the list. Criterion for mastery is 12 out of 14 correct.

feet	*keep*	
meet	deep	weed
sweet	peep	need
feel	sheep	seed
wheel	sleep	seen
	weep	seem

■ DIRECTING THE LEARNER'S ATTENTION   The purpose of this task is to help the learner recognize the regular pronunciation of the double *e* in the medial position and to transfer this and his knowledge of consonant substitution to the analysis of unknown words. This task is similar to that described in IB 7 of this chapter, and you should select your teaching activity from among the storehouse of techniques described there. When teaching this skill, you must be certain that the learner attends to the pronunciation of the key word, to the sound value of the double *e* in the medial position, to the initial and final letter(s) of the succeeding words, and to the sounds that the initial and final letter(s) produce.

■ THE POSTTEST   The pretest can be used for the posttest. The procedure and criterion for mastery remain the same.

IVB 3

■ THE PERFORMANCE OBJECTIVE   Given a known one-syllable word ending in a vowel, the learner pronounces other one-syllable words ending in a vowel.

■ THE PRETEST   Use the lists of words provided below. The first word in each list has been taught previously as a sight word or as a word that was analyzed in previous objectives. Read the first word in the list and ask the learner to pronounce the remaining words. Criterion for mastery is 10 out of 11 correct.

me	*no*	*my*	
we	so	by	sky
be	go	why	dry
		cry	try
		fly	

■ DIRECTING THE LEARNER'S ATTENTION   The purpose of this task is to help the learner recognize the regular spelling patterns of one-syllable words ending in a vowel and to transfer this knowledge and his knowledge of initial sounds to the analysis of unknown words. This task is similar to that described in IB 7 of this chapter, and you should select your teaching activity from among the storehouse of techniques described there. When teaching this skill, you must be certain that the learner attends to the directions, to the pronunciation of the key word, to the initial letter(s) in the succeeding words, and to the sound the initial letter(s) produces.

■ THE POSTTEST   The pretest can be used for the posttest. The procedure and criterion for mastery remain the same.

IVB 4

■ THE PERFORMANCE OBJECTIVE   Given a known one-syllable word ending with the *ay* combination, the learner pronounces other one-syllable words ending with the *ay* combination.

■ THE PRETEST   Use the list of words provided below. The first word (*day*) has been taught previously as a sight word. Have the learner identify this word, and then ask him to pronounce the remaining words in the list. Criterion for mastery is 10 out of 12 correct.

		day	
pay	may	play	
say	lay	stay	
way	hay	clay	
	gay	tray	
		gray	

■ DIRECTING THE LEARNER'S ATTENTION   The purpose of this task is to help the learner recognize the regular spelling pattern of a one-syllable word ending in *ay* and to transfer this knowledge and his knowledge of initial consonant substitution to the analysis of unknown words. As such, the task is similar to that described in IB 7 of this chapter, and you should select your teaching activity from among the storehouse of techniques described there. When teaching this skill, you must be certain that the learner attends to the oral directions, to the pronunciation of the key word, to the sound value of the *ay* combination, to the initial letter(s) in the succeeding words, and to the sound that the initial letter(s) produces.

■ THE POSTTEST   The pretest can also be used as the posttest. The procedure and criterion for mastery remain the same.

■ THE PERFORMANCE OBJECTIVE Given a known one-syllable word ending in the *ell* or *ill* combination, the learner pronounces other words
ending in the *ell* or *ill* combination.

■ THE PRETEST Use the lists of words provided below. The first word
in each list has been taught previously as a sight word. Have the learner
identify the first word in each list and then ask him to pronounce the
remaining words in the list. Criterion for mastery is 17 out of 19 correct.

	well			*will*		
tell	bell	smell	hill	bill	frill	spill
fell	shell	swell	kill	chill	grill	still
sell	spell		fill	drill	skill	

■ DIRECTING THE LEARNER'S ATTENTION The purpose of this task is to help
the learner recognize the regular spelling pattern of one-syllable words
ending in *ell* or *ill* and to transfer this knowledge and his knowledge of
initial consonant substitution to the analysis of unknown words. This
task is similar to that described in IB 7 of this chapter, and you should
select your teaching activity from among the storehouse of activities described there. When teaching this skill, you must be certain that the
learner attends to the directions, to the pronunciation of the key word, to
the sound value of *ell* and *ill*, to the initial letter(s) in the succeeding
words, and to the sound that the initial letter(s) produces.

■ THE POSTTEST The pretest can also be used as the posttest. The procedure and criterion for mastery remain the same.

IVB **6**

■ THE PERFORMANCE OBJECTIVE Given a known one-syllable word ending
in *all*, the learner pronounces other one-syllable words ending in *all*.

■ THE PRETEST Use the list of words provided below. The first word
(*all*) has been taught previously as a sight word. Have the learner identify it, and ask him to pronounce the remaining words in the list. Criterion for mastery is 7 out of 8 correct.

	all		
ball	hall	tall	small
call	fall	mall	stall

■ DIRECTING THE LEARNER'S ATTENTION   The purpose of this task is to help the learner recognize the regular spelling pattern of one-syllable words ending in *all* and to transfer this knowledge and his knowledge of initial consonant substitution to the analysis of unknown words. This task is similar to that described in IB 7 of this chapter, and you should select your teaching activity from among the storehouse of techniques described there. When teaching this skill, you must be certain that the learner attends to the directions, to the pronunciation of the key word, to the sound value of *all*, to the initial letter(s) in the succeeding words, and to the sound the initial letter(s) produces.

■ THE POSTTEST   The pretest can also be used as the posttest. The procedure and criterion for mastery remain the same.

IVB **7**

■ THE PERFORMANCE OBJECTIVE   Given a word he has analyzed previously or learned to recognize at sight, the learner adds the structural endings *'s*, *est*, *ly*, *er*, or *y* and pronounces the new word.

■ THE PRETEST   Use the following list of words. Have the learner pronounce each word in turn. Criterion for mastery is 9 out of 10 correct.

boy's	deepest	player	chilly	quietly
your's	tallest	older	jumpy	newly

Can your learners do today the skill you taught them last week? Are you periodically reviewing previously taught skills to make certain of retention?

■ DIRECTING THE LEARNER'S ATTENTION   The purpose of this task is to help the learner pronounce new words that are composed of a known root and the *'s*, *est*, *ly*, *er*, or *y* endings. This task is similar to that described in IB 13 of this chapter, and you should select your teaching activity from among the storehouse of techniques described there. When teaching this skill, you must be certain that the learner attends to the root word, to the form of the ending, and to the pronunciation of the ending.

■ THE POSTTEST   The procedure and criterion for mastery remain the same. Use the following words.

brother's	sweetest	walker	milky	gladly
girl's	fastest	flyer	tricky	friendly

SIGHT WORDS

■ THE PERFORMANCE OBJECTIVE   Given a flash presentation of each of the following words, the learner pronounces each word within one second. The words to test are:

read	once	slow	should	miss	done	also	point
school	shoe	near	listen	nice	felt	believe	together
own	bird	match	money	air	heavy	catch	wild
car	break	mice	most	because	love	ear	tried
only	drink	ride	next	careful	poor	lion	

■ THE PRETEST   Print each of the above words on flash cards. Then flash each word to the learner, giving him only a second or less to examine the word. Criterion for mastery is 100 percent. *Note*: Keep track of the words missed on the pretest because only the words missed need to be taught.

■ DIRECTING THE LEARNER'S ATTENTION   The purpose of this task is to teach the learner to recognize instantly each of the above words when they are printed on cards. This task is similar to that described in IIIA 6 in Chapter 4, and you should select your teaching activity from among the storehouse of techniques described there. When teaching this skill, you must be certain that the learner attends to the visual form of the word and to its distinguishing characteristics.

■ THE POSTTEST   The procedure and criterion for mastery remain the same as for the pretest.

■ THE PERFORMANCE OBJECTIVE   Given a flash presentation of each of the frequently confused words *where–there*, *would–could–should*, and *now–how*, the learner pronounces each word within one second.

■ THE PRETEST   The procedure and criterion for mastery are the same as for the pretest of the previous objective.

■ DIRECTING THE LEARNER'S ATTENTION The purpose of this task is to teach the learner to recognize instantly each of the above easily confused words when they are presented on cards. This task is similar to that described in IA 2 of this chapter, and you should select your teaching activity from among the storehouse of techniques described there. When teaching this skill, you must be certain that the learner attends to the visual discriminator that acts as the cue for contrasting the easily confused words.

■ THE POSTTEST The procedure and criterion for mastery remain the same as for the pretest.

VA 3

■ THE PERFORMANCE OBJECTIVE Given words he recognizes at sight, the learner creates and reads stories using these words.

■ THE PRETEST Provide the learner with cards, on each of which is printed a word he recognizes instantly. Follow the same procedure as described in the previous objectives of this nature (see IIIA 3 of this chapter), directing the learner to tell a story using the words he has. Criterion for mastery is the combination of any number of words that are grammatically accurate and that make sense. When the learner has formed his story, have him read it back to you. Encourage him to make any changes he desires in the word order or the word choice. The story can be of any length.

■ DIRECTING THE LEARNER'S ATTENTION The purpose of this task is to help the learner use the individual words he knows to produce and read stories. This task is similar to that described in IIIA 10 in Chapter 4, and you should select your teaching activity from among the storehouse of techniques described there. When teaching this skill, you must be certain that the learner attends to the oral directions, to the idea or message he wishes to convey, to the individual words, and to the order in which the words are placed in the sentences.

■ THE POSTTEST The procedure and criterion for mastery remain the same as for the pretest.

VB

WORD ANALYSIS

VB **1**

■ THE PERFORMANCE OBJECTIVE Given a known word illustrating the silent *e* vowel principle, the learner pronounces other words illustrating this principle.

■ THE PRETEST Use the list of words provided below. The first word in the list has been taught previously as a sight word. Have the learner identify the first word and then ask him to pronounce the remaining words. Criterion for mastery is 45 out of 50 correct.

		ride		
hide	cake	hole	nose	smile
five	came	home	note	stone
fake	rope	joke	plate	take
wake	drive	late	rake	these
wave	fine	like	rode	those
while	game	live	time	use
white	gate	made	shine	ate
woke	gave	make	side	line
bake	mile	save	skate	shake
wide	same	name	slide	smoke

■ DIRECTING THE LEARNER'S ATTENTION The purpose of the task is to help the learner recognize the regular pronunciation of one-syllable words ending in the silent *e* and to transfer this knowledge to unknown words. When teaching this skill, you must be certain that the learner attends to the directions, to the pronunciation of the known key word, to the vowel in the medial position, to the sound value of the medial vowel, to the initial and final consonants of the words, and to the sounds the initial and final consonants produce. *Caution:* Some silent *e* words, such as *have*, will not fit the generalization. Be prepared to teach such words by sight.

At what time today are your learners going to read just for the fun of it?

179

■ TEACHING ACTIVITIES / *The model activity* If the learner is unable to perform the task in the pretest, use the following arrangement of words:

ride	*white*	*ate*	*cake*	*home*
wide	while	late	bake	hose
side	smile	plate	wake	nose
slide	mile	skate	fake	close
hide	file	mate	make	rose
hive	fine	gate	rake	rope
live	shine	game	take	rode
five	line	gave	shake	
drive	like	save		
	lime	wave		
	time			

With the words arranged in this manner, direct the learner to pronounce each list of words by using his knowledge of consonant substitution. Because only one consonant sound is changed from one word to another in each list, the learner should be able to use what he has learned in previous objectives to pronounce each word. As he completes the pronunciation of each list, have him examine the words in that list again, noting the sound that the medial vowel produces and the letter that ends each word. Questions such as the following would be appropriate: "What vowel letter is in the middle of each word? What sound does this letter make in each one of the words? What letter is at the end of each word? Does the letter at the end make any sound in these words?" Repeat the same procedure for the words in the other lists, leading the learner to generalize that when a one-syllable words ends in a silent *e*, the preceding vowel makes its own sound—that is, makes the long sound of the vowel.

/ *Suggestions for reteaching and/or practice*

1 If the learner has difficulty with this task because he is unable to substitute initial consonants, redirect him to previous objectives that develop this skill and provide him with additional instruction. Then return to the model teaching activity above and use his skill in consonant substitution to develop an understanding of the silent *e* principle.
2 If the learner is able to pronounce the words through consonant substitution, but is unable to see the similarities in the words, use a more directed version of the model activity. Instead of asking questions that require him to examine the word lists, take his finger and direct it to the similarities in the words as you *tell* him what these similarities are.
3 If persistent difficulty continues because the learner is unable to remember the sounds of the vowels, review the letters of the alphabet and emphasize that all the vowels in these words "say their name."
4 If the learner has difficulty remembering the manner in which the

silent *e* affects the preceding vowel, direct him to examine the following arrangements of words:

| not | Tim | mad | hid | shin | rid | rod | slid |
| note | time | made | hide | shine | ride | rode | slide |

Have him note the similarities and differences in these words, help him to pronounce each pair of words, and direct him to state how the silent *e* changes the pronunciation.

■ THE POSTTEST The pretest can be used as the posttest. The procedure and criterion for mastery remain the same.

VB 2

■ THE PERFORMANCE OBJECTIVE Given a known word illustrating the two vowels together principle, the learner pronounces other words illustrating this principle.

■ THE PRETEST Use the list of words provided below. The first word in the list has been taught previously as a sight word. Have the learner identify the first word and then ask him to pronounce the remaining words. Criterion for mastery is 22 out of 27 correct.

read

boat	eat	meat	plain	seat	wheat
clean	suit	nail	real	tail	rain
coat	train	paint	road	teach	fruit
each	leaves	weak	sea	wait	goat
east	mail	trail			

■ DIRECTING THE LEARNER'S ATTENTION The purpose of this task is to help the learner recognize the regular pronunciation of one-syllable words that illustrate the principle of two vowels together and to transfer this knowledge to unknown words. When teaching this skill, you must be certain that the learner attends to the directions, to the pronunciation of the known key word, to the two vowels that stand together, to the consonants in the words, and to the sounds that the consonants produce. *Caution*: Some two vowels together words, such as *break*, will not fit this generalization. Be prepared to teach such words by sight.

■ TEACHING ACTIVITIES / *The model activity* If the learner has difficulty with the task during the pretest, rearrange the words for him in the following manner:

tail			*suit*	*eat*				*boat*
trail	wait	mail	fruit	each	read	sea	weak	coat
plain	nail	laid		east	real	seat	wheat	goat
rain	paint	train		meat	clean	teach	leaves	road

Using the words as they are arranged above, pronounce the first word in each list for the learner. Ask him, "What sound did you hear in the middle of this word?" (This question should be changed to "What sound did you hear at the beginning of the word" when using the words *eat*, *each*, and *east*.) Then say, "How many sounds do you hear in the middle? How many letters are in the middle?" Lead the learner to note that there is only one sound but that there are two letters. Then ask, "Which letter makes the sound you hear? What is that sound? Does the second letter make any sound?" Then have the learner say the sound that is produced in the medial position. Move on to the next word in the list and have the learner point out to you the same two letters. Have him say the sound heard in the middle of the word, and then have him pronounce the whole word. Continue in this fashion through the list of words and on to the subsequent lists, leading him to generalize that when two vowels are together, usually the first vowel says its name and the second is silent.

/ Suggestions for reteaching and/or practice

1 If the learner has difficulty with this task because he is unable to see the similarities in the vowel arrangements from word to word, use a more directed version of the model teaching activity, taking the learner's finger and directing it to the similarities as you *tell* him what these similarities are.

2 If the learner understands the vowel principle but is having difficulty inserting the consonants into the word, rearrange the word list again so that he can employ his knowledge of consonant substitution. For example, you might use the following sequence of words: *rain, pain, train, plain*; or *meat, seat, wheat*. Once he can insert the consonants in this fashion, you can return to the pattern used in the model activity and, ultimately, to the pattern used in the pretest.

3 If the learner has difficulty because he is unable to remember the sounds of the long vowel, review the letters of the alphabet and emphasize that the first vowel in the two vowels together principle says its own name.

■ THE POSTTEST The pretest can be used as the posttest. The procedure and criterion for mastery remain the same.

VB 3

■ THE PERFORMANCE OBJECTIVE Given a known word illustrating the two vowels together principle as it applies to the *ow* combination, the learner pronounces other words illustrating this principle.

■ THE PRETEST   Use the list of words provided below. The first word in the list has been taught previously as a sight word. Have the learner identify the first word and then ask him to pronounce the remaining words. Criterion for mastery is 7 out of 8 correct.

slow

row	flow
show	snow
mow	crow
grow	blow

■ DIRECTING THE LEARNER'S ATTENTION   The purpose of this task is to help the learner apply his understanding of the two vowels together principle to those *ow* words that illustrate this principle and to transfer this knowledge to unknown words. When teaching this skill, you must be certain that the learner attends to the directions, to the pronunciation of the key words, to the *ow* combination, to the consonants in the words, and to the sounds the consonants produce.

■ TEACHING ACTIVITIES / *The model activity*   If the learner is unable to pronounce the words in the pretest, you must help him see the similarity between this task and the one he completed in Objective VB 2. To do so, review some of the words taught in that objective, directing the learner to explain the function of the two vowels together. Then tell him that the *w* sometimes acts as a vowel, which would also make the words in this objective illustrative of the two vowels together principle. Ask him, "If the *ow* in *slow* acts as two vowels, then how many sounds will you hear? Which vowel will make the sound that you hear? What sound will the first vowel (the *o*) make? How will the word be pronounced if the sound you hear is the sound of the long *o*?" Then, using this principle, have him pronounce the other words in the list.

/ *Suggestions for reteaching and/or practice*

1   If the learner has persistent difficulty with the two vowels together principle, return to the previous objective and reteach.
2   If the learner is having persistent difficulty with this task for reasons other than confusion of the vowel principle itself, use the appropriate alternate activity described in the previous objective.

■ THE POSTTEST   The pretest can be used as the posttest. The procedure and criterion for mastery remain the same.

VB **4**

■ THE PERFORMANCE OBJECTIVE   Given words illustrating the *ou* and *ow* diphthongs, the learner pronounces other words containing these diphthongs.

■ THE PRETEST   Use the lists of words provided below. The first word in each of the two lists has been previously taught as a sight word. Have the learner identify the first word in the list and then have him pronounce the succeeding words. Criterion for mastery is 9 out of 11 correct, with no more than one error in each list.

out		*how*			
mouse	loud	bow	clown	town	brown
count	mouth	cow	down	now	

■ DIRECTING THE LEARNER'S ATTENTION   The purpose of the task is to help the learner recognize the sound of the *ou* and *ow* diphthongs, to associate this sound with the letter symbols, and to use his knowledge of these diphthongs to analyze and pronounce other words containing the *ou* and *ow* diphthongs. When teaching this skill, you must be certain that the learner attends to the sound of the *ou* and *ow* diphthongs, to the *ou* and *ow* letters, to the other letters surrounding the diphthongs, and to the directions.

Name six conditions of learning. If you cannot do it, see Chapter 3.

■ TEACHING ACTIVITIES / *The model activity*   If the learner is unable to read the words in the pretest, follow this procedure: Have the learner close his eyes while you pronounce the words, directing him to listen to the sound he hears in the middle of the word (or, in the case of words such as *out* and *cow*, the sound he hears at the beginning or the end). Have him reproduce the sound he hears in the medial position by asking him the question, "Say the sound you hear in the middle of the word." After he has repeated the correct sound several times, have him open his eyes and use your finger to direct his attention to the letters *ou* or *ow* that produce the sound in each word. Say, "Look where my finger is pointing. These letters say the sound you heard when I said these words. As I point to the letters, you say the sound the letters produce." When the learner appears to have made the sound–symbol connection between the letters *ou* and *ow* and their diphthong sound, present the learner with a whole word containing the *ou* or *ow* diphthong and have him pronounce it, inserting the correct diphthong sound in the appropriate place. *Caution:* It would be wise to point out to the learner that in the case of the *ow* combination, he will have to try pronouncing it as both a diphthong and as a two vowels together combination (see Objective VB 3) before being sure of how it is used in a particular word. To be sure that he does this, you should present him with *ow* words that illustrate both phonetic principles (*cow–snow*) and require him to try both pronunciations before deciding which one is appropriate.

/ Suggestions for reteaching and/or practice

1 If the learner has difficulty in hearing the sound of the *ow* and *ou* diphthongs, plan activities modeled after the suggestions provided in IIB 2 and IIB 3 in Chapter 4.

2 If the learner has difficulty in making the sound–symbol connection between the letters *ou* and *ow* and the sound of the diphthongs, plan activities for him modeled after the suggestions provided in IIB 5 in Chapter 4.

■ THE POSTTEST   The pretest may also be used for the posttest. The procedure and criterion for mastery remain the same.

VB 5

■ THE PERFORMANCE OBJECTIVE   Given spoken stimulus words ending with the *nd, nt,* or *nk* sounds and a group of three other words one of which ends with the *nd, nt,* or *nk* sounds, the learner pairs the two words that end with the same sound.

■ THE PRETEST   Using the word sets listed below, say to the learner, "Here are three words. Listen carefully." (Say the three words.) "Which one sounds like (say the stimulus word) at the end? (Repeat the three original words.) Criterion for mastery is 5 out of 6 correct.

bank / pond / best	Which one sounds like *land* at the end? Repeat the first three words.
thin / rack / pink	Which one sounds like *tank* at the end? Repeat the first three words.
sent / send / spent	Which one sounds like *hunt* at the end? Repeat the first three words.
take / think / tanned	Which one sounds like *tank* at the end? Repeat the first three words.
plant / plate / plank	Which one sounds like *hunt* at the end? Repeat the first three words.
last / found / flank	Which one sounds like *land* at the end? Repeat the first three words.

■ DIRECTING THE LEARNER'S ATTENTION   The purpose of this task is to help the learner distinguish between the ending sounds produced by the letters *nd, nt,* and *nk* and other ending sounds. This task is similar to that described in IIB 3 in Chapter 4, and you should select your teaching activity from among the storehouse of techniques described there. When teaching this skill, you must be certain that the learner attends to the oral directions and to the final sounds in each word in the spoken sequence.

■ THE POSTTEST   The procedure and criterion for mastery remain the same as for the pretest. Use the following word sets.

wink / wind / lamp	Which one sounds like *land* at the end? Repeat the first three words.
tent / hug / hunk	Which one sounds like *hunt* at the end? Repeat the first three words.
blind / blink / blimp	Which one sound like *tank* at the end? Repeat the first three words.
meant / mark / hurt	Which one sounds like *hunt* at the end? Repeat the first three words.
stick / stink / stand	Which one sounds like *tank* at the end? Repeat the first three words.
lank / found / flake	Which one sounds like *land* at the end? Repeat the first three words.

VB 6

■ THE PERFORMANCE OBJECTIVE   Given three cards, one with the letters *nd*, one with *nt*, and the third with *nk* printed on it, and a spoken stimulus word that ends in either the *nd*, the *nt*, or the *nk* sounds, the learner points to the letter card that has printed on it the letters with which the word ends.

■ THE PRETEST   Give the learner three cards with the letters *nd*, *nt*, or *nk* printed on them. Say the following words, directing the learner to point to the card that has printed on it the letters with which the spoken word ends. Criterion for mastery is 100 percent.

stand	plant	thank	pink	round	sent

■ DIRECTING THE LEARNER'S ATTENTION   The purpose of this task is to help the learner establish a sound–symbol connection between the letters *nd*, *nt*, and *nk* and words that end with these sounds. This task is similar to that described in IIB 5 in Chapter 4, except that the focus here is on ending sounds rather than on beginning sounds. You should select your teaching activity from among the storehouse of techniques described in IIB 5. When teaching this skill, you must be certain that the learner attends to the sound at the end of each spoken word and simultaneously looks at the letters that produce the sound.

■ THE POSTTEST The procedure and criterion for mastery remain the same as for the pretest. Use the following words:

| hunt | found | stink | think | bent | sand |

VB 7

■ THE PERFORMANCE OBJECTIVE Given a word he pronounced in previous objectives, the learner replaces the final consonant letter of the word with the *nd, nt,* or *nk* letters and pronounces the new word.

■ THE PRETEST Use the word lists provided below. The first word in each list has been taught previously. Have the learner identify the first word, and then ask him to pronounce the remaining words in each list. Criterion for mastery is 17 out of 19 correct, with no ending sound being missed more than once.

sat	*pot*	*wit*	*mouse*	*thin*	*ten*
sand	pond	wind	mound	think	tent
land			sound	thank	sent
band			found	pink	bent
stand			round	stink	went
			ground		

■ DIRECTING THE LEARNER'S ATTENTION The purpose of this task is to help the learner use the principle of consonant substitution as a means of identifying words ending with the *nd, nt,* or *nk* letter combinations. This task is similar to that described in IB 7 of this chapter, and you should select your teaching activity from among the storehouse of techniques described there. When teaching this skill, you must be certain that the learner attends to the directions, to the pronunciation of the key word, to the similarities and differences in succeeding words, and to the sound values produced by the letter combinations *nd, nt,* and *nk.*

■ THE POSTTEST The pretest can be used for the posttest. The procedure and criterion for mastery remain the same.

VB 8

■ THE PERFORMANCE OBJECTIVE Given known sight words, the learner pronounces these words when they are prefixed by *dis* and *un.*

■ THE PRETEST   Use the following word lists. Have the learner identify the first word in each list, first without the prefix, and then with it. Next, direct him to pronounce the other words in the list. Criterion for mastery is 7 out of 8 correct.

please/displease	happy/unhappy
like/dislike	just/unjust
color/discolor	kind/unkind
trust/distrust	like/unlike

■ DIRECTING THE LEARNER'S ATTENTION   The purpose of this task is to help the learner analyze and pronounce words composed of known sight words and the prefixes *un* and *dis*. This task is similar to that described in IB 13 of this chapter, and you should select your teaching activity from among the storehouse of techniques described there. When teaching this skill, you must be certain that the learner attends to the root word, to the form of the prefix, and to the pronunciation of the prefix.

■ THE POSTTEST   The pretest can be used for the posttest. The procedure and criterion for mastery remain the same.

VIA

SIGHT WORDS

■ THE PERFORMANCE OBJECTIVE   Given a flash presentation of each of the following words, the learner pronounces each word within one second. The words to test are:

post	field	board	move	floor
voice	held	caught	both	clothes
war	already	early	bowl	paw
warm	quick	fire	uncle	quite
wonder	always	hello	egg	animal
breakfast	roar	hair	hurt	every
feather	arrow	honey	climb	turn
else	bump	piece	end	kept
umbrella	country	roll	circus	large
nothing	elephant	turtle	kind	noise

■ THE PRETEST   Print each of the above words on flash cards. Flash each word to the learner, giving him only a second or less to examine the word. Criterion for mastery is 100 percent. *Note*: Keep track of the words missed on the pretest because it is only the missed words that need to be taught.

■ DIRECTING THE LEARNER'S ATTENTION   The purpose of this task is to teach the learner to recognize instantly and remember the words listed in the objective when they are printed on cards. This task is similar to that described in IIIA 6 in Chapter 4, and you should select your teaching activity from among the storehouse of techniques described there. When teaching this skill, you must be certain that the learner attends to the visual form of the word and to its distinguishing characteristics.

■ THE POSTTEST   The procedure and criterion for mastery on the posttest remain the same as for the pretest.

VIA 2

■ THE PERFORMANCE OBJECTIVE   Given a flash presentation of each of the frequently confused words *he–her–she* and *these–those*, the learner pronounces each word within one second.

■ THE PRETEST   The procedure and criterion for mastery are the same as for the pretest in the preceding objective, except that the words *he–her–she* and *these–those* are used.

Do you teach *before the learners practice?*

■ DIRECTING THE LEARNER'S ATTENTION   The purpose of this task is to teach the learner to recognize instantly each of the above easily confused words when they are presented on cards. This task is similar to that described in IA 2 of this chapter, and you should select your teaching activity from among the storehouse of techniques described there. When teaching this skill, you must be certain that the learner attends to the visual discriminator that acts as the cue for contrasting each of the easily confused words.

■ THE POSTTEST   The procedure and criterion for mastery remain the same as for the pretest.

VIA 3

■ THE PERFORMANCE OBJECTIVE   Given words he recognizes at sight, the learner creates and reads stories using these words.

■ THE PRETEST   Provide the learner with cards, each of which has printed on it a word that he recognizes instantly. Follow the same procedure as described in the pretest for Objective IIIA 3 of this chapter, directing the learner to tell a story using the words he has. Criterion for mastery is the combination of any number of words that are grammatically accurate and that make sense. When the learner has formed his story, have him read it back to you, encouraging him to make any changes he desires in word order or word choice. The story can be of any length.

■ DIRECTING THE LEARNER'S ATTENTION   The purpose of this task is to help the learner use the individual words he knows to produce and read stories. This task is similar to that described in IIIA 10 in Chapter 4, and you should select your teaching activity from among the storehouse of techniques described there. When teaching this skill, you must be certain that the learner attends to the directions, to the idea or message he wishes to convey, to the individual words, and to the order in which the words are placed in the sentences.

■ THE POSTTEST   The procedure and criterion for mastery remain the same as in the pretest.

VIB

WORD ANALYSIS

■ THE PERFORMANCE OBJECTIVE   Given known words illustrating the short double *o* and the long double *o* sounds, the learner pronounces other words containing these combinations.

■ THE PRETEST   Use the lists of words provided below. The first word in the list has been taught previously as a sight word. Have the learner identify the first word and then ask him to pronounce the remaining words. Criterion for mastery is 10 out of 12 correct, with neither vowel sound being missed more than once.

	too		*look*
root	room	book	took
food	soon	wood	foot
roof	zoo	cook	stood

■ DIRECTING THE LEARNER'S ATTENTION   The purpose of the task is to help the learner differentiate between the two double *o* sounds and to help him analyze and pronounce words containing the double *o*. The teacher must be certain that the learner attends to the directions, to the pronunciation of the key word, to the two sounds produced by the double *o*, and to the consonant letters that precede and follow the double *o* letters. *Caution*: The pronunciation of double *o* words varies from dialect to dialect. Don't count a word incorrect because of a dialect difference.

How many of your learners still need apples, raisins, or M&M's as encouragement to perform? Can some of them be moved to more intrinsic rewards?

■ TEACHING ACTIVITIES / *The model activity*   If the learner is unable to pronounce the words in the pretest, follow this procedure: Have the learner close his eyes while you pronounce the words, directing him to listen to the sound he hears in the middle of the word. Pronounce two words having the same double *o* vowel sound (such as *stool* and *food*), asking him, "Do these two words have the same sound in the middle?" Then pronounce two words having different double *o* vowel sounds (such as *soon* and *cook*), asking him, "Do these two words have the same sound in the middle?" This discrimination of the two sounds of *oo* is normally a difficult one for children to make. If your learner is still confused after the previous directions, try this technique. Say, "I am going to say a word. I want you to copy what I say, *just like I say it*." Here, choose any *oo* word, such as *cook*. Say, "Cook." After he has responded, look at him with disbelief and say, "Did you say 'cook'?" changing the *oo* to match the *oo* in *zoo*. The learner will *always* say, "No, I said 'cook'." He will give it correctly. Again look at him with doubt and say, "Oh, you said 'cook'." Here again you pronounce the *oo* as in *zoo*. This is usually enough illustration to clearly differentiate what you mean by the two sounds of *oo*. Once you have determined that the learner is differentiating between the two sounds of the double *o*, pronounce another pair of double *o* words, such as *food* and *book*, and ask him to reproduce the two different double *o* sounds he hears. Finally, show him the printed form of *food* and *book* and say, "This word is *book*. This word is *food*. Listen to the middle part of the words. Do they both have the same sound in the middle? Say the sound you hear in the middle of *book*. Say the sound you hear in the middle of *food*. Are the sounds the same or different? Now look at the words. Do they have the same letters in the middle? What are these letters?" Continue this line of questioning, leading the learner to generalize that the double *o* combination can make two sounds. Then present the following arrangement of words to him and direct him to use his skill in initial consonant substitution to pronounce the words.

	too			*look*	
toot	roof	zoom		book	took
root	room	zoo		cook	shook

Next present a list of words such as the following, in which the different sounds of the double *o* are mixed together. Direct the learner to pronounce the words, telling him that if he does not know the word instantly, *he must try both sounds of the double o in the middle position to see which one belongs.*

foot	soon	stood	room	stool

/ Suggestions for reteaching and/or practice

1 If the learner has difficulty in hearing the sounds of the double *o* letters, plan activities modeled after the suggestions provided in IIB 3 and IIB 4 in Chapter 4.

2 If the learner has difficulty in making the sound–symbol connection between the double *o* letter combination and the two sounds, plan activities modeled after the suggestions provided in IIB 5 in Chapter 4.

■ THE POSTTEST   The pretest can be used for the posttest. The procedure and criterion for mastery remain the same.

KEY OBJECTIVE VIB **2**

■ THE PERFORMANCE OBJECTIVE   Given a known word that illustrates the vowel-consonant–consonant-vowel principle of syllabication in which both medial consonants are sounded, the learner pronounces other words illustrating this principle.

■ THE PRETEST   Use the list of words provided below. The first word in the list has been taught previously as a sight word. Have the learner identify the first word and then ask him to pronounce the remaining words. Criterion for mastery is 6 out of 7 correct.

after	
almost	until
basket	kitchen
picnic	ticket
window	

■ DIRECTING THE LEARNER'S ATTENTION   The purpose of this task is to help the learner analyze and pronounce two-syllable words that illustrate the vowel-consonant–consonant-vowel principle. This is the first of a series of objectives designed to help the learner identify unknown words of more than one syllable. This is a crucial task for the learner if he is to become independent as a reader, for many of the words he will encounter will be long and will require that he use the principles of syllabication in an attempt to break them down into manageable sound units.

To teach a learner to use syllabication principles, you first must be sure that he distinguishes the number of sound units auditorally. Then you must see that he visually distinguishes the pattern of vowels and consonants in the word that provides the clue for determining where the syllable break occurs. Finally, you must be certain that he uses his previous knowledge of letter–sound association in sounding out the syllabicated units. When teaching this skill, then, you must be certain that the learner attends to the number of sound units in each word when it is spoken for him, to the arrangement of letters in the word that signals where syllables divide, and to the letter combinations that make up the independent syllables and their sound values.

Key objective for developing skill in
syllabication.

■ TEACHING ACTIVITIES / *The model activity* Have the learner close his
eyes while you pronounce words illustrating the syllable principle, directing him to listen to the number of sound units (or the number of
vowel sounds) he hears. Pronounce each word, exaggerating slightly the
syllable break. After pronouncing each word, ask the learner to tell you
how many sound units he heard. Clapping your hands for each syllable
can facilitate his understanding of this principle. Once you have determined that he is hearing each unit of sound, ask him to repeat the
word after you, emphasizing slightly the syllable break so that you can
be sure he is dividing the pronunciation at the correct place. Again, hand
claps are appropriate directors. Finally, show him the printed form of
the word, saying, "This word is *after*. Listen for the number of sound
units you hear as I pronounce it. Af——ter. How many sound units did
you hear? Now say the word as you look at the printed form. What is
the last sound you hear in the first sound unit? What letter in *after*
stands for that sound? Mark the place in the word where the first sound
unit ends and the second one begins." Repeat this procedure until you
have several similar words marked according to the syllable break. Then
direct the learner to look at the place where the words are divided,
helping him to formulate a syllabication principle for words following
that pattern. Go through the other words, asking him to make the
syllable division and to pronounce the words.

/ *Suggestions for reteaching and/or practice*

1 If the learner has difficulty hearing the number of sound units in the
words, you can say a two-syllable word and clap for each syllable. Then
clap without speaking the word and say, "How many times did I clap?
How many sounds in the word?" Then say another two-syllable word,
hold the learner's hands, and repeat the above process. Then provide
another two-syllable word, and let the learner clap by himself in accordance with the number of sounds heard. Finally, provide a two-syllable
word and ask the learner to tell the number of sounds without the aid
of clapping.
2 Other activities designed to help the learner hear the number of
sound units in words are provided in IB 6 in Chapter 4.
3 If the learner has difficulty in identifying the last letter sound heard
in a particular syllable or in associating that sound with the appropriate
letter symbol, you should return for reteaching to the objectives that
originally taught the auditory discrimination and sound–symbol correspondence for those letters.

4 If the learner has difficulty in providing the appropriate vowel sound for any particular syllable, he should be returned to the objective in which that vowel unit was originally introduced. For example, in the word *after*, the first vowel sound was taught in IB 7 of this chapter and the *er* combination was taught in IVB 7 of this chapter. When he has mastered the vowel unit, he can return to this objective and be asked to apply that knowledge as a part of pronouncing two-syllable words.

5 Play riddle games with learners in which syllabication plays a part. For example, you can ask: "I am a big animal. I have a trunk and tusks. You see me in the zoo. I have three syllables in my name. Who am I?"

6 Learners who have difficulty with syllabication should be provided with instruction in syllabicating compound words. Because we always divide compounds between the two words, their syllabication is often easier for learners to grasp.

7 Write a list of multisyllable words on the board. Pronounce each word aloud, tapping on the chalkboard to signal each syllable. Have the learners pronounce each word following your model and tapping out the number of syllables on their desks as they do so. Learners who have particular difficulty with this can be aided if you take their hand, say the word with them, and guide their hand to tap for each syllable.

8 Present the learner with a group of two-syllable words that all utilize a known prefix. A list such as the following might be appropriate:

unlike   unjust   unkind   unwise

Say each word for the learner, directing him to listen for the number of sound units he hears. The similarity of the prefix from word to word may help him to focus more clearly on the sound units and thereby help him make the transition to performing the task described in the model activity above.

9 Provide the learner with two-syllable words that he knows at sight. Have him pronounce these aloud, directing him to draw a line through the vowels in each word as they are sounded. Then have him compare the number of vowel sounds with the number of syllables in each word, helping him to see that for every vowel sound heard there is one syllable division.

10 Play games with the learner in which he must use aspects of syllabication. For example, use a gameboard device in which a learner progresses space-by-space toward some goal. His progress along the board toward this goal is dependent upon his ability to tell how many sound units are heard in the word you say orally or upon his ability to correctly pronounce a word using one or more of the syllable principles you have taught him.

■ THE POSTTEST   The pretest can also be used for the posttest. The procedure and criterion for mastery remain the same.

VIB ③

■ THE PERFORMANCE OBJECTIVE   Given a known word that illustrates the vowel-consonant–consonant-vowel principle of syllabication in which only one medial consonant is sounded, the learner pronounces other words illustrating the principle.

■ THE PRETEST   Use the list of words provided below. The first word in the list has been taught previously as a sight word. Have the learner identify the first word and then ask him to pronounce the remaining words. Criterion for mastery is 100 percent.

hello

follow   kitten   rabbit   often

■ DIRECTING THE LEARNER'S ATTENTION   The purpose of this task is to help the learner analyze and apply the vowel-consonant–consonant-vowel principle of syllabication to words in which only one medial consonant is sounded. This task is similar to that described in VIB 2 of this chapter, and you should select your teaching activity from among the storehouse of techniques described there. When teaching this skill, you must be certain that the learner attends to the directions, to the number of sound units he hears in the words, to the double consonants that visually signal syllable division, and to the syllable units and their sound values.

■ THE POSTTEST   The pretest can also be used for the posttest. The procedure and criterion for mastery remain the same.

VIB ④

■ THE PERFORMANCE OBJECTIVE   Given a known two-syllable word ending in *er*, the learner pronounces other two-syllable words ending in *er*.

■ THE PRETEST   Use the list of words provided below. The first word in the list has been taught previously as a sight word. Have the learner identify the first word and then ask him to pronounce the remaining words. Criterion for mastery is 9 out of 10 correct.

bigger

sister	supper	letter	butter	under
summer	matter	better	dinner	winter

■ DIRECTING THE LEARNER'S ATTENTION   The purpose of this task is to help the learner apply his knowledge of the vowel-consonant–consonant-vowel principle of syllabication to those two-syllable words that end in *er*. This task is similar to that described in VIB 2 of this chapter, and you should select your teaching activity from among the storehouse of techniques described there. When teaching this skill, you must be certain that the learner attends to the directions, to the vowel-consonant–consonant-vowel arrangement of letters, to the syllable division, and to the letters and sound values of each syllable, particularly the *er* unit.

■ THE POSTTEST   The pretest can also be used for the posttest. The procedure and criterion for mastery remain the same.

VIB 5

■ THE PERFORMANCE OBJECTIVE   Given a known word containing the *ar* or *or* combination, the learner pronounces other words containing these combinations.

■ THE PRETEST   Use the word lists provided below. The first word in each list has been taught previously as a sight word. Have the learner identify the first word and then ask him to pronounce the other words listed. Criterion for mastery is 19 out of 21 correct, with neither combination being missed more than once.

	car			*for*	
arm	dark	jar	lard	corn	or
bark	far	garden	star	horn	short
farm	part	hard	yard	north	
barn	farmer	park	start		

■ DIRECTING THE LEARNER'S ATTENTION   The purpose of this task is to help the learner analyze and pronounce words containing the *ar* and *or* combinations. The teacher must be certain that the learner attends to the sound value of *ar* and *or*, to the letters that produce these two sounds, and to the sound values of the other letters in the words to be pronounced.

■ TEACHING ACTIVITIES / *The model activity*   To teach the *ar* combination, direct the learner to close his eyes and listen to the last sound of the word you are going to pronounce. Then pronounce the word *car*. Say to the learner, "What sound did you hear at the end of that word? Say the sound you heard at the end." When you are sure that the learner hears the sound accurately, direct him to look at the letters *ar* as you pronounce the word *car*. Say, "What sound did you hear at the end? What letters are at the end of the word? The letters *ar* make the sound you hear at the end of the word *car*." Then let the learner apply his knowledge of the sound–symbol association for *ar* by directing him to pronounce the following words arranged so that he can use his knowledge of consonant substitution as an aid:

bark	park	star	far
dark	part	jar	farm

Repeat the same procedure for the *or* letter combination.

/ Suggestions for reteaching and/or practice

1 If the learner has difficulty in hearing the sound of *ar* or *or*, plan activities for him modeled after the suggestions provided in IIB 2 and IIB 3 in Chapter 4.

2 If the learner has difficulty in making the sound–symbol connection between the letters and the sounds, plan activities modeled after the suggestions provided in IIB 5 in Chapter 4.

■ THE POSTTEST   The pretest can be used as the posttest. The procedure and criterion for mastery remain the same.

VIB **6**

■ THE PERFORMANCE OBJECTIVE   Given a known word containing the soft *c* sound, the learner pronounces other words containing this sound.

■ THE PRETEST   Use the words provided below. The first word in the list has been previously taught as a sight word. Have the learner identify the first word and then ask him to pronounce the other words listed. Criterion for mastery is 100 percent.

*circus**

cent	dance	face	fence	place	race	ice

■ DIRECTING THE LEARNER'S ATTENTION   The purpose of the task is to help the learner analyze and pronounce words containing the soft *c* sound. The teacher must be certain that the learner attends to the sound value of the soft *c* and to the other letters in the word and their sound values.

■ TEACHING ACTIVITIES / *The model activity*   To teach the soft *c* sound, direct the learner to close his eyes and listen to the sound he hears at the begining of *cent* and *cat*. When the learner has identified the sound at the beginning of *cent* as the *s* sound and the sound at the beginning of *cat* as the *k* sound, direct him to open his eyes. Show him the printed form of *cent* and *cat*, emphasizing slightly the initial sound as you point to the initial letter in each word. Ask the learner, "What sound do you hear at the beginning of *cent?* What letter does *cent* begin with? What sound do you hear at the beginning of *cat?* What letter does *cat* begin with? How many sounds can the letter *c* make? What are the two sounds it can make?" Lead the learner to generalize that the letter *c* can sound like either an *s* or a *k*. Show him the sight word *circus*, and have him explain the sounds the two *c*s make in this word. Then direct the learner to look at the words used in the pretest, telling him to look at the *c* in each word as you pronounce it. After each word is pronounced, ask the learner, "What sound did the letter *c* make in this word? What letter follows the letter *c* in this word?" When you have pronounced the entire list, help the learner to generalize that we pronounce the letter *c* as an *s* when it is followed by *e* or by *i* (as in *cent*). Then show him the words on the pretest again, have him pronounce each word in the list, inserting the soft sound of *c* in the proper place in each word.

/ *Suggestions for reteaching and/or practice*

1 If the learner has difficulty in hearing the sounds of the hard and soft *c*, plan activities modeled after the suggestions provided in IIB 2 and IIB 3 in Chapter 4.
2 If the learner has difficulty recognizing the fact that the soft *c* sound is heard when it is followed by the letter *e* or *i*, you may want to color code the letter that follows the *c* to help him focus his attention on this discriminator.

■ THE POSTTEST   The pretest may be used for the posttest. The procedure and criterion for mastery remain the same.

VIB **7**

■ THE PERFORMANCE OBJECTIVE   Given a compound word composed of two known words, the learner pronounces the compound word.

■ THE PRETEST   Print the following words on cards. Present the cards to the learner one at a time, encouraging him to analyze and pronounce each word. Criterion for mastery is 100 percent. The words are:

afternoon	everything	inside	sometime
airplane	grandfather	milkman	sunshine
barnyard	grandmother	outside	himself
bedroom	herself	peanut	policeman
birthday			

■ DIRECTING THE LEARNER'S ATTENTION   The purpose of this task is to help the learner identify unknown compound words by isolating and identifying the known words that form the compound. This task is similar to that described in IB 13 of this chapter, and you should select your teaching activities from among the storehouse of techniques described there. When teaching this skill, you must be certain that the learner attends to the two known words that form the compound.

■ THE POSTTEST   The pretest may be used for the posttest. The procedure and criterion for mastery remain the same.

VIIA

SIGHT WORDS

■ THE PERFORMANCE OBJECTIVE Given a flash presentation of each of the following words, the learner pronounces each word within one second. The words to test are:

wolf	splash	buy	watch	monkey
world	spring	dear	cross	people
worm	station	through	engine	log
cried	turkey	thought	front	build
pennies	soup	tomorrow	bear	soft
cabbage	squirrel	brought	calf	beautiful
cage	wear	enough	deer	care
heard	cover	head	eye	year
learn	across	lie	bear	vegetable
carry	bottom	answer	left	great
sign	automobile	balloon	minute	picture

■ THE PRETEST Print each of the above words on flash cards. Then flash each word to the learner, giving him only a second or less to examine the word. Criterion for mastery is 100 percent. *Note*: You should keep track of the words missed on the pretest because only the missed words need to be taught.

■ DIRECTING THE LEARNER'S ATTENTION The purpose of this task is to teach the learner to recognize instantly each of the above words when they are printed on cards. As such, the task is similar to that described in IIIA 6 in Chapter 4, and you should select your teaching activity from among the storehouse of techniques described there. When teaching this skill, you must be certain that the learner attends to the visual form of the word and its distinguishing characteristics.

■ THE POSTTEST The procedure and criterion for mastery remain the same as for the pretest.

VIIA ■2

■ THE PERFORMANCE OBJECTIVE   Given a flash presentation of each of the frequently confused words *so–soon–some* and *much–must,* the learner pronounces each word within one second.

■ THE PRETEST   The procedure and criterion for mastery are the same as for the pretest of the previous objective except that the words *so–soon–some* and *much–must* are used.

■ DIRECTING THE LEARNER'S ATTENTION   The purpose of this task is to help the learner recognize instantly each of these easily confused words when they are presented on cards. This task is similar to that described in IA 2 of this chapter, and you should select your teaching activities from among the storehouse of techniques described there. When teaching this skill, you must be certain that the learner attends to the visual discriminator that acts as the cue for contrasting these words.

■ THE POSTTEST   The procedure and criterion for mastery remain the same as for the pretest.

VIIA ■3

■ THE PERFORMANCE OBJECTIVE   Given words he recognizes at sight, the learner creates and reads stories using these words.

■ THE PRETEST   Provide the learner with a list that contains the words he recognizes at sight. Follow the some procedure as described in the pretest for IIIA 3 of this chapter, with the exception that you tell the learner to write a story (rather than tell it) and to use the words on the list (rather than use word cards). Criterion for mastery is the combination of any number of words that are grammatically accurate and that make sense. When the learner has written his story, have him read it to you, encouraging him to make any changes he desires in word order or word choice. The story can be of any length. Spelling, handwriting, punctuation, and other aspects of composition are not to be considered here.

■ DIRECTING THE LEARNER'S ATTENTION   The purpose of this task is to help the learner to write and read stories using the individual words he knows. This task is similar to that described in IIIA 10 in Chapter 4, and you should select your teaching activity from among the storehouse of techniques described there. When teaching this skill, you must be certain that the learner attends to the directions, to the idea he wishes to convey in the story, to the individual word forms, and to the order in which the words are placed in the sentences of the story.

■ THE POSTTEST   The procedure and criterion for mastery remain the same as for the pretest.

VIIB

WORD ANALYSIS

■ THE PERFORMANCE OBJECTIVE   Given a known word illustrating the vowel-consonant-vowel principle of syllabication in which the first vowel is long, the learner pronounces other words illustrating this principle.

■ THE PRETEST   Use the list of words provided below. The first word in the list has been taught previously as a sight word. Have the learner identify the first word and then ask him to pronounce the remaining words. Criterion for mastery is 10 out of 12 correct.

over

began	music	paper	even	behind	beside
tiger	open	begin	became	belong	between

■ DIRECTING THE LEARNER'S ATTENTION   The purpose of this task is to help the learner analyze and pronounce two-syllable words illustrating the vowel-consonant-vowel principle in which the first vowel is long. This task is similar to that described in VIB 2 of this chapter, and you should select your teaching activity from among the storehouse of techniques described there. When teaching this skill, you must be certain that the learner attends to the directions, to the number of sound units heard in the word, to the vowel-consonant-vowel arrangement of letters in the middle of the word, to the syllable break after the first vowel, to the sound value of the first vowel, and to the letter units and sound value of each syllable.

■ THE POSTTEST   The pretest may also be used as the posttest. The procedure and criterion for mastery remain the same.

■ THE PERFORMANCE OBJECTIVE   Given a known word illustrating the vowel-consonant-vowel principle of syllabication in which the first vowel is short, the learner pronounces other words illustrating this principle.

■ THE PRETEST   Use the list of words provided below. The first word in the list has been previously taught as a sight word. Have the learner identify the first word and then ask him to pronounce the remaining words. Criterion for mastery is seven out of eight correct.

never

river   robin   seven   visit   wagon   finish   ever   present

■ DIRECTING THE LEARNER'S ATTENTION   The purpose of this task is to help the learner analyze and pronounce two-syllable words with the vowel-consonant-vowel arrangement, but in which the sound of the first vowel is short, rather than long (as it was in the words taught in the previous objective). This task is similar to that described in VIB 2 of this chapter, and you should select your teaching activity from among the storehouse of techniques described there. When teaching this skill, you must be certain that the learner attends to the directions, to the vowel-consonant-vowel arrangement of letters in the middle of the word, to the syllable break before the second vowel, to the sound of the first vowel in the vowel-consonant-vowel arrangement, and to the other syllable and its sound value. *Note*: It is important to teach a learner who is faced with breaking a vowel-consonant-vowel arrangement that he may have to try syllabicating the word using the principles described both in this objective and the previous one.

■ THE POSTTEST   The pretest may be used also as the posttest. The procedure and criterion for mastery remain the same.

VIIB **3**

■ THE PERFORMANCE OBJECTIVES   Given a known word illustrating the short *y* principle, the learner pronounces other two-syllable words ending with the short *y*.

■ THE PRETEST   Use the list of words provided below. The first word in the list has been taught previously as a sight word. Have the learner identify the first word and then ask him to pronounce the remaining words. Criterion for mastery is 11 out of 13 correct.

baby

candy	happy	party	puppy	story	every	pony
city	lady	bunny	sleepy	cooky	hungry	

■ DIRECTING THE LEARNER'S ATTENTION   The purpose of this task is to help the learner analyze and pronounce two-syllable words that have the short sound of *y* at the end. This task is similar to that described in VIB 2 of this chapter, and you should select your teaching activity from among the storehouse of techniques described there. When teaching this skill, you must be certain that the learner attends to the directions, to the letter *y* and its preceding consonant (which together create the final syllable), to the sound value associated with the letter *y* when it appears at the end of a two-syllable word, and to the other syllable unit of the word and its sound value.

■ THE POSTTEST   The pretest may be used for the posttest. The procedure and criterion for mastery remain the same.

VIIB 4

■ THE PERFORMANCE OBJECTIVE   Given a known two-syllable word having an unaccented *a* in the initial position, the learner pronounces other two-syllable words illustrating this principle.

■ THE PRETEST   Use the list of words provided below. The first word in the list has been taught previously as a sight word. Have the learner identify the first word and then ask him to pronounce the remaining words. Criterion for mastery is 100 percent.

about

afraid   alone   along   around   asleep

■ DIRECTING THE LEARNER'S ATTENTION   The purpose of this task is to help the learner analyze and pronounce two-syllable words that have an unaccented *a* in the initial position. This task is similar to that described in VIB 2 of this chapter, and you should select your teaching activity from among the storehouse of techniques described there. When teaching this skill, you must be certain that the learner attends to the directions, to the letter *a* in the initial position, to the sound value associated with this unaccented vowel, and to the number of syllables in the word and their sound values.

■ THE POSTTEST   The pretest may be used also as the posttest. The procedure and criterion for mastery remain the same.

VIIB 5

■ THE PERFORMANCE OBJECTIVE   Given a known word composed of the *ew* combination, the learner replaces the initial consonant with another consonant, blend, or digraph and pronounces the new word.

■ THE PRETEST   Use the list of words provided below. Have the learner identify the first word in the list and then ask him to pronounce the remaining words. Criterion for mastery is 100 percent.

new

few   flew   grew   stew   blew   crew   chew

■ DIRECTING THE LEARNER'S ATTENTION   The purpose of this task is to help the learner analyze and pronounce words composed of the *ew* combination, using his knowledge of consonant substitution. This task is similar to that described in IB 7 of this chapter, and you should select your teaching activity from among the storehouse of techniques described there. When teaching this skill, you must be certain that the learner attends to the directions, to the pronunciation of the key word, to the initial consonant letter, blend, or digraph, to the sound associated with this initial letter or letters, and to the *ew* combination.

■ THE POSTTEST   The pretest may also be used as the posttest. The procedure and criterion for mastery remain the same.

VIIB 6

■ THE PERFORMANCE OBJECTIVE   Given a spoken stimulus word beginning with the sound produced by the *str* or *thr* consonant combination and a group of three words one of which begins with the sound of *str* or *thr*, the learner pairs the two words beginning with the same sound.

■ THE PRETEST   Using the word sets listed below, say to the learner, "Here are three words. Listen carefully." (Say the words.) "Which one sounds like (say the stimulus word) at the beginning?" (Repeat the three original words.) Criterion for mastery is 5 out of 6 correct.

saw / straw / shawl   Which one sounds like *street* at the beginning?
                             Repeat the first three words.

throw / mow / tree   Which one sounds like *three* at the beginning?
                             Repeat the first three words.

tall / this / threat   Which one sounds like *three* at the beginning?
                             Repeat the first three words.

stand / strand / chant   Which one sounds like *street* at the beginning?
                             Repeat the first three words.

strap / slap / swap   Which one sounds like *street* at the beginning?
                             Repeat the first three words.

mesh / tee / thresh   Which one sounds like *three* at the beginning?
                             Repeat the first three words.

Do you smile? It's a great reinforcer for some learners.

■ DIRECTING THE LEARNER'S ATTENTION   The purpose of this task is to cue the learner to the importance of listening to the beginning sounds of words and to help him distinguish the *str* and *thr* sounds from other consonant sounds. This task is similar to that described in IIB 2 in Chapter 4, and you should select your teaching activity from among the storehouse of techniques described there. When teaching this skill, you must be certain that the learner attends to the directions and to the beginning sounds of the words in each spoken sequence.

■ THE POSTTEST   The procedure and criterion for mastery remain the same. Use the following word sets.

through / thumb / tea	Which one sounds like *three* at the beginning? Repeat the first three words.
sharp / start / stress	Which one sounds like *street* at the beginning? Repeat the first three words.
stay / stray / steep	Which one sounds like *street* at the beginning? Repeat the first three words.
theft / then / thrift	Which one sounds like *three* at the beginning? Repeat the first three words.
thrive / tie / thimble	Which one sounds like *three* at the beginning? Repeat the first three words.
stuck / strut / stub	Which one sounds like *street* at the beginning? Repeat the first three words.

VIIB 7

■ THE PERFORMANCE OBJECTIVE   Given spoken words beginning with the *str* or *thr* sounds, the learner identifies the beginning letters in each word.

■ THE PRETEST   Give the learner two cards, one with *str* and the other with *thr* printed on it. Say the following words, directing the learner to point to the card on which the letters beginning the word are written. Criterion for mastery is 100 percent.

stride   throb   struck   strife   throng   thrush

■ DIRECTING THE LEARNER'S ATTENTION   The purpose of this task is to help the learner establish a sound–symbol connection between the letters *str* and *thr* and words that begin with these sounds. This task is similar to that described in IIB 5 in Chapter 4, and you should select your teaching activity from among the storehouse of techniques described there. When teaching this skill, you must be certain that the learner attends to the sound at the beginning of each spoken word and simultaneously looks at the card containing the correct letter combination.

■ THE POSTTEST The procedure and criterion for mastery remain the same as for the pretest. Use the following words.

through   thresh   stray   stroll   thrive   strut

VIIB 8

■ THE PERFORMANCE OBJECTIVE Given a written sentence with one word missing and cued for the missing word by the letter combination (*str* or *thr*) with which the word begins, the learner says a word beginning with the letter combination that fits the context of the sentence.

■ THE PRETEST Give the learner the following sentences. Say, "Each of these sentences has one word missing. Read the sentence, look at the letter combination that begins the missing word, and say a word beginning with that combination and which will finish the sentence." Use the following sentences. Criterion for mastery is 5 out of 6 correct.

The football player was big and str——.

In the baseball game the umpire said, "Str—— one!"

The queen sat on her thr——.

The man was fishing in the str——.

My mother fixed the rip with her needle and thr——.

The boy thr—— the ball to me.

■ DIRECTING THE LEARNER'S ATTENTION The purpose of this task is to help the learner use his knowledge of both context and the letter–sound correspondence for the *str* and *thr* combinations to identify unknown words. This task is similar to that described in IIB 12 in Chapter 4, and you should select your teaching activity from among the storehouse of techniques described there. When teaching this skill, you must be certain that the learner attends to the directions, to the sentence context, and to the letter combinations and their sound values.

■ THE POSTTEST The procedure and criterion for mastery remain the same as for the pretest. Use the following sentences.

When I use a ruler, I can draw a str—— line.

The jar was up high. I had to str—— to reach it.

The drink was hot, and it burned my thr——.

"Winning the game was my biggest thr——," said the baseball player.

I lost my kite because the str—— broke.

You only have one pet, but I have thr——.

VIIB 9

■ THE PERFORMANCE OBJECTIVE   Given a word beginning with *str* or *thr* in combination with other known phonetic elements, the learner pronounces the word.

■ THE PRETEST   Put each of the following words on cards. Show a card to the learner and ask him to pronounce the word. *Note*: This is not to be a flash presentation. The learner may examine each word carefully before pronouncing it. Criterion for mastery is 12 out of 14 correct.

street	strong	three	throat
strap	strike	threw	thrash
string	strive	throw	thrill
strip		throne	

■ DIRECTING THE LEARNER'S ATTENTION   The purpose of the task is to help the learner use his knowledge of *str* and *thr* and his knowledge of other phonetic elements to analyze and pronounce unknown words. When teaching this skill, you must be certain that the learner attends to the directions, to the *str* and *thr* combinations and their sound values, and to the other phonetic elements in the words.

■ TEACHING ACTIVITIES / *The model activity*   If the learner is unable to perform this task, it is probably due to one of two reasons. Either he has not yet established the sound–symbol connection for *str* and *thr* or he is unable to pronounce the other phonetic elements of the word. If the problem is the former, return to the previous three objectives and reteach the *str* and *thr* combinations. If the problem is the latter, the learner must be returned to the objectives in which the phonetic elements causing the difficulty were originally taught.

/ *Suggestions for reteaching and/or practice*

If the learner has persistent difficulty with this task, it may be helpful to return to the concept of consonant substitution. For example, if he has established a sound–symbol correspondence for *str* and knows the word *meet* at sight, you can arrange the words *meet* and *street* one under the other, have the learner point out how the two words are relatives, and help him to pronounce *street* by replacing the *m* with the *str*.

■ THE POSTTEST The pretest may be used as the posttest. The procedure and criterion for mastery remain the same.

VIIB 10

■ THE PERFORMANCE OBJECTIVE Given a known word containing the silent letters *gh*, *k*, or *b*, the learner pronounces other words containing these silent letters.

■ THE PRETEST Use the following lists of words. The first word in each list has been taught previously as a sight word. Have the learner identify the first word in each list and then ask him to pronounce the other words. Criterion for mastery is 8 of 9 correct.

	right	*know*	*climb*
high	night	knew	lamb
light	straight	knock	crumb
might			

■ DIRECTING THE LEARNER'S ATTENTION The purpose of this task is to teach the learner to recognize that the letters *gh*, *k*, and *b* are sometimes silent and to help him analyze and pronounce words in which these silent letters appear. When teaching this skill, you must be certain that the learner attends to the silent letter or letters in each word and to the other phonetic elements of the word.

■ TEACHING ACTIVITIES / *The model activity* Have the learner close his eyes and listen to the sounds in the words you will pronounce. Say the word *right* and ask the learner to identify the sounds. If he correctly identifies the sounds of *r*, *i*, and *t*, have him open his eyes and direct him to examine the printed form of the word. Have him identify the letters *r*, *i*, and *t*, and lead him to state that the letters *gh* are silent. Repeat the same procedure for the word *high*. Then direct the learner to independently analyze and pronounce the other words having the silent *gh* combination. Repeat the same procedure for the silent *k* and silent *b*.

/ *Suggestions for reteaching and/or practice*

1 Have the learner examine the names of the pupils in the class to discover how many names contain silent letters. Relate this to the pronunciation of the names.

2 List on the chalkboard a group of words that contain silent letters. Direct the learner's attention to the board as you pronounce the words. Ask him to examine each word, decide which letters are not heard, and draw a line through these unheard letters.

3 Direct the learner to listen to the word you are going to say and to spell it just the way he hears it. Then say, "The word is *right*." The learner spells, "R-i-t" or "R-i-t-e." You say, "Yes, that is just the way the word sounds when we hear it, but this is the way it looks when we see it." Then erase the learner's spelling of the word and replace it with the correct spelling.

4 If you wish to teach a word containing silent letters, such as the word *right*, you can color code (or identify in some other distinctive way) the sounded letters. Teach the learner to pronounce only those letter sounds that are colored. As he becomes more familiar with the word, gradually remove the color code and let him recognize the word without this aid.

■ THE POSTTEST   The pretest can be used as the posttest. The procedure and criterion for mastery remain the same.

CHAPTER SIX / IF THE LEARNER PRONOUNCES WORDS BUT DOES NOT UNDERSTAND

Skill Objectives for Teaching Comprehension

The successful reader is the person who can do two things simultaneously. First, he knows how to turn those inscrutably silent scribbles on a paper page into spoken words and, second, he thinks about what the words are saying to him. If either of these operations is in any way defective, he is a poor reader in direct proportion to the magnitude of the defect. Thus, the teacher of reading must always carry in her head an awareness of this duality in the reading process.

Chapters 4 and 5 of this book provide the scope and sequence of skills necessary for teaching the learner how to get the words off the page and into his ear. This is the necessary first step to successful reading achievement, and if you will follow the program given in these chapters creatively, you will succeed in teaching your learner a basic sight vocabulary and a generalized understanding of the English decoding system. But you are still left with the second task—teaching him to get meaning as he reads. This is the purpose of Chapter 6.

THE DIFFICULTIES OF MEANING

Getting meaning while reading or listening is a thought-gathering process, and the problems involved in teaching a learner to think are formidable—formidable for him and formidable for you. There are at least two major reasons for this. First, a learner responds to the words he reads and hears from a very egocentric position. What he thinks of as he reads or listens is the sum total of his own unique involvement with the words that come to him from the page or through the air. He may or may not have had the necessary prerequisite experiences to match or parallel the experiences the author is reconstructing. The realities that the author speaks from may not be the realities the learner listens from. You can well appreciate the possibilities for error. They appear staggering.

The second difficulty, almost as confounding as the first, relates to a learner's ability to process the input of thoughts and ideas by using what is often called higher-level thinking skills. We know that with the reader who understands what he reads, thinking does take place, but what and how it takes place is open to question. There are no certified road maps that guarantee readers who think! By now you are probably ready to throw up your hands in dispair. Don't. Even though knowledge of the thinking process is theoretical and full of unknowns, experience does suggest guidelines and activities that produce thinking behavior even when we cannot explain why.

This chapter focuses on three thinking experiences that are appropriate to the reading act: the ability to conceptualize, or develop concepts; the ability to classify, that is, find relationships between and among concepts; and the ability to do inferential thinking, such as answer questions, see implications, and acquire purposeful knowledge. These three thinking skills form a developmental hierarchy: the learner must have concepts before he can classify, and he must be able to classify before he can make accurate inferences. Each of these thinking skills requires some degree of abstract reasoning and, like the problem of experience background, is fraught with instructional difficulties.

This is not to say that you cannot directly improve a learner's thinking skills. You can. However, to do so requires a good deal of knowledge plus thinking skills of your own. This is particularly so when you attempt to handle the first problem stated above—that of matching a learner's experience with that from which the author is writing. There is no one-shot, sure-fire solution to this teaching problem. Hopefully, the home and community environment will create an active and varied life style in the learner that in turn encourages an active and varied experience background. Hopefully, *you* will match or surpass the quantity and quality of out-of-school experiences available to the learner by creating active and varied learning experiences within your classroom that focus on firsthand, sensory activities—activities that allow a learner to *do* rather than just to *receive* experience and that can form a basis for an active, creative awareness by the learner toward his world. Because there is no way in which this book can predict with even minimal precision how a learner's experience background will differ from that needed for understanding a particular author's writing, you must take the responsibility for this aspect of thought gathering. You must first assess both the learner's experience and the prerequisite experience necessary for a successful understanding of the assigned reading, and then use this information to plan activities that minimize the experience differences you discover. Other than warning you to examine occasionally the range of pre-requisite experiences available to the learner and reminding you to make the necessary adjustments, this book offers little assistance to you in this area of thinking skills.

This chapter does, however, offer more direct assistance with the second problem. There are things you can do to help the learner develop concepts, manipulate these concepts by classification and/or re-arrangement of structures and organizations, and infer meaning. Although the complex nature of thinking generally and thinking when you read particularly makes it impossible to be as precise in programming these skills as was done with the decoding skills in Chapters 4 and 5, never-theless, by following the activities and seeing their transfer value to all classroom subjects (see Appendix J), you will develop these skills in a more systematic fashion than is usual in many classrooms.

SKILLS TAUGHT IN THIS CHAPTER

■ CONCEPTS   When faced with the task of helping learners think when they read, the teacher typically turns first to problems of word meaning. This is the thinking skill involved in concept development. Words are the names given to concepts. The word *snow*, for example, names the concept of the cold, wet, white stuff that we spin our wheels in all winter long. This concept is different from the cold wet stuff we call *rain*. Each is a separate concept with a separate name. This is a logical place to begin in comprehension because concepts and the words that label them are the core element in thinking. We think as a response to the meaning words carry. What meaning they carry is the meaning component our language assigns them. Therefore, if a learner does not have the *assigned* meaning for words, both written and oral communication becomes impossible, and thinking remains confined to the very limited and personal language of the individual learner.

In order to expand the number and quality of concepts available to your learners, this chapter will show you how to teach two essential and different word-meaning skills.

The meaning in an English sentence comes from two kinds of words. One can be said to show *referent* or *content* meaning, while the other involves *functional* or *relationship* meaning. For example, in the sentence: "We see the goblins on Halloween," the content words are *We, goblins*, and *Halloween*. If a learner does not know what these words mean, that is, what concepts they name, he will not grasp the content of the sentence. The words *see, the,* and *on*, however, are *function* words that signal the relationship of the three content words to each other. The functional relationships expressed by these three little words are as im-portant, much more subtle, and less definitive than the three content words. This, then, is the problem you face in teaching word meaning skills. You must be concerned both with the concepts attached by the learner to the content words and with the learner's awareness of the relationships signaled by the function words.

The number of content words that learners need to have meaning for is tremendous. From sunup to sundown, day after day, learners are asked to receive and process oral and written messages, grasp the content of these messages, and then generate thoughts in response to the messages. Confusions are possible. A teacher had a boy in her second-grade class who went for weeks without making any answers on arithmetic drills. Daily, she would duplicate problem sheets so that the children could practice their addition and subtraction. Art's paper never had any answers on it. When she finally got around to questioning him, she found that he knew how to add and subtract but was confused by her directions. "Do your own paper, and mark the answers under each problem," was her usual direction, and Art finally screwed up enough courage to ask, "What is an answer?" His was a content-meaning problem. He did not have a concept for the word *answer*; he didn't know its meaning. In contrast, however, if Art had failed to do his work because he didn't know *where* to write his answers (didn't know the meaning of *under*), his problem would have been one of functional word meaning. He would not have had a concept for the word *under*.

There are literally thousands of content words that a learner will need meaning for, and you can surely see that any attempt in this book to anticipate all of these must necessarily meet with failure. Each subject you teach—language, science, social studies, math, or health—will have its own content vocabulary of concepts related to that subject, and you are responsible for directing learners in active learning of these concepts and their names. In order that you might teach this content vocabulary as effectively as possible, however, we have included one objective containing multiple learning activities that should give you a grasp of the techniques possible in this area of instruction.

Of greater immediate concern is the necessity for some directed and specific lessons involving the learner's function-word vocabulary. These are the verbal concepts signaling the various relationships within our English sentence system that must evoke immediate response and understanding on the part of the reader. He must grasp the concepts signaled by such seemingly insignificant words as *on*, *or*, *if*, *while*, *more*, *any*, and *because*. This chapter shows you how to teach the five primary classes of function words. Each of these has a teaching module that includes multiple teaching activities. Each module also contains a list of parallel concepts that should be taught along with the model.

Finally, as you teach concepts and word meaning, let this short statement be your guide: Tell me and I forget; show me and I remember; let me do and I understand.

■ CLASSIFICATION   The second group of thinking skills in this chapter teaches the learner to organize meanings in order to grasp the main idea of a selection. The learner who has a fund of concepts must be led to see that these concepts relate to one another. Concepts are not discrete. Their overlapping relationships with other concepts, if noted, allow the learner to classify and combine concepts for various purposes. This leads to the ability to order information and to group names of concepts into smaller numbers of generalized sets. This, in turn, enhances the retention of the concepts and the learner's understanding of their functions and relationships. This skill, if successfully learned, will ultimately allow the learner to extract from masses of information the main idea—the point of it all.

This skill is taught by two separate but related activities. First are those exercises designed to teach the learner to classify by creating relationships between concepts. As the learner develops proficiency in this kind of thinking activity, he is led to see that this shared commonality, or classification system, can be the main idea or focus of the concepts. This becomes the second type of exercise, helping the learner see the main idea and its relationship to the parts. The learner who can see relationships, classify them, and then transfer this skill to his reading of narrative and factual materials by making a focus that separates main idea from detail has developed powerful thinking skills.

■ FACTS AND INFERENCE This third level of thinking skill is built on two reading activities. First, it will show the learner how to look for the fact and detail of what he hears and reads. In this way, he is directed to search for purposeful knowledge and to recognize what is factual and can be proven. Second, he is shown how to think inferentially, by first knowing the fact and detail of what he reads and then by grasping implications and inferences in order to solve for what is not known. This kind of reading-between-the-lines activity requires sophisticated thinking on the learner's part. Hopefully, with these two skills he will be able to make intelligent and thoughtful judgments concerning what he reads, its accuracy, its factual validity, what implications can be drawn, what inferences made, and ultimately what decisions he might make on the basis of this thoughtful activity.

USING THIS CHAPTER

The numbering system used in this chapter is similar to that in Chapters 4 and 5. The Roman numeral designates the skill cluster: I is the cluster of skills that teach word meaning; II the cluster of skills that teach classifying–main idea; and III the cluster of skills that teach fact and inference. The capital letter designates the specific objective within the cluster. For example, IIB would be the second objective in the classifying–main idea cluster. The Key Objective format is the same as in Chapters 4 and 5 except that because every objective in this chapter should be repeated frequently using different reading material, they are *all* classified as Key Objectives.

Teaching your learner to think is a necessary goal at any stage in his reading development. The operational skills associated with word meaning, main idea, and/or fact-inference should be taught orally to five-year-old kindergarten children. Likewise, the fourth-grade reader will use these same skills when he reads his social studies lesson or math story problem. In this chapter, we have tried to include objectives and teaching activities that suggest this range of possibilities. Any activity that is described here as a prereading oral lesson, with some modification, can be taught as a reading skill in a later grade. Conversely, many of the reading exercises and objectives could be adapted for use as oral exercises. It is your responsibility to make the adaptation. Some suggestions to help you in this task are included in Appendix J.

IA KEY OBJECTIVE

■ THE PERFORMANCE OBJECTIVE   Given any content word found in reading materials used by the learner, he indicates his understanding of the conceptual meaning of the word by (1) giving a synonym for the concept, (2) using it in an appropriate context, (3) defining it in his own words, or (4) performing a physical operation indicative of the meaning.

■ THE PRETEST   In your day-to-day classroom operations, you constantly question learners to determine their understanding of various content areas (math, science, history, and geography). You should use these particular opportunities to test content vocabulary. A typical pretest situation might occur in a science class where the concept *erosion* is encountered. Here it is appropriate to ask the learner what the word means and to elicit from him an appropriate response to at least two of the four techniques above for assessing meaning. Criterion for mastery is 100 percent. Keep track of the words missed, since you need to teach only the conceptual meanings the learner does not know.

■ DIRECTING THE LEARNER'S ATTENTION   The purpose of this task is to teach content word meanings. In directing a learner to create accurate word meanings, you must do two things. First, you must develop a conceptual understanding. To do this, expose him to selected experiences that form the basis for the concept. Direct him to carefully look and listen to these illustrative experiences, no matter what the number, and to attach a word that names the concept. Now the learner has a meaning for the word. A single concept will have been developed from multiple situations. Now, redirect the learner to the specific content lesson in which the word was or will be found. (You can teach word meaning skills as they arise in the daily lessons, or you can anticipate necessary concepts and teach them prior to encountering them in the content lessons. The good teacher will do both.) Now, you must direct the learner to the meaning of the word as it is found in one specific context. The word no longer has *a* meaning, but now assumes *the* meaning appropriate to this instance. Consequently, when teaching this skill, you must be certain that the learner attends to both the conceptual meaning and the specific contextual setting in which it is found.

> **Key objective** for teaching content word meanings.

■ TEACHING ACTIVITIES / *The model activity* There are multiple ways to help learners grasp the meaning concepts that surround them in their classrooms and that leap from the printed page to bombard the ear. As a teacher, it is your responsibility to choose learning strategies and activities appropriate to the background of your learner and the word being learned. At times, you will need to develop a concept through multiple firsthand experiences with a whole series of events that lead to conceptualization. You would teach the concept of *erosion,* for example, by having your learner pour water over a slanted tray of dirt and then examine and describe the changes in the grooved mud. This activity could be followed by a visit to a local stream and some directed examination of the banks and gullies that occur there. Five minutes on a dirt playground after a rain shower would also create a condition where the concept of *erosion* could be learned. With only these experiences, your learner would have a rich understanding of the concept, its causes, definition, and effect.

Only one step removed from this vivid, firsthand experience is the creative use of audiovisual materials to teach the concept. Here, with a series of slides, a movie, or illustrated books, your learner can again move from the specific illustrations to the generalized concept of erosion.

At times, an examination of the context in which a word is found will be necessary for developing both the concept and its specific meaning. The following sentences are an example: "Erosion is one of the farmer's most pressing problems. It affects both the yield he receives from his crops, the value of his land, and the costs of planting and harvesting." Here, a learner has many options for the meaning of the word *erosion.* It could mean lack of fertilizer or type of weather, because each fits the conditions as stated in this context. However, if the next sentence reads, "To watch his good, black earth wash away in the wind and rain can be as discouraging as losing money," the learner can now conclude that in this specific instance, erosion means the moving away by wind and water of a farmer's topsoil. The concept may not be entirely clear, but the specific meaning in this context is sufficient for adequate comprehension.

Your final resource for teaching a concept or word meaning is a well-planned dictionary activity coupled to any of the three previous techniques. A dictionary definition can be used to pinpoint a specific word meaning (in the case of erosion, "the wearing away of soil or rock through the actions of climate and weather"). In addition, by listing various meanings of the word on the chalkboard, you can guide learners to the core concept of erosion, allowing them in some future lesson to quickly respond to the sentence, "An erosion of confidence in their elected officials was the principle cause for the defeat of five labor leaders seeking to head already existing unions."

/ *Suggestions for reteaching and/or practice*

1 Use both oral and written exercises in which words are replaced with synonyms. Each learner can be encouraged to supply another word that "means about the same thing." Appropriateness to the concept can be judged by class discussion and debate. Lists of such synonyms will create the conceptual meaning.

2 Teach word opposites. One sure way to discriminate a concept is by knowing not only what it is but also what it is not. If erosion is *wearing away*, what do we call *building up?* It is most appropriate to teach this concept of word opposites at the prereading or early reading stage. Play a word game where you orally give the syntactic frame, "If something is not *big*, it must be ————." Encourage the learner to supply the word that elicits the opposite condition to *big*. Either *little* or *small* would be appropriate responses. The following is a partial list of opposites that can be taught:

clean/dirty	winter/summer	big/little
above/below	good/bad	on/off
left/right	before/after	in/out
stop/go	open/close	long/short
sick/well	front/back	up/down
push/pull	first/last	over/under
noisy/quiet	wide/narrow	boy/girl
right/wrong	young/old	man/woman
top/bottom	buy/sell	happy/sad
friend/enemy		

3 Encourage learners to associate a word meaning or concept with a mental picture of that meaning or concept. Let each learner explain his mental picture—the source of meaning or memory strategy that helps him know and remember the concept.

4 Teach the use of a thesaurus. This can be done by having learners, individually or as a class project, note on 3- by 5-inch cards the key concepts and various synonyms created from class discussions. In this way, you build not only meaning vocabulary but also a synonym source for use by the class in writing assignments.

5 Develop an interest in the origin of words. Why do the words *pig* and *pork* refer to a similar concept but have such different connotations? The answer to this kind of meaning problem lies in word origin and cultural associations. Learners can be introduced to this area of study by finding the meaning originally associated with their family names. Help learners invent a new machine, such as one that would be useful in space for the exploration of Venus. Have them create a name for their machine by combining words they know into compounds or by using common Latin or Greek roots. They might even draw on characters from mythology as a source for new names. Illustrate these meanings with such common words as *zenith, radio, television,* or *helicopter.*

6 Teach the meanings available in compound words. What are the meanings of the simple words? What new concepts are created when two or more simple words are made into one compound word?

7 As learners' reading horizons widen, teach common prefixes and suffixes as a technique for giving meaning to words created through the use of these affixes. The following list constitutes the most utilitarian affixes for learners operating at the level described in this book.

	The prefix	Its meaning	Sample word
	dis	apart	disbelieve
	ex	out from	export
Prefixes:	in	not	incorrect
	un	not	unhappy
	sub	under	subway
	pre	before	preview

	The suffix	Its meaning	Sample word
	less	without	senseless
Suffixes:	al	having to do with	national
	ly	in what way or in what manner	happily
	ful	full of	joyful

■ THE POSTTEST The suggestions provided for the pretest should be adapted and used for the posttest.

IB ❶ KEY OBJECTIVE

■ THE PERFORMANCE OBJECTIVE   Given any function word found in reading materials used by the learner, he indicates his understanding of the functional meaning by (1) performing a physical operation that indicates its meaning or (2) stating the sentence relationship it signals. Your learner should understand the function words that signal the following five essential meaning relationships common to English sentences:

1. Prepositions that signal both positional and time relationships.
2. Pronouns and their antecedents.
3. Words that signal contrast–comparison relationships.
4. Words that signal chronological sequences.
5. Words that signal cause–effect relationships.

There are three teaching activities in this set of objectives. The first tests and teaches prepositions; the second, pronouns; and the third covers contrast–comparison relationships, chronological sequences, and cause–effect relationships. In effect, then, the five meaning relationships are covered in three objectives.

Though these meaning relationships are arranged in order of difficulty, there is no prescribed time when they should be taught. A kindergarten teacher, for example, might teach both the preposition and pronoun skills *orally* to six year olds. A first- or even fourth-grade teacher might find it advantageous to review these skills as *reading* activities. Both lessons could be appropriate to the meaning skills needed in these grades. You should examine the five objectives and their teaching activities to see what is appropriate for your learners. If a lesson is modeled orally, could you produce a written one for a later grade? If modeled as a reading activity, could you make it into an oral learning activity for younger learners? These should be your considerations as you read the five function word objectives.

Key objective for teaching function word meanings.

■ THE PRETEST (PREPOSITIONS) Give the learner a simple direction containing a prepositional phrase. Direct him to perform the direction, thereby indicating his understanding of the prepositional concept. For example, place in front of your learner a shoe box containing three blocks; one red, one blue, and one yellow. Give the following oral directions to see if he grasps the operations signaled by the prepositions italicized in the following sentences.

Take the blue block *out* of the box.

Put the red block *over* the blue one.

Put the red block *between* the blue and yellow ones.

Put the yellow block *under* the blue one.

Put the yellow block *beside* the blue one.

Take the blue block *off* the yellow one.

Put it *on* the table.

Put three blocks *into* the shoe box.

Your learner should be able to do these operations with 100 percent accuracy and at a rapid rate.

Devise further directions to test your learner for these additional prepositions:

about	around	but	like	to
across	at	down	near	until
after	before	for	of	up
against	beneath	from	outside	upon
along	by	in	since	with
among	beyond	inside	through	without

■ DIRECTING THE LEARNER'S ATTENTION This activity can be done either orally or while reading. When teaching this skill, you must be certain that the learner is cued to the preposition being learned, the rest of its phrase, and its connective relationship to the rest of the sentence.

■ TEACHING ACTIVITIES / *The model activity* The relationships and functions signaled by prepositions can be taught and learned most easily through game-type activities. Only a few minutes a day of directed instruction will give your learner an accurate response to prepositional signals. For example: "Here is a penny. What can I do with this penny? I can hide the penny *inside* my desk." Here you put the penny in a desk drawer. "Who can think of something else we can do with the penny?" Here you are asking your learners to think of prepositional situations. This will be difficult for them because they will want to stop their ideas with the verb, "We can *spend* the penny." You must be ready to add a prepositional phrase to such responses. If a learner says, "We can spend the penny," you can continue with such additions as "*at* the store," or "*for* candy." This encourages them to produce the necessary related function word objectives.

/ *Suggestions for reteaching and/or practice*

Create simple sentences like the following:
a. The bell rings at 11.
b. Moles burrow under the ground.
c. After the game we went home.

Give a Ditto copy of each lesson to your learners with the following directions: "Circle the words in each sentence that answer the question I ask." Then say, "Which words in the first sentence tell when the bell rings? Circle them. Which word connects rings with 11? Circle it." Here you are giving learners practice with both prepositional phrases and the connecting functions of the preposition.

THE POSTTEST The suggestions for the pretest can be used also for the posttest.

IB 2

■ THE PRETEST (PRONOUNS) Give the learner sentences such as, "Little children should never play with sharp objects. *They* can hurt eyes and ears." Direct him to indicate how the pronoun *they* could refer to (1) eyes and ears or (2) little children. A group of five such sentences should be constructed and used. Criterion for mastery is 100 percent.

■ DIRECTING THE LEARNER'S ATTENTION Direct the learner to the pronoun being taught. Say, "This word can stand for and means the same as some other words in the last sentence. Can you find those words?"

The level of difficulty of this task is relatively high. It would best be taught as a reading activity so that the learner can refer back to the previous sentences without having to carry all the words in his head as would be the case in an oral presentation. When teaching this skill, you must be certain that the learner recognizes all the words, understands your directions for the task, and sees the possibility for two antecedents to the pronoun being taught.

---

*Are you putting this to work? Tell me, I forget; show me,
I remember; let me do, I understand.*

■ TEACHING ACTIVITIES / *The model activity* Make a list of five common pronouns: *they, he, himself, our, it.* Put them on the board with the direction, "These are five common, everyday words. We use them all the time. What do they mean?" Focus learners on the fact that these words only have meaning when they stand for other concrete referents named in a sentence or selection. Say "What does *they* mean? Can someone make *they* mean something?" Here you are asking that learners create an antecedent for this pronoun. One might say, "My parents bought a new car. *They* paid for it with cash." Now, the word *they* has meaning. It stands for *parents*.

/ Suggestions for reteaching and/or practice

1 Ditto short sentences in which a pronoun has a clear antecedent. Circle each pronoun, and ask the learner to draw a line from the pronoun to the word for which it stands.
2 Reverse the preceding activity by circling the antecedent and directing the learner to draw a line to the pronoun that stands for the antecedent.
3 Put a pronoun on the board. Ask the learner to name in one minute as many things as he can think of that the pronoun could stand for. A variation of this technique would be to ask for things the pronoun could stand for that begin with *s* or *l* or *z*. This limits the antecedents and makes the activity more compact.

■ THE POSTTEST The suggestions provided for in the pretest may be used also for the posttest.

IB **3**

■ THE PRETEST (CAUSE–EFFECT, CHRONOLOGY, AND CONTRAST–COMPARISON)
Give the learner a sentence or group of sentences containing cause–effect, chronological, or comparison–contrast relationships. Ask him to name each relationship and identify the function word or words that signal the relationship.

Use the following four paragraphs in the order presented. Explain that the first paragraph is a simple listing of events. This is the base paragraph against which the other three are to be measured and compared. Next, direct him to read the second paragraph and explain how it differs from the first. What is told in the second paragraph that is not told in the first one? He should see that the second paragraph has a sequence of events that is not a part of the first one; that it has a chronological or time relationship. Next, ask him to find the key words that signal this relationship. They are: *during, after, later,* and *finally.*

Continue this same activity with the third and fourth paragraphs. Paragraph 3 is a *contrast* relationship signaled by the words *much more than.*

Paragraph 4 is a *cause-effect development* signaled by the words *because* and *were able*. Criterion for mastery is 100 percent.

1 During our visit to the museum, we saw a collection of old silverware, an absorbing display of old-fashioned wedding gowns, a room filled with Indian relics, and the first Stars and Stripes ever carried in battle.

2 During our visit to the museum, we saw the first Stars and Stripes ever carried in battle; after that we enjoyed a collection of old silverware, later wandered into the room filled with Indian relics, and finally found ourselves absorbed in a display of old wedding gowns.

3 During our visit to the museum, we enjoyed seeing the first Stars and Stripes ever carried in battle and the absorbing display of old-fashioned wedding gowns much more than we did the room filled with Indian relics and the collection of old silverware.

4 Because, on our visit to the museum, we had seen the first Stars and Stripes ever carried in battle, a room full of Indian relics, a display of old silverware, and a collection of old-fashioned wedding gowns, we were able to present a successful class program in which we compared relics of the past with their modern equivalents.[1]

■ DIRECTING THE LEARNER'S ATTENTION   When teaching this skill, you must be certain that the learner attends to two variables. First, he must identify the function words that signal the meaning relationships; second, he must understand the relationship expressed by each function word.

■ TEACHING ACTIVITIES / *The model activity*   Create a series of simple sentences or statements, connecting them with the word *and*. Example: *I catch many fish,* and *I fish at night*. Explain that you have written two related ideas on the board. They are equal relatives. You want to change them into other relationships as simply as possible. How can I change these into a cause–effect relationship? How can I make one statement into a cause or why situation, while the other statement becomes a what or result statement? The simplest modification would be: *If* I fish at night, I catch fish. Here the signal word for a cause–effect relationship is *if*. A similar relationship can be established with the words *because* or *since*.

Next, ask your learners for a comparison or contrast relationship. Here additions must be made to the simple statements. Example: I catch *more* fish at night *than* I do during the daytime. The key words are *more* and *than*. Other key word possibilities would include *either, or, nor, although, like,* and *different*. All can signal a comparison or contrastive pairing of ideas.

[1] O. S. Niles, "Comprehension Skills," in *Reading Instruction: Dimensions and Issues*, William K. Durr (ed.), Boston, Houghton Mifflin, 1967, pp. 130–131.

Finally, direct your learners to make a chronological relationship from these simple statements. An example is: During the afternoon I fished very hard, and *later* I caught some fish. *Later* signals the time change from afternoon to sometime following the afternoon. Other key words could include: *then, after, first, when,* and *until.*

/ Suggestions for reteaching and/or practice

1 Put on the chalkboard words that can signal chronological relationship, such as *first, then,* and *later.* Have the learner think of a sequence of events that could be signaled with these words. Write this sequence on the board.

2 This same technique can be used with the comparison–contrast and cause-effect structures.

3 Examine a section of a science text that explains a science experiment. The explanation will often be paragraphed according to chronological relationship. Have the learner number the sequence and circle each key function word.

4 Examine arithmetic story-problems for the key words that signal the computation to be performed. Have learners circle these words and determine the arithmetic operation to be performed.

5 Play the "if–then" game. Say, "I am going to say a sentence that *could be true.* When I finish, you tell what will happen next."

a. If the bell doesn't ring for class, ...

b. Because Tommy was late to class, ...

c. Since winter is here, ...

Each of the responses will be an effect signaled by the causal statement given. This game also can be used to create simple deductive cause–effect relationships using the *not* meaning frames. Example:

a. If a book is *not* read (red), ...

b. Because a boy is *not* little, ...

■ THE POSTTEST The suggestions provided for the pretest can be adapted and used for the posttest.

IIA KEY OBJECTIVE

■ THE PERFORMANCE OBJECTIVE Given four pictures, two of which are related through use, sequence, composition, or cause and effect, the learner pairs the pictures thus related and states the relationship.

■ THE PRETEST Collect a picture of a hammer, some nails, a pencil, and a sheep. Place the pictures in front of your learner, saying, "Can you tell me what these are?" The learner should identify each picture correctly. If corrections are needed, you make them. Next, say "Two of these go together. Can you name (point to or otherwise identify) the two that go together." The learner should indicate the hammer and nails as going together. If he makes this relationship, you should then ask him, "Why do they go together?" His answer could be: "You hit nails with a hammer," or "You use a hammer and nails to build," or, "I have a hammer and nails." These responses, while not equal, do indicate that he sees a relationship based on use. Devise four other examples for use in testing. Criterion for mastery is 100 percent.

■ DIRECTING THE LEARNER'S ATTENTION The purpose of this task is to teach the learner to make relationships among concepts. The ability to see meaningful relationships between concepts is absolutely necessary if he is to comprehend at a higher level what he reads or hears. This objective and the one that follows are both prerequisites to the final objective in this cluster, that of teaching the learner to extract the main idea of a paragraph. As a prerequisite, this objective directs the learner to assign an accepted concept to each of four discrete meaning units (in this objective, the units are pictures, although at a higher skill level they could also be words), and then to search among the four concepts for whatever relationships his experience with them allows. When teaching this skill, you must be certain that the learner's attention is directed at two levels. He must have a frame of meaning for each of the pictures, and then he must be able to relate them through the associations he has gained by experiences with them.

Key objective for developing skill in making meaning relationships.

■ TEACHING ACTIVITIES / *The model activity* Although the objective requires the learner to find a relationship between two of four concepts,
when teaching this skill at beginning levels, you can create activities that
call for only two concepts at a time. For example, hold up a piece of
paper and a scissors. Say, "What is this —— and this?" Direct your
learner to name the two objects. Then ask, "In what way are paper and
scissors alike?" The most immediate conection between paper and
scissors is that scissors cut paper. This is a relationship based on use, and
when a learner verbalizes this relationship, it indicates he can relate these
concepts in this way.

Oral presentations such as the above can get the learner thinking about
the task of relating experiences with other experiences. A little five-
minute drill each day will create the set necessary for the next higher-
level objectives.

Other model frames for this activity are:

1 "In what way are first and last alike?" This calls for a relationship
based on sequence.

2 "In what way are matches and fire alike?" This calls for a relationship based on cause and effect.

3 "In what way are a pin and a doorknob alike?" This calls for a relationship based on composition; both are metal.

Caution: Learners will create numerous relationships between two
objects. Some of these will be totally idiosyncratic and without real
thinking value. An example of this would be the response, "I have a
hammer and a nail," to the relationships indicated in the pretest. Such
an answer does relate two objects, but without any real cognitive effort
to manipulate the objects in varied ways. You will have to use your
judgment in deciding whether to accept and reinforce a response or
whether to reject and extinguish it.

/ *Suggestions for reteaching and/or practice*

1 Collect a set of pictures depicting the action of a story. After reading
or hearing the story, ask the learner to arrange the pictures in the proper
sequence of events, thus establishing a relationship based on time.
2 Sentences can be divided into subject and predicate phrases and the
learner directed to put them together in the proper relationships. Example: Even a tiny rabbit/will eat the farmer's carrots.
3 Most reading readiness tests contain a section called Relationships.
Each unit usually has four or more pictures, two of which go together.
Use these ideas to make Dittoed exercises in which the learner draws a
line between, or colors, the ideas that go together.
4 Put the following numbers on the board. Ask your learners what
number comes next: 1-3-5-7-9-( ). A variation of this asks for the missing number: 2-4-( )-8-10-12.

5 Create paradigms such as the following with words, figures, or pictures:

a. Red is to rose as ——— is to grass.
b. Motor is to car as ——— is to lawnmower. [grass/boy/dog]

For either of these exercises, you may choose to illustrate each relationship with pictures rather than with words, thus permitting learners who are not yet reading to perform relationship thinking. *Note:* The level of difficulty of these two illustrations is different. Whether you supply clues to the relationship (as in the motor–car item) or leave the response open-ended (as in the red–rose item) will depend upon the skills of your learner.

■ THE POSTTEST   The suggestions provided in the pretest can be adapted and used for the posttest.

Are you using the comprehension exercises in this chapter in your daily instruction in the content areas? See also Appendix J.

IIB

CLASSIFICATION SKILLS

■ THE PERFORMANCE OBJECTIVE   Given a box of objects, the learner groups those that belong together and explains his system for classifying them.

■ THE PRETEST   Collect a series of models and figures that includes models of cars, buses, and trains, animals, doll clothes, colored blocks, and cardboard letters such as *A, B, C, D, E*. Your collection should have a minimum of 20 pieces. Place these in a shoe box and ask the learner to name as many of the objects as he can. Then say, "Some of these things belong together. Can you collect the things that belong together?" You may find it necessary to model what you mean, by selecting two of the objects that are part of a set and by saying, "See, the *A* and the *B* go together *because they are both letters*. Can you find other things that belong together?" After the learner has grouped as many objects as he can, have him tell you why he put them together—that is, what is his basis for classifying them, or what is the common denominator for each group? Ideally, he will group the above objects into: colors, letters, transportation or vehicles, clothes, and animals. These are not the only possibilities, however. He might group by color, by weight, or even by beginning sounds. As his teacher, you must judge two things. First, does he grasp the concept of classification—that is, that things can be grouped into sets according to some shared quality or construction—and, second, does his classification show sophisticated thinking. You must be aware of and remember that many creative learners will discover some weird classification systems. Encourage this diversified thinking while showing them more typical responses. Criterion for mastery is 100 percent.

■ DIRECTING THE LEARNER'S ATTENTION   The purpose of this task is to teach learners to observe and label the world not as disconnected and mutually exclusive objects and events but as experienced realities related to other realities, which can be grouped according to selected similarities or excluded because of some unacceptable contrast. By giving this task to the learner, you are helping him grasp the relationship of the part to the whole or the whole to the part. This is an intermediate step in teaching the learner to see details in relation to the main idea. The learner who can create classifying systems is well on his way to seeing the point of a paragraph or larger selection.

When teaching this skill, you must direct the learner's attention to the concepts defined by each of the objects and then to the search for a common denominator by which all the concepts can be grouped.

Key objective for developing classifying skills.

■ TEACHING ACTIVITIES / *The model activity* The classifying task can create both deductive and inductive reasoning. An excellent oral exercise is to say to learners, "Listen very carefully. I'm going to try to fool you. I'm going to say some words. When I finish, I want you to tell me what all the words are. These are the words: *Chevrolet, Ford, Plymouth, Dodge, Buick, Mercury*, and *Cadillac*. What are they?" You are directing the learners to the logical conclusion that you have named seven *cars*. These seven words (concepts) can be grouped under the denominator *cars* or *automobiles*. To give this answer, a learner must create a classification system that fits all the words.

/ *Suggestions for reteaching and/or practice*

1 This thinking process can be reversed by saying, "Listen while I try to fool you. I will say a word. Can you give me examples of that word? Here is the word: *car*." Now the learners are given the generalized classification and asked for specific instances that fit within that classification. Answers would be: *Ford, Buick, Chevrolet, Rambler*, etc.
2 Once learners are able to handle this task effectively, modify the game slightly by saying, "This time I really will fool you. Listen while I say some words. Which one *doesn't belong?* Here are the words: *Ford, Buick, Chevrolet, bicycle, Dodge, Cadillac*." Now the task is to classify and to spot concepts that don't belong to the classification system.
3 Create sentences like: "Jack collects many things, such as butterflies, rocks, matchbooks, model airplanes, and arrowheads." Direct the learner to divide this sentence in half; *Jack collects* is one half, the list of objects is the other. Construct a sample outline such as:

a. Jack collects
b. butterflies
   rocks
   matchbooks
   model airplanes
   arrowheads

This is a combined relationship and classification skill. It allows the learner to group like concepts and arrange the total meaning into a dual relationship.

4   Explain to the learners that you are going to say 12 words. Each word will be said just once. When you stop, they are directed to write or recite as many of the words as they can remember. The words are:

ruby	pearl	sapphire	diamond
deer	boat	tiger	car
airplane	elephant	lion	sled

Let each member of the class read or say as many of the words as he can remember. The learner who remembers the most has usually grouped these words into three classifications; *precious stones, transportation,* and *animals.* Point this out to the class and demonstrate this classification technique with the above words. Repeat the exercise with a new list and see how many more words are remembered.

■ THE POSTTEST   The suggestions provided for the pretest can be adapted and used for the posttest.

IIC KEY OBJECTIVE

■ THE PERFORMANCE OBJECTIVE Given a short informational paragraph, the learner states the main idea and remembers the details that support the idea.

■ THE PRETEST Select a short informational paragraph appropriate to the reading achievement level of the learner. Direct him to read it carefully. Supply any word that he doesn't recognize. Then ask, "Can you tell me what this paragraph is about *in one word*?" This usually will prove difficult but serves to zero the learner in on the task. Next say, "Can you tell me what this paragraph is about using less than six words." The choice *six* is an arbitrary decision that must be made in order to limit the learners only to the main idea or point of the selection. Finally say, "What are the facts that support or add to your main idea?" These might be listed on paper or written on the board. The learner should be allowed to reread the selection to find any details he might have missed. Criterion for mastery is your judgment regarding how well he has grasped the main idea.

■ DIRECTING THE LEARNER'S ATTENTION The purpose of this task is to teach the learner to pick out the main idea in a paragraph. With this exercise, you are asking him to use the same thinking skills as taught in the preceding objective, but at a much more difficult level and with many more distractors. He must be directed first to read the total paragraph, and then through a classification procedure to extract the common denominator—the point of it all, the main idea. Once this is accomplished, the specific details will appear as parts to the whole, and the learner needs to be directed only to remember and list these parts. When teaching this skill, you must be certain that the learner attends to the total paragraph and to the common denominator that holds the paragraph together.

Key objective for developing skill in picking out the main idea.

■ TEACHING ACTIVITIES / *The model activity* Select a well-written informational paragraph. In such a paragraph, the first sentence usually will be the topic sentence. Number each detail and write it in a short phrase. Put these phrases on the blackboard, and direct the learners to examine each phrase and then make their own phrase that expresses the part common to the others.

Example: Brushing teeth regularly
Bathing frequently
Eating nutritious, well-balanced meals
Getting sufficient rest
Getting sufficient exercise

A good main idea for these details would be *good health habits*. Have the learner read the original paragraph, underline the topic sentence, and number each of the details as they occur.

/ *Suggestions for reteaching and/or practice*

1 Select a well-written informational paragraph and write each sentence on a separate piece of paper. Direct your learner to arrange these sentences in the correct order. *Caution*: The topic sentence (main idea) can be either the *first* or the *last* sentence and is equally appropriate in either position.

2 Many times, authors will use certain word clues that help guide the reader to the main idea and sequence of details. Words like *first, last, then*, and *next* usually point out specific detail. Collect such paragraphs and teach the use of these words in organizing the selection.

Example: There are good reasons for Denmark's success. First, the government encourages adult education. Second, it has established a reputation for excellent dairy products. A third reason is found in the cooperative farm.

3 Use the "telegram" technique. Direct your learners to read the paragraph and decide what words could be omitted without losing the meaning. Explain that they are going to send the paragraph as a telegram and will have to pay for each word. What is left will be a selection of the main idea and essential supporting details.

4 Main idea can be taught in narration or story writing. Here you have the learner read the story and create a good title. If carefully thought out, this title will be the main idea or point to the story.

5 Outlining is an aid to teaching the main idea of an informational selection. Even as early as second grade, your learners can be told, "There are three important ideas in this reading lesson. See if you can find them as you read." Later, you can put these on the board and discuss how each learner determined what an important idea was. *Caution*: If you are using a formal outline technique with your class, remember to teach only those outlining skills that are important. Ask these questions: Does the outline separate main idea clearly from detail? Is it short and concise? Is it in the learner's own words or just copied from the book?

6   Make "stand-up" paragraphs. They can be fun and they can teach main idea–detail skills. Select a learner to stand in front of the class and think up a key topic sentence. (This might have to be "planted" at first.) Other members of the class think up details that elaborate on the topic sentence. As each adds an important detail, he stands behind the learner who made the topic sentence. The paragraph becomes a row of learners starting at the front of the room. When all the "sentences" have taken their places, have them repeat their sentences one after the other and then construct the paragraph. Don't be afraid to have sentences rearranged or even omitted if they do not belong.

7   Ask a question: "Did you have a good time over the weekend?" Answers should be either oral or written, giving reasons one, two, three, and so forth. The sentence that answers the question is the main idea, and the listed reasons are the supporting detail.

8   Teach learners to anticipate where the main idea is likely to occur. For example, at the lower reading levels, the main idea is invariably the first or last sentence. If the structure of such paragraphs is analyzed and graphically illustrated for learners, they will have a strategy for finding the main idea. That is, they will look at the first and last sentences and see if this communicates the point of it all in the paragraph. One good way to graphically illustrate paragraph structure is to compare paragraphs to triangles; paragraphs with the main idea first are structured

as $\triangle$ and those with the main ideas last are structured as ∇ .

■ THE POSTTEST   The suggestions provided for the pretest may be adapted to the posttest.

IIIA

FACT SKILLS

■ THE PERFORMANCE OBJECTIVE Given either a story or short informative selection, the learner answers factual questions related to the material.

■ THE PRETEST Select a story or article that is appropriate to the reading ability of the learner. Direct him to read the material carefully. If it contains words he does not recognize, pronounce them for him. When he has completed his reading, ask him five questions whose answers may be found in the selection. These questions should be of the *who, what, when,* or *where* type. Criterion for mastery is 80 percent. *Note*: If the learner is not yet able to read, this objective can be converted to a listening task.

Sample paragraph:

In the spring and early summer, butterflies appear as if by magic. Most of them emerged from cocoons that were attached to weeds and bushes during the last year's fall. However, one of the most colorful butterflies, the Monarch, didn't spend the cold winter in a cocoon. Instead it migrated, like the birds, to warm southern California and there spent a cozy winter. In the spring it flew north, again bringing spring color to signal the end of winter.

Sample factual questions:

1. What butterflies migrated to the north in spring?
2. Where does this butterfly spend the cold winter?
3. When does the butterfly return to the north?
4. To what are cocoons usually attached?
5. What besides the butterfly migrates south for the winter?

■ DIRECTING THE LEARNER'S ATTENTION The purpose of this task is to teach the learner to read for factual information. Reading has many purposes, but one of the most important is to acquire information. Without knowledge gained from factual input, either through reading or listening, response to the word becomes a function of chance rather than reason. Options for behavior disappear and are replaced by either passive indifference or emotional tantrums. Therefore, one of your important reading jobs is to help your learners gain knowledge through reading.

When teaching this skill, you must be certain that the learner attends to the facts and details of what he reads—that is, to the information in a selection that can be verified by specific words or sentences. A key device in insuring such attention is that of purpose setting, giving the learner specific cues regarding what to look for. Reading for fact and detail is a memory task: The learner is rewarded not for thinking, but for remembering. He will remember best those things he knows you are looking for. Hence, the purpose-setting cues are essential.

Key objective for teaching learners to read for factual information.

■ TEACHING ACTIVITIES / *The model activity*   Before reading a selection from a textbook or reader, put the following purpose-setting formula on the board:

Who?   Where?   When?   How many?   What happens?

Ask the learner to use this formula as a guide in his reading. Such a guide invariably will produce the details of a selection.

/ *Suggestions for reteaching and/or practice*

1   Before directing a learner to read a selection, set a purpose by asking him to see how many things he can learn during his reading. Direct him to make a tally mark on a paper as he reads, each mark standing for something he learned while reading. Each mark will usually stand for a factual detail in the selection.

2   Before assigning a reading lesson, list key words from the selection on the board. Set the purpose by directing the learner to "find information about these words."

3   Prior to assigning a specific reading task, list several factual questions on the chalkboard as purpose setters. Direct the learner to find the answers to these specific questions as he reads.

4   Teach the learner how to set purposes for himself by asking his own questions as he reads. In the pretest selection on the Monarch butterfly, for example, train the learner to anticipate factual information by listing for himself some questions that he thinks he should be able to answer after having read the selection. At the conclusion of his reading, he checks to see how many of his questions he can answer, how many were not answered by the selection, and how many facts he had not anticipated in his questions.

5   Teach the learner to use the SQ3R technique. This is a systematic purpose-setting study technique that is particularly effective with content textbooks. The five steps are: *Survey, Question, Read, Recite,* and *Review.* Before beginning his reading, the learner is taught to *survey* a chapter or selection to get an idea of what it is about. He then examines the material, particularly the headings and subheadings, and poses *questions* for himself, which he should be able to answer when he has finished reading. He then *reads* to answer his questions, *recites* to see if he is now able to answer the questions, and *reviews* to find information relative to any question he was unable to answer. The first two steps in this technique, survey and question, are particularly appropriate to purpose setting because the learner is actively involved in determining what he is trying to learn. He sets the goals. It is *his* questions that guide his reading. This creates a relevance for learning that can be missing from other types of purpose setting.

■ THE POSTTEST   The suggestions provided in the pretest may be adapted and used in the posttest.

Did you remember to point out key words in those arithmetic story-problems to help your learners set up the mathematical computations?

IIIB KEY OBJECTIVE

■ THE PERFORMANCE OBJECTIVE Given either a story or short informative selection, the learner answers *inferential* questions related to the material.

■ THE PRETEST Select a story or article appropriate to the reading ability of the learner. Direct him to read the material carefully. If it contains words he does not recognize, pronounce them for him. When he has completed the reading, ask him five questions that can be answered by making inferential judgments about the information given in the selection. These questions will not follow a specific pattern but will require that you lead the learner between the lines and beyond the page in his search for understanding. Criterion for mastery is 80 percent. *Note*: If the learner is not yet able to read, this objective can be converted to a listening task.

Sample paragraph:

Annie took her little kitty out to play. "We will play here," she said. "We will have fun." Then the little kitty saw a robin hopping on the grass. He ran to play with it. "Silly kitty," said Annie. "Birds do not play with kittens. You come back and play with me."

Sample inferential questions:

1. What will Annie do next?
2. Which of the following sentences might be true according to the story?
   a. Annie's kitty is black and white.
   b. Annie has a pet robin.
   c. The robin flew away.
3. Why was the robin hopping on the grass?
4. Why did Annie play with her kitty?

■ DIRECTING THE LEARNER'S ATTENTION Making an inference requires the learner to think beyond the literal meaning found in the material. He must ask himself, "What do the facts suggest? What do I know from my experience about these facts? What implications are possible?" Such thinking requires interpretations, evaluations, and judgments on his part. You can best help learners make the leap from literal to interpretative thinking by developing sophisticated questioning techniques.

Such questions must require *thought*. Their answers are subject to verification only by inductive or deductive reasoning and logic. When a learner has answered an inferential question and is asked to explain how he knew that answer, he will have to respond by saying, "Well, it says this and it says this and, therefore, that has to be." (Given this fact and that fact, this result must follow.) The result is *not* stated on the page. It comes only after the learner examines the facts, is prodded by an inferential question, and thinks about the question in terms of both what the facts say and what his experience has taught him. Such skill requires memory for the fact, an experience background related to this topic, and thought.

When teaching this skill, then, you must be certain that the learner attends to the facts in the selection, to the question you pose, and to what he knows from experience about the topic in question.

> **Key objective** for teaching learners
> to read for inferences.

■ TEACHING ACTIVITIES / *The model activity*   Readers will not learn to infer meanings from the printed page unless you pose questions that force them to look for implied meanings. The key instructional technique, then, is to ask the right questions. To do this, first examine the material being read to determine what is stated. Then assess the learner, asking yourself, "With the experience background he possesses, what could I reasonably expect him to infer from the facts?" Then pose your questions, always making sure that the answer is not stated and that the learner possesses experience that will allow him to make judgments about the question. Questions should avoid *yes* and *no* answers, and a one-word answer to a genuine inferential question would be a rarity. Most inferential questions will begin with the word *why*, and you can often test the extent to which you are requiring inferential thinking by countering the number of times you pose *why* questions.

/ Suggestions for reteaching and/or practice

1   You can develop inferential thinking by following inferential questions with other questions, guiding learners to apply their experience to the problem. For the first question posed in the sample pretest, for example, you can ask the follow-up questions, "What would *you* do next if you were Annie? What would you do if you were in that situation?" For the third question in the pretest sample, you might ask follow-up questions such as, "Have you seen robins hopping on the grass? What are they looking for? What do you suppose *this* robin was looking for?" You are providing a model here which shows the learner that by asking himself similar questions he can answer inferential questions.

2   Adapt some of the purpose-setting techniques described in Objective

IIIA of this chapter to the inferential thinking task. For example, include inferential questions among those you put on the chalkboard prior to reading, or include the question *why* as one of the key words you put on the board to guide reading.

3 If you know you will be asking inferential questions requiring a certain type of experience background, prepare your learners for such questions by providing at some prior time a film, story, or discussion that develops the necessary experience background. This prior experience then becomes the basis for the inferential thinking, because you can now ask, "Why was the robin in the film hopping on the grass? Why do you suppose *this* robin is hopping on the grass?"

4 Copy the first sentence from a story or factual selection. Direct the learner to read the sentence and to then hypothesize concerning what the rest of the story is about. Building these hypotheses requires not only imagination but also inferential logic. This is a particularly good activity for learners who find it difficult to read for any purpose other than to remember the facts and details of a selection.

5 A good way to help learners infer meanings is to provide them with paragraphs and direct them to ask you, or each other, questions about the paragraph that do not have answers clearly stated in the passage itself. It is sometimes necessary to model such questions for learners at the early stages, but they soon are able to build their own. The more they build questions, the more they gain skill in inferential thinking.

■ THE POSTTEST   The suggestions provided for the pretest can be adapted and used for the posttest.

Have you asked your learners to think today?

CHAPTER SEVEN /
DEVELOPING
THE READING HABIT

This book focuses on the skills needed to read; its basic premise is that unless the learner possesses these skills, he will not read. However, as has been pointed out, skills are not the entire reading program. Other aspects of reading must be developed also. The most important of these is the development of the reading habit.

One of the biggest dangers of a skills approach is that we will become so busy teaching skills that we neglect to develop readers. That is, we will produce learners who *can* read but who *don't* read. To combat this eventuality, we must develop in learners an enthusiasm for reading, producing avid, as well as skillful, readers. The best way to achieve this is to organize a recreational reading program to complement the skills program.

THE CONCEPT OF RECREATIONAL READING

Recreational reading is just what its name implies—reading for the fun of it. As such, the recreational reading program must be structured to make reading enjoyable. It should be presented as a respite from the rigors of the regular school day, as relaxation, and as an activity having inherent value for the learner. It should never take on the connotation of "work," nor should the learner ever be put in the position of reading a book simply to complete a book report assignment.

This program should be concurrent with, *not in place of*, the systematic skill development program. The success of recreational reading depends largely on the effectiveness of the skill program because the learner will be unable to read recreationally unless he possesses the skills needed to handle the book and has achieved success in the skill tasks associated with reading. Consequently, the skills program is the foundation for the recreational program, whereas recreational reading is where the learner applies his skills and where he learns that reading is an enjoyable and rewarding act.

DEVELOPING A RECREATIONAL READING PROGRAM

The implementation of a recreational reading program requires conscious effort and commitment on your part. You must somehow find the time, provide the materials, structure a supportive environment, and plan related activities.

Finding the time / In teaching school, time is always a factor. There are so many things to teach and only so much time in the school day. However, we always find time for the important things, and developing the reading habit certainly is important. A good way to do this is to schedule recreational reading at the beginning of the school day, so that you *know* you will have time for it. Other techniques are to use recreational reading as one of the learners' independent activities when they are not working directly with you during the skill instruction period or as one of your safety valve activities (see Chapter 3). In the latter regard, however, you must be careful not to relegate recreational reading to the status of something-you-do-when-all-your-other-work-is-done because this implies that everything is more important than reading.

In any case, recreational reading must occur frequently. Although the time periods devoted to it can be short, they should be part of the regular schedule, so that the learners can anticipate them. Avoid the traditional practice of confining recreational reading to the last period on Friday when the learners are eager to go home, and do not look at the recreational reading period as something you schedule only when you need to complete your attendance register or other pressing paperwork.

Providing the materials / For a recreational reading program to succeed, there must be something to read. Books are obviously your major source of materials, but you should not confine yourself to books alone. Magazines, newspapers, comics, brochures, pamphlets, and any other printed matter having any interest to your learners should be provided. The collection should reflect a wide range of interests, consistent with the assortment of individuals you are serving. Room libraries, consisting of books borrowed from the central school library or from the local public library, should be on constant display, with one collection of books frequently replacing another. Trade books should be used in the subject-matter areas, with both fictional and informational books relating to units under study available for the learner's use. All this reading material is of little value, however, if the learner never has time to use it. Consequently, you must frequently encourage the learners to browse through and read the material being displayed.

Obtaining the reading materials is often a problem. Since schools rarely have the money these days to purchase them, we must find alternative ways to obtain such materials. The most obvious of these is the library system in your local community. Although librarians are a frequent target of abuse, it has been our experience that most are anxious to help and when informed of what you are trying to do, they will gladly provide you with many books. Another source is the paperback book clubs that provide learners with the opportunity to purchase some of the best children's books at a very low cost (see Appendix C). You can then encourage each learner to leave his books on the shelf in the room so that they can be read by others. Another source of reading materials is local newstand dealers, who frequently save torn copies of paperback books, magazines, and comics and happily donate these upon request. The learners themselves can be involved in gathering materials by soliciting book and magazine donations from the neighborhood; by running cake sales, paper drives, or other fund-raising projects in which the proceeds are used to purchase reading materials; and by contributing the books they have at home to the room library. Finally, you must be a beggar, a borrower, and a saver yourself, collecting reading material from any source available and storing it in your classroom for use by your learners. In providing materials, the best guide is, I can never have too much!

Structuring a supportive environment / The classroom environment plays a crucial role in developing the reading habit. Not only must the room have many books as discussed above, it should also reflect the focus on books in other ways. Bulletin boards, for example, should present recommended booklists, books on a single theme, information on book award winners and authors' backgrounds, children's art depicting book scenes, and children's evaluations of books they have read. Films and recordings of fables, folk tales, poetry, and picture books should be available for use. Finally, a place should be designated in the classroom for relaxed reading. This can be a corner of the room where you have laid an old second-hand rug, scattered about some throw pillows, and perhaps placed an old easy chair or rocker. The intent is to provide an appealing place in the room where children can relax with a book.

In the final analysis, however, the most important element of a supportive environment is *you*. If you want your learners to be readers, you must be a model for them. You yourself must be interested in reading, and you must constantly seek to convey this attitude to the class. You should become familiar with all kinds of children's books, make frequent references to children's literature in your teaching, and show that it is important to you that learners enjoy their reading. Most important of all, however, you should make obvious your own enjoyment of the act by reading a book of your choice while the learners are themselves engaged in recreational reading. Nothing will impress your learners more than your eagerness to practice what you preach in regard to recreational reading.

Related activities / The reading habit must also be developed through book-related activities. You should read orally to your learners and allow them to share books they have read.

The daily activities of *all* classrooms, sixth grade as well as kindergarten, should include oral reading of children's literature by the teacher. Such reading, especially when it emphasizes highly recommended books the learners are unlikely to read by themselves, is probably more effective than any other single technique in building a love of literature and in starting learners toward the reading habit. This activity requires some preparation on your part, however, because you must be familiar with the book and practice reading it aloud if you are to read it well. It should be emphasized, also, that this activity is designed to be enjoyable. Any discussion following the oral reading should be casual and nonintimidating, not a testing session.

Learner sharing of books they have read also stimulates interest in reading and helps develop the reading habit. The emphasis, however, must be on sharing and not on reporting, because reporting has a coercive connotation we want to avoid in recreational reading. Consequently, the decision to share a book with others should be left to the learner. When he reads a book he really enjoys, encourage him to share it as a means of getting one of his peers interested in reading it. Such sharing may take the form of book talks, audience reading, book fairs, puppetry, dramatization, or any other activity in which learners discuss a book with the intention of interesting others in it.

■ OTHER COMMON CONCERNS   Teachers in the field often have questions relating to the development of the reading habit that have not been answered in this chapter. Some of these, together with their answers, are listed below.

1   What kind of book should we encourage the learner to read?

There are really only two considerations regarding the kind of books a learner should read. The first is, "Does he *want* to read it?" That is, does the book interest him? The second is, "*Can* he read it?" That is, does he possess the reading skills necessary to handle the book or is it too hard for him? If he both wants to read the book and is able to read it, it is a good book for him.

2   How do we involve the very slow reader in a recreational reading program?

Because a learner is unable to read does not mean he cannot participate in the recreational reading program. He can be provided with picture books and picture magazines that interest him and that he *is* able to handle. You can also make booklets out of interesting material cut from old editions of *My Weekly Reader, Jack and Jill, Children's Digest,* and other sources containing material commensurate with his ability. Comic books are another source for such learners. Using such easy material, he can read for relaxation in the same manner as more advanced learners, and he will not feel like a dummy unless your attitude toward him *makes* him feel like one. If you accept his reading material as being worthwhile, so will he.

3 Should we outlaw comic books in the classroom?

As has been implied in the statement above, we are not opposed to comic books per se. For children who have much difficulty with reading, it is better that they read comic books than nothing at all. However, it is doubtful that comics help develop the reading habit, and learners should be weaned away from them and guided to books as soon as they possess the necessary skills. These first books should possess the same characteristics that attracted them to comics in the first place; low readability, adventure, action, and colorful pictures. It is helpful to remember, also, that the most effective way to eliminate the appeal of comics is to make them readily available. As soon as you ban them, they attain the aura of forbidden fruit and their appeal soars.

4 Should we be concerned about the learner who reads only Dr. Seuss stories or who reads only horse stories?

In recreational reading, our primary concern is to create an interest in reading. Initially, any kind of book will do. We are not immediately concerned with what the learner reads as long as he *does* read. Once the reading habit has become established, however, you may wish to encourage learners to vary their interests and enrich their tastes.

5 Should we have contests in our classroom to see who can read the most books.

Definitely not. In the first place, we want to encourage children to read because it is an enjoyable and rewarding act in itself, not because it will win a prize. Secondly and more important, such contests motivate only those who need no motivation while frustrating those who need to be encouraged the most; only the good readers have a chance to win the prize. If you feel that some form of reward is needed to encourage learners to begin reading books, make it a personal thing between you and the learner, rather than a competition in which he has no chance to win.

CONCLUSION

This book has emphasized the development of reading skills, and it is not intended in this chapter to hedge on this position. Rather, it is intended as a realistic appraisal of the task we face. Skills canot be taught in isolation and then forgotten. Instead, there must be a structured and systematic attempt to transfer these skills to the reading act—to put the skills to work with books. The recreational reading program provides the means for such application.

Of equal importance, however, is the fact that the ultimate goal of reading instruction is the development of learners who not only are able to read but who *do* read. This goal will be realized only if learners are provided both with the necessary skills *and* with a program in which the reading of interesting and stimulating materials is an integral part of the school day. Attention to both aspects of reading results in the development of the reading habit.

APPENDIX A / A SEQUENTIAL LIST OF THE SKILLS INCLUDED IN THIS BOOK

CHAPTER 4:   If the Learner Cannot Read at All

Cluster 1

A. What the Learner Looks at

1. Given three geometric figures that are exactly alike and one that is clearly different, the learner marks the one that is different.

THIS IS THE KEY OBJECTIVE FOR NOTING VISUAL DIFFERENCES.

2. Given a few seconds to examine a geometric figure, the learner reproduces from memory a figure just like it, to the satisfaction of the teacher.

THIS IS THE KEY OBJECTIVE FOR VISUAL MEMORY.

3. Given three letters that are exactly alike and one that is clearly different, the learner marks the one that is different.

4. Given a few seconds to examine a letter, the learner reproduces the letter from memory, to the satisfaction of the teacher.

5. Given three numerals that are exactly alike and one that is clearly different, the learner marks the one that is different.

6. Given a few seconds to examine a numeral, the learner reproduces it from memory, to the satisfaction of the teacher.

7. Given three words that are exactly alike and one that is clearly different, the learner marks the one that is different.

8. Given a few seconds to examine a short word, the learner reproduces the word from memory, to the satisfaction of the teacher.

B. What the Learner Listens to

1. When directed to close his eyes and listen to a sound produced by the teacher or from the immediate classroom environment, the learner names the sound.

2. Given sounds in pairs that are either the same or different, the learner identifies the pairs as being the same or different.

3. When directed to close his eyes and listen to taped rhythms produced by the teacher, the learner reproduces the rhythms.

4. When directed to close his eyes and listen to three words spoken by the teacher, the learner reproduces the words in the sequence in which they are spoken.

5. When directed to close his eyes and listen to three words spoken by the teacher, the learner repeats the first and the last words.

6. Given a multisyllable word spoken by the teacher, the learner tells the number of syllable units in the word.

7. Given multisyllable words spoken by the teacher, the learner repeats the first sound unit and the last sound unit in each word as directed.

Cluster II

A. What the Learner Looks at

1. Given a manuscript model of his own name, the learner makes an acceptable copy, as determined by teacher judgment.

2. Given a list of five names of students in his class, the learner identifies his name by drawing a circle around it.

3. Given a lower-case manuscript model of the words *yes* and *no*, the learner makes an acceptable copy of these words, as determined by teacher judgment.

4. Given a list of 10 words of which *yes* and *no* are two of the words, the learner identifies first the word *yes* and then the word *no* by drawing a circle around it as directed.

5. Given a random group of alphabet letters in lower case, the learner points to and names each letter in turn.

6. Given a random group of numerals, the learner points to and names each numeral in turn.

7. Given a stimulus lower-case letter, the learner matches it with its upper-case counterpart.

8. Given cards with the words *yes, no,* and his name printed on them, the learner, when directed, points to the first letter in each of these words.

THIS IS THE KEY OBJECTIVE FOR LETTER–SOUND SEQUENCING.

B. What the Learner Listens to

1. Given spoken words in pairs that are either the same or different, the learner identifies the pairs as being the same or different.

2. Given spoken pairs of words, the learner says "Yes" if the words begin alike and "No" if they do not.

THIS IS THE KEY OBJECTIVE FOR NOTING AND IDENTIFYING BEGINNING SOUNDS

3. Given spoken words in pairs that either rhyme or do not rhyme, the learner says "Yes" if the pair rhymes and "No" if it does not.

THIS IS THE KEY OBJECTIVE FOR NOTING AND IDENTIFYING ENDING SOUNDS

4. Given a spoken stimulus word beginning with either the *m* or *d* sound and a group of three other words one of which begins with the *m* or *d* sound, the learner pairs the two words beginning with the same sound.

5. Given spoken words beginning with *m* or *d* sounds, the learner identifies the beginning letter as *m* or *d*.

THIS IS THE KEY OBJECTIVE FOR CONNECTING LETTERS AND SOUNDS.

6. Given a spoken stimulus word beginning with either the *l* or hard *c* sound and a group of three other words one of which begins with the *l* or hard *c* sound, the learner pairs the two words beginning with the same sound.

7. Given spoken words beginning with the *l* or hard *c* sounds, the learner identifies the beginning letters as *l* or *c*.

8. Given a spoken stimulus word that begins with either the *s* or the *h* sound and a group of three other words one of which begins with the *s* or the *h* sound, the learner pairs the two words beginning with the same sound.

9. Given spoken words beginning with *s* or *h* sounds, the learner identifies the beginning letter as being either *s* or *h*.

10. Given a spoken incomplete sentence, the learner adds words necessary to make a complete and grammatically sensible sentence unit.

11. Given a spoken sentence in which one word is missing, the learner supplies a word in the missing spot to make a complete and sensible sentence unit.

12. Given an oral sentence with one word missing and cued for the missing word with a card having printed on it the first letter of that word (*m, d, l, c, s, h*), the learner says a word that fits the context and begins with that letter sound.

THIS IS THE KEY OBJECTIVE FOR USING CONTEXT AND LETTER–SOUND CORRESPONDENCE.

Cluster III

A. What the Learner Looks at

1. Given three letters that are exactly alike and one that is somewhat similar, the learner marks the one that is different.

2. Given a few seconds to examine a letter that is easily confused with other letters, the learner reproduces the letter from memory, to the satisfaction of the teacher.

3. Given three words that are exactly alike and one word that is somewhat similar, the learner marks the word that is different.

4. Given a few seconds to examine a word that is easily confused with other words, the learner reproduces the word from memory, to the satisfaction of the teacher.

5. Given a few seconds to examine a word, the learner picks out another word having the same initial consonant from among a group of four words.

6. Given a fraction of a second to examine each of 10 flash cards with words he selected as wanting to learn to read printed on them, the learner pronounces each word within one second.

THIS IS THE KEY OBJECTIVE FOR RECOGNIZING WORDS INSTANTLY.

7. Given a fraction of a second to examine flash cards with the words: *I, and, the, a, to, was, in, it, of, my,* and *he* printed on them, the learner pronounces each word within one second.

8. Given cards with words he has learned to pronounce at sight printed on them, the learner, when directed, points to the first letter and then to the last letter in each of these words.

9. Given sentence frames spoken by the teacher and words he recognizes printed on individual cards, the learner points to the card containing the word that completes the sentence frame.

10. Given words he recognizes instantly, the learner creates and reads a single-sentence story using these words.

THIS IS THE KEY OBJECTIVE FOR CREATING AND READING STORIES.

B. What the Learner Listens to

1. Given a spoken stimulus word beginning with the *t, b,* or *p* sounds and a group of three other words one of which begins with the *t, b,* or *p* sound, the learner pairs the two words beginning with the same sound.

2. Given spoken words beginning with the *t, b,* or *p* sounds, the learner identifies the beginning letters as *t, b,* or *p*.

3. Given a spoken stimulus word beginning with the *w, r,* or *f* sounds and a group of three other words one of which begins with the *w, r,* or *f* sound, the learner pairs the two words beginning with the same sound.

4. Given spoken words beginning with the *w, r,* or *f* sounds, the learner identifies the beginning letters as *w, r,* or *f*.

5. Given a spoken stimulus word beginning with the *k, j, n,* or hard *g* sound and a group of three other words one of which begins with the *k, j, n,* or hard *g* sound, the learner pairs the two words beginning with the same sound.

6. Given spoken words beginning with the *k, j, n,* or hard *g* sounds, the learner identifies the beginning letters as *k, j, n,* or *g*.

7. Given an oral sentence with one word missing and cued for the missing word with a card having printed on it the first letter of the missing word (*t, b, p, w, r, f, g, k, j,* and *n*), the learner says a word beginning with the letter that fits the context of the sentence.

8. Given a stimulus word ending with an *m, d, l,* or voiceless *s* sound and a group of three other words one of which ends with an *m, d, l,* or the voiceless *s* sound, the learner pairs the two words *ending* with the same sound.

9. Given spoken words ending with *m, d, l,* or voiceless *s* sound, the learner identifies the ending letters as *m, d, l,* or *s.*

Cluster IV

A. What the Learner Looks at

1. Given a fraction of a second to examine flash cards having printed on them the words *here, fast, to, me, at,* or *come,* the learner pronounces each word within one second.

2. Given a sentence frame spoken by the teacher and words he recognizes at sight printed on individual cards, the learner points to the card with the word printed on it that completes the sentence frame.

3. Given a fraction of a second to examine flash cards with the words *see, help, home,* and *work* printed on them, the learner pronounces each word within one second.

4. Given a sentence frame spoken by the teacher and the words *see, help, home,* and *work* printed on individual cards, the learner points to the card with the word printed on it that completes the sentence frame.

5. Given five known words in which the first letter is printed in lower case, the learner matches each word with the same word when the first letter is printed in upper case.

6. Given a page of writing and directed to point to the first word and last word in a line of print and to the first word and last word on a page, the learner instantly does so.

7. Given a fraction of a second to examine flash cards having printed on them the words *down* and *up,* the learner pronounces each word within one second.

8. Given a fraction of a second to examine flash cards with the color words *white, black, red, blue, green,* and *yellow* printed on them, the learner pronounces each word within one second.

9. Given a fraction of a second to examine flash cards with the number words *one* to *ten* printed on them, the learner pronounces each word within one second.

10. Given words he recognizes instantly, the learner creates and reads multiple-sentence stories using these words.

B. What the Learner Listens to

1. Given a spoken stimulus word beginning with the *sh* or voiceless

th sound and a group of three other words one of which begins with the *sh* or voiceless *th* sound, the learner pairs the two words beginning with the same sound.

2. Given spoken words beginning with the *sh* or voiceless *th* sounds, the learner identifies the beginning letters as *sh* or *th*.

3. Given an oral sentence with one word missing and cued for the missing word with a card with the *sh* or *th* digraph printed on it, the learner says a word beginning with the digraph that fits the context of the sentence.

CHAPTER 5:   If the Learner Knows Some Words but Does Not Read Fluently

Cluster 1

A. Sight Words

1. Given a flash presentation of certain words, the learner pronounces each word within one second.

2. Given a flash presentation of each of the frequently confused words *on–no*, *was–saw*, and *the–then*, the learner pronounces each within one second.

THIS IS THE KEY OBJECTIVE FOR RECOGNIZING EASILY CONFUSED WORDS.

3. Given words he recognizes at sight, the learner creates and reads stories using these words.

B. Word Analysis

1. Given a spoken stimulus word beginning with the *q, v, y,* or *z* sound and a group of three other words one of which begins with the *q, v, y,* or *z* sound, the learner pairs the two words beginning with the same sound.

2. Given a spoken word beginning with the *q, v, y,* or *z* sound, the learner identifies the beginning letter as *q, v, y,* or *z*.

3. Given an oral sentence with one word missing and cued for the missing word with a card having printed on it the first letter of that word (*q, v, y,* or *z*), the learner says a word beginning with the letter that fits the context of the sentence.

4. Given a spoken stimulus word beginning with the *ch, wh* or voiced *th* sound and a group of three other words one of which begins with the *ch, wh,* or voiced *th* sound, the learner pairs the two words beginning with the same sound.

5. Given spoken words beginning with the *ch, wh,* or voiced *th* sounds, the learner identifies the beginning letters as *ch, wh,* or *th*.

6. Given an oral sentence with one word missing and cued for the missing word with a card having printed on it the digraph with which the word begins (*ch, wh,* or *th*), the learner says a word beginning with the digraph that fits the context of the sentence.

7. Given known words composed of the vowel–consonant phono-

grams *at, et, it, ot, ut,* the learner replaces the first consonant with another consonant or digraph and pronounces the new word.

THIS IS THE KEY OBJECTIVE FOR USING PATTERNS TO ANALYZE WORDS.

8. Given words he pronounced in Objective IB 7, the learner replaces the final consonant with another consonant or digraph and pronounces the new word.

9. Given key words either introduced in Objectives IB 7 and IB 8 or identified during the course of this objective, the learner changes either the beginning or the ending of the words and pronounces the new words.

10. Given a spoken stimulus word ending with the *ck* sound and a group of three other words one of which ends with the *ck* sound, the learner pairs the two words that end with the *ck* sound.

11. Given a spoken word, the learner points to the letters *ck* if the word ends with the *ck* sound.

12. Given words he pronounced in previous objectives, the learner replaces the final consonant in these words with *ck* and pronounces the new word.

13. Given a word he has previously analyzed or learned to recognize at sight, the learner adds the structural ending *ed, ing,* or *s* and pronounces the new words.

THIS IS THE KEY OBJECTIVE FOR ANALYZING WORD PARTS.

Cluster II

A. Sight Words

1. Given a flash presentation of certain words, the learner pronounces each word within one second.

2. Given a flash presentation of each of the frequently confused words *it–if* and *they–then–the–them,* the learner pronounces each word within one second.

3. Given words he recognizes at sight, the learner creates and reads stories using these words.

B. Word Analysis

1. Given a spoken stimulus word beginning with the sound produced by the consonant blend *br, cr, dr, fr, gr, tr,* or *pr* and a group of three other words one of which begins with the sound of *br, cr, dr, fr, gr, tr,* or *pr,* the learner pairs the two words beginning with the same sound.

2. Given spoken words beginning with the *br, cr, dr, fr, gr, tr,* or *pr* sounds, the learner identifies the beginning letters in each word.

3. Given an oral sentence with one word missing and cued for the missing word with a card having printed on it the blend with which

the word begins (*br, cr, dr, fr, gr, tr,* or *pr*), the learner says a word beginning with the letter blend that fits the context of the sentence.

4. Given a word he has learned previously, the learner substitutes the blends *br, cr, dr, fr, gr, tr,* and *pr* in the initial position and pronounces the new word.

5. Given a word learned in a previous objective, the learner changes either the beginning or the ending of the word and pronounces the new word.

6. Given a spoken stimulus word beginning with the sound produced by the consonant blend *bl, cl, fl, pl, gl,* or *sl* and a group of three other words one of which begins with the sound of *bl, cl, fl, pl, gl,* or *sl*, the learner pairs the two words beginning with the same sound.

7. Given spoken words beginning with the *bl, cl, fl, pl, gl,* and *sl* sounds, the learner identifies the beginning letters of each word.

8. Given an oral sentence with one word missing and cued for the missing word by a card having printed on it the blend with which the word begins (*bl, cl, fl, pl, gl,* or *sl*), the learner says a word beginning with the letter blend that fits the context of the sentence.

9. Given a word he has learned previously, the learner substitutes the blends *bl, cl, fl, pl, gl,* or *sl* in the initial position and pronounces the new word.

10. Given a spoken stimulus word ending with the *ng* sound and a group of three other words one of which ends with the *ng* sound, the learner pairs the two words that end with the *ng* sound.

11. When given a spoken word, the learner points to the letters *ng* if the word ends in the *ng* sound.

12. Given a word he pronounced in previous objectives, the learner replaces the final consonant in the word with the letters *ng*, substitutes an initial sound he knows, and pronounces the new word.

13. Given compound words composed of two known words, the learner pronounces the compound words.

Cluster III

A. Sight Words

1. Given a flash presentation of certain words, the learner pronounces each word within one second.

2. Given a flash presentation of each of the frequently confused words *then–when* and *here–were*, the learner pronounces each word within one second.

3. Given words he recognizes at sight, the learner creates and reads stories using these words.

B. Word Analysis

1. Given a known word composed of the vowel–consonant phono-

grams *en, in,* or *an,* the learner replaces the initial consonant in each word with another consonant, digraph, or blend he knows and pronounces the new word.

2. Given a spoken stimulus word beginning with the sound produced by the consonant blend *sk, sw, sm, sn, sp,* or *st,* and a group of three other words one of which begins with the sound of *sk, sw, sm, sn, sp,* or *st,* the learner pairs the two words beginning with the same sound.

3. Given spoken words beginning with the *sk, sw, sm, sn, sp,* and *st* sounds, the learner identifies the beginning letters in each word.

4. Given an oral sentence with one word missing and cued for the missing word with a card having printed on it the blend with which the word begins (*sk, sw, sm, sn, sp,* or *st*), the learner says a word beginning with the letter blend that fits the context of the sentence.

5. Given a word learned in previous objectives, the learner changes either the beginning or the ending of the word and pronounces the new word.

6. Given a spoken stimulus word ending with the *st* sound and a group of three other words one of which ends with the *st* sound, the learner pairs the two words that end with the *st* sound.

7. Given a spoken word, the learner points to the letters *st* if the word ends in the *st* sound.

8. Given a word he pronounced in previous objectives, the learner replaces the final consonant with the letters *st,* substitutes an initial sound he knows, and pronounces the new word.

9. Given the contractions *I'm, can't, won't, I'll, don't, isn't, he's, it's, I've, you're, we've,* and *let's* printed on cards, the learner pronounces each contraction and identifies the two words that make up the contraction.

Cluster IV

A. Sight Words

1. Given a flash presentation of certain words, the learner pronounces each word within one second.

2. Given a flash presentation of each of the frequently confused words *his–has* and *what–that,* the learner pronounces each word within one second.

3. Given words he recognizes at sight, the learner creates and reads stories using these words.

B. Word Analysis

1. Given known words ending with the phonograms *and, end, ight, old,* or *ind,* the learner replaces the initial consonant with another

consonant, consonant blend, or digraph and pronounces the new word.

2. Given a known word containing a double *e* in the medial position, the learner pronounces other words containing the double *e* in this position.

3. Given a known one-syllable word ending in a vowel, the learner pronounces other one-syllable words ending in a vowel.

4. Given a known one-syllable word ending with the *ay* combination, the learner pronounces other one-syllable words ending with the *ay* combination.

5. Given a known one-syllable word ending in the *ell* or *ill* combination, the learner pronounces other words ending in the *ell* or *ill* combinations.

6. Given a known one-syllable word ending in *all*, the learner pronounces other one-syllable words ending in *all*.

7. Given a word he has analyzed previously or learned to recognize at sight, the learner adds the structural endings *s*, *est*, *ly*, *er*, or *y* and pronounces the new word.

Cluster V

A. Sight Words

1. Given a flash presentation of certain words, the learner pronounces each word within one second.

2. Given a flash presentation of each of the frequently confused words *where–there*, *would–could–should*, and *now–how*, the learner pronounces each word within one second.

3. Given words he recognizes at sight, the learner creates and reads stories using these words.

B. Word Analysis

1. Given a known word illustrating the silent *e* vowel principle, the learner pronounces other words illustrating this principle.

2. Given a known word illustrating the two vowels together principle, the learner pronounces other words illustrating this principle.

3. Given a known word illustrating the two vowels together principle as it applies to the *ow* combination, the learner pronounces other words illustrating this principle.

4. Given words illustrating the *ou* and *ow* diphthongs, the learner pronounces other words containing these diphthongs.

5. Given spoken stimulus words ending with the *nd*, *nt*, or *nk* sounds and a group of three other words one of which ends with the *nd*, *nt*, or *nk* sound, the learner pairs the two words that end with the same sound.

6. Given three cards that have the letters *nd* printed on one, *nt* on another, and *nk* on the third and a spoken stimulus word that ends in either the *nd*, *nt*, or *nk* sound, the learner points to the letter card having printed on it the letters with which the word ends.

7. Given a word he pronounced in previous objectives, the learner replaces the final consonant letter of the word with the *nd*, *nt*, or *nk* letters and pronounces the new word.

8. Given known sight words, the learner pronounces these words when they are prefixed by *dis* and *un*.

Cluster VI

A. Sight Words

1. Given a flash presentation of certain words, the learner pronounces each word within one second.

2. Given a flash presentation of each of the frequently confused words *he–her–she* and *these–those*, the learner pronounces each word within one second.

3. Given words he recognizes at sight, the learner creates and reads stories using these words.

B. Word Analysis

1. Given known words illustrating the short double *o* and the long double *o* sounds, the learner pronounces other words containing these combinations.

2. Given a known word that illustrates the vowel-consonant–consonant-vowel principle of syllabication in which both medial consonants are sounded, the learner pronounces other words illustrating this principle.

THIS IS THE KEY OBJECTIVE FOR SYLLABICATION.

3. Given a known word that illustrates the vowel-consonant–consonant-vowel principle of syllabication in which only one medial consonant is sounded, the learner pronounces other words illustrating this principle.

4. Given a known two-syllable word ending in *er*, the learner pronounces other two-syllable words ending in *er*.

5. Given a known word containing the *ar* or *or* combination, the learner pronounces other words containing these combinations.

6. Given a known word containing the soft *c* sound, the learner pronounces other words containing this sound.

7. Given a compound word composed of two known words, the learner pronounces the compound word.

Cluster VII

A. Sight Words

1. Given a flash presentation of certain words, the learner pronounces each word within one second.

2. Given a flash presentation of each of the frequently confused words *so–soon–some* and *much–must*, the learner pronounces each word within one second.

3. Given words he recognizes at sight, the learner creates and reads stories using these words.

B. Word Analysis

1. Given a known word illustrating the vowel–consonant–vowel principle of syllabication in which the first vowel is long, the learner pronounces other words illustrating this principle.

2. Given a known word illustrating the vowel–consonant–vowel principle of syllabication in which the first vowel is short, the learner pronounces other words illustrating this principle.

3. Given a known word illustrating the short *y* principle, the learner pronounces other two-syllable words ending with the short *y*.

4. Given a known two-syllable word having an unaccented *a* in the initial position, the learner pronounces other two-syllable words illustrating this principle.

5. Given a known word composed of the *ew* combination, the learner replaces the initial consonant with another consonant, blend, or digraph and pronounces the new word.

6. Given a spoken stimulus word beginning with the sound produced by the *str* or *thr* consonant combination and a group of three words one of which begins with the sound of *str* or *thr*, the learner pairs the two words beginning with the same sound.

7. Given spoken words beginning with the *str* or *thr* sounds, the learner identifies the beginning letters in each word.

8. Given a written sentence with one word missing and cued for the missing word by the letter combination with which that word begins (*str* or *thr*), the learner says a word beginning with the letter combination that fits the context of the sentence.

9. Given a word beginning with *str* or *thr* in combination with other known phonetic elements, the learner pronounces the word.

10. Given a known word containing the silent letters *gh*, *k*, or *b*, the learner pronounces other words containing these silent letters.

CHAPTER 6: If the Learner Can Pronounce Words but Does Not Understand

Cluster 1

A. Content Word Meaning

Given any content word found in reading materials used by the learner, he indicates his understanding of the conceptual meaning of the word by (a) giving a synonym for the concept, (b) using it in an appropriate context, (c) defining it in his own words, or (d) performing a physical operation indicative of the meaning.

THIS IS THE KEY OBJECTIVE FOR CONTENT WORD MEANING.

B. Function Word Meaning

Given any function word found in reading materials used by the learner, he indicates his understanding of the functional meaning by (a) performing a physical operation that indicates its meaning or (b) stating the sentence relationship it signals. The types of function words included are (1) prepositions that signal both positional and time relationships, (2) pronouns and their antecedents, and (3) words that signal contrast–comparison relationships, words that signal chronological sequences, and words that signal cause–effect relationships.

THIS IS THE KEY OBJECTIVE FOR FUNCTION WORD MEANING.

Cluster II

A. Meaning Relationships

Given four pictures, two of which are related through use, sequence, composition, or cause–effect, the learner pairs the pictures thus related and states the relationship.

THIS IS THE KEY OBJECTIVE FOR RELATIONSHIPS.

B. Classification Skills

Given a box of objects, the learner groups those that belong together and explains his system for classifying them.

THIS IS THE KEY OBJECTIVE FOR CLASSIFYING SKILLS.

C. Main Idea and Detail Skills

Given a short informational paragraph, the learner states the main idea and remembers the details in the paragraph that support the idea.

THIS IS THE KEY OBJECTIVE FOR MAIN IDEA.

Cluster III

A. Fact Skills

Given either a story or short informative selection, the learner answers factual questions related to the material.

THIS IS THE KEY OBJECTIVE FOR REMEMBERING FACTUAL INFORMATION.

B. Inference Skills

Given either a story or a short informative selection, the learner answers inferential questions related to the material.

THIS IS THE KEY OBJECTIVE FOR READING FOR INFERENCE.

APPENDIX B/
SOURCES OF
PRACTICE MATERIALS

The following is a list of programs, workbooks, games, references, and other commercial material that you can use to supplement the practice activities provided in this book. The list is selective, rather than exhaustive, including only those materials considered to be most useful in a reading skills program.

Two cautions regarding the use of this material are in order. First, do not use practice material as teaching material. Claims of the publisher notwithstanding, the materials included in this list *do not teach* the reading skills; they provide only the practice and repetition needed to make habitual a response taught previously. Directing the learner to use any practice material without first developing with him an understanding of what he is learning will result in partial learning at best and in total confusion at worst.

Second, do not give one or more of the following materials to a learner and direct him to complete the whole book. Such a strategy is both inefficient and dangerous. A learner seldom *needs* practice on all exercises in a particular book, and it is inefficient to demand that he do them all. Also, the skills practiced in many of these books are haphazardly or incorrectly arranged, so it is dangerous to demand that he do them in order. A far better practice is to clip the pages from workbooks and other materials, filing them according to the skills taught in this book. Then, when a learner needs practice on a particular skill, go to the file folder containing the workbook exercises for that skill and select one for use. By covering the page with acetate and directing the learner to write answers directly on the acetate with a grease pencil, you will be able to reuse the workbook page many times.

PRACTICE MATERIALS	SOURCES
Adventures in Discovery An early childhood education program using structured activities and books to develop concepts of time, size, etc.	Western Publishing Company, Inc. 850 Third Avenue New York, New York 10022
Basic Phonics Program A useful series of workbooks on phonetic analysis.	Reardon Publishing Company 19220 Miles Avenue Cleveland, Ohio 44128
Breaking the Sound Barrier An effective workbook approach to basic instruction in phonetics.	The Macmillan Company 866 Third Avenue New York, New York 10022
Chandler Language-Experience Readers Individual pupil workbooks and paperback experience readers.	Chandler Publishing Company 124 Spear Street San Francisco, California 94105
Engelmann, Siegfried. *Preventing Learning Failure in the Primary Grades*, 1969. Contains valuable exercises for language and concept development and for sound-symbol drills.	Science Research Associates 259 East Erie Street Chicago, Illinois 60611
Farquhar, Carolyn, Bettye Jennings, and Elaine Weber. *Personalized Approach to Reading* Provides a multitude of instructional strategies for teaching specific reading skills.	Pendell Publishing Company Midland, Michigan
Frostig Program for the Development of Visual Perception A kit of exercises in five areas of perceptual development.	Follett Publishing Company 201 North Wells Street Chicago, Illinois 60606
Herr, Selma. *Learning Activities for Reading*, Second Edition, 1970. Provides a multitude of directed activities in teaching selected reading skills.	William C. Brown Company, Publishers 135 South Locust Street Dubuque, Iowa 52001
Junior Listen and Hear Books Helps develop skills of auditory discrimination.	Follett Publishing Company 201 North Wells Street Chicago, Illinois 60606
Macmillan Reading Spectrum— Spectrum of Skills Programmed books on various levels teaching selected reading skills.	The Macmillan Company 866 Third Avenue New York, New York 10022
The Magic World of Dr. Spello A workbook providing a useful review of selected analysis skills.	Webster Division McGraw-Hill Book Company Manchester Road Manchester, Missouri 63011
Michigan Language Program Seventeen programmed workbooks for the severely disabled reader.	Ann Arbor-Humphrey Science Publishers, Inc. Drawer 1425 Ann Arbor, Michigan 48106

PRACTICE MATERIALS	SOURCES
New Phonics Skill Texts Four workbooks with systematic exercises and useful activities in phonetics.	Charles E. Merrill Publishing Company 1300 Alum Creek Drive Columbus, Ohio 43216
New Webster Word Wheels A kit of word wheels emphasizing beginning digraphs, blends, prefixes, and suffixes.	Webster Division McGraw-Hill Book Company Manchester Road Manchester, Missouri 63011
Paper Bag Puppet Patterns Useful device for developing language usage and placement of events in logical sequence.	McGraw-Hill Book Company 330 West 42nd Street New York, New York 10036
Peabody Language Laboratory This program teaches vocabulary development and sentence structure to young children.	George Peabody Teachers College Nashville, Tennessee
Phonics Game Kit Games useful in practicing word analysis.	Lyons & Carnahan 407 East 25 Street Chicago, Illinois 60616
Phonic Lotto This and many other similar games are available and can be used to practice selected word analysis skills. Some of the other games include *Group Word Teaching Game, Group Sounding Game, What the Letters Say,* and *The Syllable Game.*	Garrard Publishing Company 1607 North Market Street Champaign, Illinois 61820
Phonic Quizmo This and other similar games are available and can be used to practice selected word analysis skills. Some of the other games include *Phonetic Word Wheel* and *Make-a-Word Game.*	Beckley-Cardy Company 1900 North Narragansett Ave. Chicago, Illinois 60639
Phonic Rummy This and many other similar games are available and can be used to practice selected word analysis skills. Some of the other games include *ABC Game* and the *Doghouse Game.*	Kenworthy Educational Service, Inc. 138 Allen Street Buffalo, New York 14201
Phonics We Use Series of workbooks on phonetic analysis. Useful if selected pages are used with the appropriate skill taught in this book.	Lyons & Carnahan 407 East 25 Street Chicago, Illinois 60616
Phonics Workbooks A series of five workbooks containing exercises for practice in phonetic analysis.	Webster Division McGraw-Hill Book Company Manchester Road Manchester, Missouri 63011

PRACTICE MATERIALS	SOURCES
Programmed Reading A series of workbooks printed as programs.	Buchanan-Sullivan Associates and Webster Division McGraw-Hill, Inc. Princeton Road Hightstown, New Jersey 08520
Reading Aids Through the Grades A listing of 300 reading activities.	Bureau of Publications Teachers College Columbia University New York, New York 10027
Reading Games A sourcebook of games to be used in conjunction with reading instruction.	Teachers Publishing Corp. 22 West Putnam Avenue Greenwich, Connecticut 06830
Reading with Phonics A series of exercises useful in reinforcing some of the skills taught in this book.	J. B. Lippincott Company East Washington Square Philadelphia, Pennsylvania 19105
Resources in Teaching Reading Contains specific suggestions for activities and exercises for reading.	Reading Laboratory University of Florida Gainesville, Florida 32601
School Readiness Treasure Chest Useful in developing oral language skills and ability to put events in sequence.	Harper & Row, Publishers 49 East 33 Street New York, New York 10016
Skilstarters A personalized, game-oriented program of reading readiness.	Random House, Inc. 201 East 50 Street New York, New York 10022
Sounds I Can Hear Records that help develop rudimentary auditory discrimination skills.	Scott, Foresman and Company 1900 East Lake Avenue Glenview, Illinois 60025
Source Materials for the Improvement of Reading A reference list of sources of material. Request Bureau of Educational Research Bulletin No. 37.	Board of Education City of New York 110 Livingston, Street Brooklyn, New York 11201
Speech to Print Phonics A strong program in auditory discrimination, useful in practicing tasks similar to many of those taught in this book.	Harcourt Brace Jovanovich, Inc. 757 Third Avenue New York, New York 10017
Spelling and Writing Patterns A series of spelling workbooks stressing a multisensory, sound–symbol relationship approach. The activities can be easily and usefully adapted to reading tasks.	Follett Publishing Company 201 North Wells Street Chicago, Illinois 60606
Spice A collection of reading-related activities.	Educational Service Box 112 Benton Harbor, Michigan 49022

PRACTICE MATERIALS	SOURCES
SRA Basic Reading Series and Satellites Reading selections useful in reinforcing instruction in phonetics.	Science Research Associates, Inc. 259 East Erie Street Chicago, Illinois 60611
Structural Reading Series A series of workbooks and other materials useful in teaching decoding skills.	L. W. Singer Company, Inc. Division of Random House 501 Madison Avenue New York, New York 10022
Systems for Success A series of two workbooks designed for use with adolescent and adult illiterates.	Follett Publishing Company 201 North Wells Street Chicago, Illinois 60606
Vowel Dominoes A game useful in practicing vowel sounds. Other games are also available from this source.	Remedial Education Center 1321 New Hampshire Avenue, N.W. Washington, D. C. 20036
Word Attack and Comprehension Two workbooks developing visual, auditory, contextual, and comprehension skills.	Ann Arbor-Humphrey Science Publishers, Inc. Drawer 1405 Ann Arbor, Michigan 48106

APPENDIX C / SOURCES OF APPEALING READING MATERIALS

The following is a list of sources of appealing reading materials you can use to develop the reading habit among your learners. The list is divided into two sections. The first lists high-interest, easy-to-read books and where they may be obtained. The second lists sources of book lists that can be used as guides in selecting reading materials for your learners.

HIGH INTEREST, EASY-TO-READ BOOKS	SOURCES
Archway Paperbacks Large selection of paperback books ranging as low as third grade in difficulty.	Washington Square Press Div. of Simon & Schuster, Inc. 630 Fifth Avenue New York, New York 10020
Aviation Readers A graded series of books on aviation.	The Macmillan Company 866 Third Avenue New York, New York 10022
Basic Vocabulary Series Stories written by E. W. Dolch stressing the most common sight words.	Garrard Publishing Company 1607 North Market Street Champaign, Illinois 61820
Beginner Books A group of individually sold, easy-to-read trade books on a variety of topics.	McGraw-Hill Book Company 330 West 42 Street New York, New York 10036
Break Through! Paperback series of high-interest, easy-reading selections of a multi-ethnic nature.	Allyn and Bacon, Inc. 470 Atlantic Avenue Boston, Massachusetts 02210
Button Books A series of easy-to-read stories about the Button family.	Beckley-Cardy Company 1900 North Narragansett Ave. Chicago, Illinois 60639

HIGH INTEREST, EASY-TO-READ BOOKS	SOURCES
Childhood of Famous American Series Many titles of a low reading level.	The Bobbs-Merrill Co., Inc. 4300 West 62 Street Indianapolis, Indiana 46268
Cowboy Sam Series Easy-to-read ranch stories of special interest to boys.	Beckley-Cardy Company 1900 North Narragansett Ave. Chicago, Illinois 60639
Discover Books A paperback book club associated with *My Weekly Reader*.	Discover Books Education Center Columbus, Ohio 43216
E & R Book Clubs A club from which learners can order different paperback releases each month.	E & R Book Clubs Vandalia Road Jacksonville, Illinois 62650
I Can Read Books Easy-to-read, attractive books for the beginning reader.	Harper & Row, Publishers 49 East 33 Street New York, New York 10016
Let's Find Out Books High-interest beginning reading books about a variety of topics including biography and science.	Franklin Watts, Inc. 845 Third Avenue New York, New York 10022
Little Wonder Books Small booklets at low reading levels on topics of interest to children.	Charles E. Merrill Publishing Company 1300 Alum Creek Drive Columbus, Ohio 43216
Paperback Classroom Library Collections of 100 paperback books for each of the six elementary grades and kindergarten.	Educational Reading Service, Inc. 64 East Midland Avenue Paramus, New Jersey 07652
Pleasure Reading Series A series of well-known stories rewritten with special attention to vocabulary control.	Garrard Publishing Company 1607 North Market Street Champaign, Illinois 61820
Reader's Digest Skill Builders High-interest, low-level materials modeled after the regular edition of *Reader's Digest*.	Reader's Digest Association Pleasantville, New York 10570
Scholastic Book Clubs Source of a variety of children's books. Clubs include the See Saw Club (K-1), Lucky Book Club (2-3), Arrow Book Club (4-6), and others.	Scholastic Book Services 50 West 44 Street New York, New York 10036
The True Books Informational books on a wide range of topics.	Childrens Press 1224 West Van Buren Street Chicago, Illinois 60607
Viking Paperbound Books Inexpensive paperbound editions of excellent children's literature selections.	The Viking Press, Inc. 625 Madison Avenue New York, New York 10022

HIGH INTEREST, EASY-TO-READ BOOKS	SOURCES
Walt Disney Story Books A series of easy-to-read books featuring familiar cartoon characters.	The Macmillan Company 866 Third Avenue New York, New York 10022
Yearling Books Paperback editions of children's classics.	Dell Publishing Company, Inc. 750 Third Avenue New York, New York 10017

LISTS OF SUITABLE READING MATERIALS	SOURCES
Aids in Selecting Books for Slow Readers Lists both sources and criteria for selecting books for disabled readers.	American Library Association 50 East Huron Street Chicago, Illinois 60611
Allen, Patricia (compiler). *Best Books for Children,* Revised Edition, 1964. A list of 3300 selected titles.	R. R. Bowker Company 1180 Ave. of the Americas New York, New York 10036
A Basic Book Collection for Elementary Grades. An annotated list of essential books.	American Library Association 50 East Huron Street Chicago, Illinois 60611
A Bibliography of High-Interest, Low-Vocabulary Books for Retarded Readers A valuable source list.	Colorado Department of Education Denver, Colorado
A Bibliography of Reading Lists for Retarded Readers A source of books suitable for disabled readers. Request Extension Bulletin, College of Education Series No. 37.	State University of Iowa Iowa City, Iowa 52240
Carr, Constance. "Substitutes for the Comic Books." *Elementary English,* XXVIII (April-May, 1951), 194–200. Suggests books possessing much of the appeal of comics.	
Condit, M. A. *Trade Books for Beginning Readers,* 1960. Books for children in grades K-3.	H. W. Wilson Company 950 University Avenue New York, New York 10452
Dunn, Anita, Mabel Jackson, and J. Newton. *Fare for the Reluctant Reader,* 1964. A standard source for appealing reading material.	Capitol Area School Development Association State University of New York Albany, New York 12203
Eakin, Mary K. *Subject Index to Books for Intermediate Grades,* 1963. Cross-indexes the contents of 1800 books.	American Library Association 50 East Huron Street Chicago, Illinois 60611

LISTS OF SUITABLE READING MATERIALS	SOURCES
Eakin, Mary K., and Eleanor Merritt. *Subject Index to Books for Primary Grades*, 1961. Cross-indexes the contents of nearly 1000 books.	American Library Association 50 East Huron Street Chicago, Illinois 60611
Fry, Edward, and Warren Johnson. "Booklist for Remedial Reading." *Elementary English*, XXXV (October, 1958), 373-380. Includes approximately 100 books useful with retarded readers.	
Guide to Children's Magazines, Newspapers, and Reference Books, Revised Edition. An excellent source for reading materials.	Association for Childhood Education International Washington, D. C. 20016
Kress, R. (compiler). *A Place to Start: A Graded Bibliography for Children with Reading Difficulties.* A source list of suitable books for remedial readers.	Reading Center Syracuse University Syracuse, New York
Library Books for Retarded Readers. A listing of high-interest, low-level library books.	Illinois Reading Service Box 277 Bloomington, Illinois 61702
Library Materials for Remedial Reading A list of suggested materials. Request Bibliography No. 3, Instructional Materials Bulletin, June, 1959.	College Library Iowa State University Cedar Falls, Iowa 50613
Lundeen, Alma, and Margaret Prendergrass. "Books for Retarded Readers." *Illinois Library*, XLIII (April, 1961), 271-87. Provides a list of recommended books.	
McConnell, M. L., and D. H. West (compilers). *Children's Catalog.* A primary and essential source of classified and graded lists of children's books.	H. W. Wilson Company 950 University Avenue New York, New York 10452
Spache, George. *Good Reading for Poor Readers*. Revised Edition, 1966. A comprehensive list of printed materials for poor readers.	Garrard Publishing Company 1607 North Market Street Champaign, Illinois 61820

APPENDIX D / A PLAN FOR ORGANIZING A READING CLASS

The following is a seven-step strategy for organizing your class for skill instruction in reading. The steps range from what you do before school opens in September through the sixth week of school. The suggestions follow those made regarding the efficient management of instruction in Chapter 3, and each step in the enclosed plan is keyed to direct you back to the place in the book where each element is described in detail.

STEP 1:   Prior to the Opening of School

A / Develop many on-going safety-valve ideas (see Chapter 3).

B / Develop a basic plan for independent activity that will involve the balance of the class meaningfully while you are working with the skill groups (see Chapter 3).

C / Make an instructional plan that strikes a balance between systematic skill instruction and developing the reading habit (see Chapter 7).

D / Develop a system of record keeping that will make certain that the skill progress of each child is accurately recorded while not demanding an excess of teacher time (see Chapter 3).

E / Plan the physical organization of the room so that seating arrangements and interest centers effectively support your basic instructional plan (see Chapter 3).

F / Develop a plan for systematic positive reinforcement. How will pupils be rewarded for successful performance in reading? (see Chapter 3).

G / Steal, beg, borrow, make, and buy any and all practice-type material, cut it up, and file it according to skill objectives (see Appendix B).

H / Steal, beg, borrow, or buy any and all types of reading material that can be used in a recreational reading program (see Chapter 3, Chapter 7, and Appendix C).

STEP 2: First Week of School

No formal reading instruction. Systematically teach the basic, general classroom routines that you want children to follow regularly.

STEP 3: The Second Week of School

A / Administer the placement test (see Appendix E).

B / Teach children to use the safety-valve activities independently (see Chapter 3).

C / Begin using a buffer (see Chapter 3). Explain his function to pupils, supervise his work, and consciously strive to develop a positive class attitude toward the function of the buffer.

D / As the buffer gets used to his role, give him the opportunity to operate independently while you begin testing individual learners to determine the *level* at which they are currently reading (see Chapter 3).

STEP 4: The Third Week of School

A / Initiate the basic plan of independent activities that will involve the pupils while you are working with skill groups. Isolate the routines upon which the success of the independent activities depend and systematically teach these routines.

B / Implement your plan for reinforcement.

C / Continue to develop the role of the buffer.

D / Encourage children to use the safety-valve activities when they complete independent activities.

E / Complete your testing to determine each learner's current reading level.

F / Begin administering the pretests provided in this book. Be aware of the attention span of children and each day administer only as many pretests as the pupils can handle.

STEP 5: The Fourth Week of School

A / Continue previously established procedures relating to the basic independent activities, the safety-valve activities, and the buffer.

B / Complete the pretests for the skill objectives.

C / Record the pretest performances on your record-keeping device. Determine the number of skill groups you will have initially.

D / Make sure that you are putting the recreational reading program into operation.

STEP 6.   The Fifth Week of School

A / On Monday, teach one short skill group while the rest of the class does independent activities. Then spend the rest of the class time supervising the independent activities. At the end of the class, evaluate how the organization worked and plan necessary adjustments.

B / On Tuesday, implement any adjustments in your organization resulting from the previous day's activity. Do not teach a skill group today. Concentrate on implementing the adjustments.

C / On Wednesday, try another short skill lesson, evaluate, and make adjustments.

D / Repeat this procedure for the balance of the week, increasing the number of skill groups taught per day as the organization smooths out.

E / Check the effectiveness of your reinforcement system. Find new rewards (perhaps more material rewards) for those learners who are not responding. Begin spacing out rewards and substituting less tangible rewards for those who are responding well.

STEP 7.   The Sixth Week of School

If you feel that your organization is now thoroughly worked out, initiate the full program of independent activities, skill instruction, and development of the reading habit. If the organization is not yet sound, continue to make adjustments until it is ready.

APPENDIX E / GROUP PLACEMENT TEST FOR WORD RECOGNITION SKILLS

Even a cursory inspection of this reading skills program suggests the need for some kind of device for quickly placing a group of learners in the appropriate skill cluster. For a teacher to attempt to lead a group of learners individually through the pretests for each objective in each cluster would be very difficult. It might be Christmas before you started teaching! Consequently, the following placement test is provided to assist you in rapidly placing each learner in terms of his approximate word recognition skill level. The thinking skills taught in Chapter 6 are omitted from this placement test because they do not lend themselves to a developmental hierarchy but are, rather, a small group of skills repeated frequently in a spiral fashion.

PROCEDURES

This test is designed for use with your total class. It is composed of cumulative objectives, or subtests, selected from each cluster. If a learner can perform on this placement test within the criterion levels established for each cluster, he probably possesses all the skills within that cluster. If the criterion levels are not met, the learner should be tested individually on each objective within that cluster to determine exactly where instruction should begin.

The testing is relatively simple, but you must do some prior preparation. The material that follows combines teacher directions with what the pupil sees on his answer sheet. To administer the test, you must Ditto an answer sheet for each learner, copying the information under "Pupil Sees" for each subtest item. Your directions can be read directly from this appendix.

In administering the test, timing is not critical except where noted in the teacher directions.

You are strongly urged to administer no more than two clusters of this placement test per day. This leisurely pace will insure adequate pupil attention span and will still allow you to complete your initial placement of each learner within one week.

CAUTION

Although this placement test is not meant to be a precision instrument, it will place your learners efficiently within a band of skills that you can quickly narrow by using the individual objective pretests. To be most effective, however, you must adhere strictly to the criterion suggested. When in doubt regarding the learner's mastery in a particular subtest or cluster, *go back to the individual pretests for that cluster*. As has been stated in the body of the book, it is better to be too careful than not careful enough.

GROUP PLACEMENT TEST FOR CHAPTER 4 SKILLS

Cluster I / The learner who makes more than two incorrect responses in this section should be pretested on each objective in Cluster I, Chapter 4.

1 Direct the group to each line in turn. Tell them to circle the word that you show on the card.

PUPIL SEES	TEACHER SHOWS
he/it/it/it	he
the/was/the/the	was
come/come/cat/come	cat

2 Direct the learners to each line in turn. Flash a card, for a count of 3, that matches one word in each line. Direct the learners to circle the matching word.

PUPILS SEES	TEACHER SHOWS
let/like/many/little	like
first/fast/fun/fat	first
want/was/weather/wants	wants

3 Speak the following words, accenting *slightly* the syllable divisions. Direct the learners to the appropriate line and ask them to circle the numeral that indicates the number of sound units heard.

PUPILS SEES	TEACHER SAYS
1/2/3/4/5	Helicopter
1/2/3/4/5	Table
1/2/3/4/5	Tree

Cluster II | The learner who makes more than two incorrect responses in this section should be pretested on each objective in Cluster II, Chapter 4.

---

1 Prepare cards having upper-case letters printed on them. Hold up these cards one at a time for examination and direct the learners to find the mate for each letter and circle it.

PUPIL SEES	TEACHER SHOWS
p/b/o/g/t	G
f/e/c/b/o	E
u/m/a/v/n	N
p/d/b/x/g	D
a/v/u/k/r	A

2 Direct the learners to each word in turn, telling them to circle the first or last letter as directed.

PUPIL SEES	TEACHER SAYS
elephant	Circle the first letter.
yes	Circle the first letter.
no	Circle the last letter.
top	Circle the first letter.
funny	Circle the last letter.

3 Speak the following pairs of words, directing the learners to circle *yes* if the words begin with the same sound and *no* if the words do not.

PUPIL SEES	TEACHER SAYS
yes/no	Shot/chew
yes/no	Pet/pit
yes/no	Stamp/champ
yes/no	Like/let
yes/no	Many/never

4 Say each word in the following list, directing the learners to circle the letter that begins each word.

PUPIL SEES	TEACHER SAYS
s/m/l/n	Many
d/t/o/b	Did
d/r/j/l	Laundry
e/r/s/c	Cabinet
m/x/s/z	Scissors
h/d/f/w	Hand

Cluster III | The learner who makes more than two incorrect responses in this section should be pretested on each objective in Cluster III, Chapter 4.

---

1 Pronounce each word in the following list, directing the learners to circle the pronounced word. Allow only five seconds for each response, and then move on to the next item.

PUPIL SEES	TEACHER SAYS
ten/tot/told/to	To
the/there/then/that	The
as/saw/was/want	Was
of/over/fun/for	Of

2 Speak the following sentences to your learners, directing them to circle on their paper the word that is omitted from the sentence. Flash a blank card to signal the omitted word as you say the sentence. These sentences may be repeated if necessary.

PUPIL SEES	TEACHER SAYS
and/he/it/to	I have a pencil _____ paper.
in/my/no/a	Can an elephant play_____piano?
and/yes/I/my	Can you see _____ coat?
he/in/and/it	I like to hide _____ the garage.

3 Read each word in the following list, directing the learners to circle the letter that begins each word.

PUPIL SEES	TEACHER SAYS
k/n/j/r	Keep
p/t/l/b	Baker
r/t/f/y	Tiger
m/d/f/r	Rainbow
i/c/j/p	Jump

4 Read each word in the following list, directing the learners to circle the letter that is heard at the end of each word.

PUPIL SEES	TEACHER SAYS
n/u/e/m	Came
f/j/t/l	Doll
s/e/z/w	Place
t/d/p/s	Lid

Cluster IV | The learner who makes more than two incorrect responses in this section should be pretested in each objective in Cluster IV, Chapter 4.

---

1 Read each word in the following list, directing the learners to circle the word pronounced in each group. Allow only five seconds for each response and then move on to the next item.

PUPIL SEES	TEACHER SAYS
don't/down/brown/doubt	Down
him/here/whelp/help	Help
fast/first/last/fist	Fast
it/to/at/all	At
sew/set/easy/see	See

2 Read each word in the following list, directing the learners to circle the letter combination that is heard at the beginning of each word.

PUPIL SEES	TEACHER SAYS
sh/ch/s/wh	Shirt
ck/sh/h/sch	Shack
t/dr/th/tl	Think
sl/wh/fr/th	Thistle

GROUP PLACEMENT TEST FOR CHAPTER 5 SKILLS

Cluster I / *The learner who makes more than two incorrect responses in this section should be pretested on each objective in Cluster I, Chapter 5.*

1 Say a word in isolation and then in a sentence, directing the learners to circle the word on their answer sheets. Allow only five seconds for each response and then move on to the next item.

PUPIL SEES	TEACHER SAYS
get/fril/little/girl	Girl/The girl went home.
after/other/attic/Africa	After/We will do it after dinner.
when/won/hoo/who	Who/Who won the game?
letter/little/liddle/fitter	Little/He was a little boy.
then/the/they/thy	They/They are going home.
saw/way/was/wasp	Was/He was going home.

2 Read each word in the following list, directing the learners to circle the letter combination that is heard at the beginning of each word.

PUPIL SEES	TEACHER SAYS
wh/th/ch	When
wh/th/ch	Chip
wh/th/ch	This

3 Direct the learners to each row of words in turn. Pronounce the first word in the row and have them circle the word you tell them to find.

PUPIL SEES	TEACHER SAYS
set/bet/wit/pet/pat	The first word is *set*. Now find and circle *bet*.
cat/fit/fat/mat/tot	The first word is *cat*. Now find and circle *fat*.
but/net/mut/nub/nut	The first word is *but*. Now find and circle *nut*.
sit/sack/sip/sect/sick	The first word is *sit*. Now find and circle *sick*.
lot/lick/lock/lush/lob	The first word is *lot*. Now find and circle *lock*.

4 Direct the learners to circle the word pronounced in each group.

PUPIL SEES	TEACHER SAYS
want/wants/wanted/wanting	Wanting
want/wants/wanted/wanting	Wants
want/wants/wanted/wanting	Wanted

Cluster II | The learner who makes more than two incorrect responses in this section should be pretested on each objective in Cluster II, Chapter 5.

---

1 Say a word in isolation and then in a sentence, directing the learners to circle this word on their answer sheets. Allow only five seconds for each response and then move on to the next item.

PUPIL SEES	TEACHER SAYS
sad/slap/said/sap	Said/I said to sit down.
for/frame/fun/from	From/He came from his house.
surprise/supper/search/soup	Surprise/I have a surprise for you.
doer/door/dock/poor	Door/He will open the door.
ben/bend/been/bin	Been/I have been at my house.
it/is/ill/if	If/Do it if you can.

2 Direct the learners to each row in turn. Pronounce the first word in the row and have them circle the word you tell them to find.

PUPIL SEES	TEACHER SAYS
sip/dip/drip/drop/gripe	The first word is *sip*. Now find and circle *drip*.
cab/crib/crop/crab/drab	The first word is *cab*. Now find and circle *crab*.
bed/sled/slip/sed/slept	The first word is *bed*. Now find and circle *sled*.
rub/clock/club/cub/slod	The first word is *rub*. Now find and circle *club*.

3 Pronounce each compound word, directing the learners to draw a line between the two words that make up the word pronounced.

PUPIL SEES		TEACHER SAYS
any	out	Anyone
some	body	Without
every	where	
with	one	

Cluster III | The learner who makes more than two incorrect responses in this section should be pretested on each objective in Cluster III, Chapter 5.

---

1 Say a word in isolation and then in a sentence, directing the learners to circle this word on their answer sheets. Allow only five seconds for each response and then move on to the next item.

PUPIL SEES	TEACHER SAYS
peas/place/please/breeze	Please/Please help me.
sing/sang/swing/song	Song/Let's sing a song.
very/marry/weary/vary	Very/This is very hard.
guest/guess/gets/guest	Guess/I will guess the answer.
where/their/there/wear	There/He is over there.
were/where/wear/here	Were/We were going home.

2 Direct the learners to each row in turn. Pronounce the first word in the row and have them circle the word you tell them to find.

PUPIL SEES	TEACHER SAYS
back/smock/smash/black/smack	The first word is *back*. Now find and circle *smack*.
him/swam/swim/dim/slim	The first word is *him*. Now find and circle *swim*.
bet/rest/beck/blest/best	The first word is *bet*. Now find and circle *best*.
lad/last/blast/lost/lack	The first word is *lad*. Now find and circle *last*.

3 Direct the learners to draw a line from the contractions on the left to the words from which each contraction is formed.

PUPIL SEES		TEACHER SAYS
don't	let us	(Directions only)
I'll	do not	
let's	would not	
won't	I will	

Cluster IV | The learner who makes more than two incorrect responses in this section should be pretested on each objective in Cluster IV, Chapter 5.

1   Say a word in isolation and then in a sentence, directing the learners to circle this word on their answer sheets. Allow only five seconds for each response and then move on to the next item.

PUPIL SEES	TEACHER SAYS
dive/giv/live/give	Give/I will give you a penny.
there/their/ther/they're	Their/It is their house.
sure/shure/chure/sur	Sure/I am sure it is right.
duz/dose/does/dos	Does/He does write well.
bread/reddy/ready/retty	Ready/I am ready to go.
that/wat/what/wut	What/What are you doing?

2   Direct the learners to each row in turn. Pronounce the first word in the row and have them circle the word you tell them to find.

PUPIL SEES	TEACHER SAYS
feet/fell/field/free/feel	The first word is *feet*. Now find and circle *feel*.
my/fly/ski/sky/sly	The first word is *my*. Now find and circle *sky*.
day/dray/tray/trae/they	The first word is *day*. Now find and circle *tray*.
will/gill/dill/grell/grill	The first word is *will*. Now find and circle *grill*.
ball/stall/still/shall/stoll	The first word is *ball*. Now find and circle *stall*.

3   Direct the learners to circle the word pronounced.

PUPIL SEES	TEACHER SAYS
new/newer/newest/newly	newly
new/newer/newest/newly	newer
new/newer/newest/newly	newest

Cluster V | The learner who makes more than two incorrect responses in this section should be pretested on each objective in Cluster V, Chapter 5.

---

1   Say a word in isolation and then in a sentence, directing the learners to circle this word on their answer sheets. Allow only five seconds for each response and then move on to the next item.

PUPIL SEES	TEACHER SAYS
should/could/would/showed	Should/We should go home now.
beneath/believe/beehive/deliver	Believe/I do not believe your story.
heady/heavy/heave/levy	Heavy/That load you are carrying must be heavy.
tried/treed/trip/treid	Tried/He tried very hard to win the game.
next/necked/net/mesh	Next/You are next in line.
when/were/where/there	Where/Where are you going?

2   Direct the learners to circle all the words in each row that say the word pronounced.

PUPIL SEES	TEACHER SAYS
bote/boat/bot/boty/boate	Find and circle all the words that can say *boat*.
bote/bout/boit/bowt/bowl	Find and circle all the words that can say *bout*.
bait/bat/baat/bate/batty	Find and circle all the words that can say *bait*.

3   Direct the learners to each row in turn. Pronounce the first word in this row and have them circle the word you tell them to find.

PUPIL SEES	TEACHER SAYS
say/sand/sank/sing/band	The first word is *say*. Now find and circle *sand*.
thin/thing/than/found/think	The first word is *thin*. Now find and circle *think*.
ten/bend/bank/bent/bunt	The first word is *ten*. Now find and circle *bent*.

4   Pronounce each word, directing the learners to draw a line between the two parts that make up the word.

PUPIL SEES		TEACHER SAYS
dis	turb	dislike
un	like	unhappy
an	happy	distrust
un	light	
dis	trust	

Cluster VI | The learner who makes more than two incorrect responses in this section should be pretested on each objective in Cluster VI, Chapter 5.

1 Say a word in isolation and then in a sentence, directing the learners to circle the word on their answer sheets. Allow only five seconds for each response and then move on to the next item.

PUPIL SEES	TEACHER SAYS
field/felled/fielded/feeled	Field/They played ball in the field.
close/clues/clothes/cloze	Clothes/He was wearing his new set of clothes.
ernest/erly/pearl/early	Early/He got up early this morning.
elephant/umbrella/underneath/umber	Umbrella/When it rains, we use an umbrella.
all ways/almost/allowed/always	Always/He is always happy.
these/those/their/toes	Those/He is going to eat those apples.

2 Pronounce the first word in each list, directing the learners to circle all other words in the list that have the same middle sound.

PUPIL SEES	TEACHER SAYS
too/food/wood/book/room	The first word is *too*. Now find and circle all other words having the same middle sound as *too*.
look/foot/stood/zoot/took	The first word is *look*. Now find and circle all other words having the same middle sound as *look*.

3 Direct the learners to look at each word in turn and to draw a line between the syllables in that word.

PUPIL SEES	TEACHER SAYS
after	(Directions only)
basket	
rabbit	
follow	
until	

4   Pronounce each compound word, directing the learners to draw a line between the two words that make up the word.

PUPIL SEES		TEACHER SAYS
each	man	Everything
every	noon	Afternoon
out	night	Outside
home	side	
after	thing	

Cluster VII | The learner who makes more than two incorrect responses in this section should be pretested on each objective in Cluster VII, Chapter 5.

---

1   Say a word in isolation and then in a sentence, directing the learners to circle this word on their answer sheets. Allow only five seconds for each response and then move on to the next item.

PUPIL SEES	TEACHER SAYS
every/enough/through/enuff	Enough/I have not had enough pie.
build/built/bought/bilk	Build/I will build a house.
through/thorough/though/thought	Thought/I thought you were at home.
anything/anniversary/answer/angel	Answer/Did you get the right answer?
energy/engine/engineer/imagine	Engine/The car has a big engine.
much/most/must/mist	Must/You must stay in the house today.

2   Direct the learners to look at each word in turn and to draw a line between the syllables in that word.

PUPIL SEES	TEACHER SAYS
began	(Directions only)
open	
music	
never	
tiger	

3 Direct the learners to each row in turn. Pronounce the first word in the row and have them circle the word you tell them to find.

PUPIL SEES	TEACHER SAYS
rip/stiff/strip/strike	The first word is *rip*. Now find and circle *strip*.
long/slong/strong/string/thong	The first word is *long*. Now find and circle *strong*.
boat/trout/throw/thoat/throat	The first word is *boat*. Now find and circle *throat*.
crash/thrash/trash/thatch/threes	The first word is *crash*. Now find and circle *thrash*.

4 Direct the learners to look at each word in turn and to cross out the letters in the word that are not sounded.

PUPIL SEES	TEACHER SAYS
high	(Directions only)
knock	
crumb	
straight	

APPENDIX F / THE DIFFERENCE BETWEEN TEACHING AND TESTING

To develop reading skills in children, you must both test and teach effectively. Testing and teaching are, however, two distinctly different types of teacher behavior, and it is crucial that you demonstrate your understanding of this difference in your classroom work.

TESTING

Testing is the diagnostic step—the point at which you determine whether the learner can perform the desired skill. Normally, it will occur in two places; prior to teaching (pretest) to determine if the learner already knows the skill and therefore needs no instruction, and following teaching (posttest) to determine whether those who failed the pretest have now achieved mastery as a result of your instruction.

Testing requires first that you specify what skill you want to assess. This is achieved by using the performance objectives provided in this book. Second, testing requires that you structure a situation in which the learner is forced to respond—that is, to perform the skill in its totality. It is not broken down or simplified for him. For example, if you are testing for sight words, you flash him the whole word and require a response to the rapid exposure; if you are testing for sound–symbol connection, you present him with a sound and require him to identify the symbol; if you are testing for his ability to analyze words by substituting initial consonants in phonograms, you present him with a list of unknown words having the same phonogram element but different initial consonants and require him to pronounce them; and if you are testing for his ability to identify the meaning of unknown words through the use of context, you give him a sentence using unknown words and require him to state the meaning of these words. In any case, testing requires little teacher effort beyond insuring that the test does indeed assess the specified skill. In this book, of course, these tests are provided for you.

TEACHING

Teaching is the instructional step—the point at which you provide the learner with the input that allows him to perform the task he was unable to perform in the pretest. Because he was unable to respond during the test to your request that he perform the total skill, it stands to reason that teaching is more than simply asking him to respond again. You, the teacher, must expend considerable energy and effort beyond that of simply asking questions—you must break the skill down into comprehensible and manageable steps.

If a learner is unable to perform a skill, it must be assumed that it is a puzzle to him. The effective teacher follows certain steps in helping the learner figure out the puzzle.

1 *The teacher analyzes the skill, identifying the separate pieces of the puzzle.* The effectiveness of any teacher can usually be determined by the degree to which he is able to identify the pieces of the puzzle. We usually label such a teacher as one who knows what he is teaching or as one who knows his field. Such teachers identify the pieces of the puzzle *prior to instruction* and structure the learning episode in a manner that allows the learner to see each piece of the puzzle and how the pieces fit together. In this book the pieces of the puzzle are provided for you in the section of each objective entitled "Directing the Learner's Attention."

2 *The teacher directs the learner's attention to the pieces of the puzzle.* As the first step in instruction, the effective teacher directs the learner to pay attention—not to the situation as a whole but, rather, to the pieces of the puzzle. These are specific directions that explicitly tell the learner what the puzzle is and what the separate pieces of the puzzle are. They let him know *exactly* what he must attend to (what he must look at, what he must listen to, or both) in order to master the skill. Failure to direct attention to each piece of the puzzle at the outset will result in the learner's not paying attention or paying attention to the wrong piece, and he will still be unable to figure out the puzzle—perform the skill— at the conclusion of the lesson.

3 *The teacher shows the learner each of the pieces of the puzzle.* Once the learner's attention has been directed, the teacher shows him each piece of the puzzle. Now the learner is not responding to the skill in its totality as he was in the test. Instead, the task has been *simplified* because it has been broken down into its essential pieces. He is shown each of the separate parts as a step toward understanding how the skill as a whole functions. As a part of this step, the teacher *dramatizes, or highlights,* the crucial pieces by color coding, by underlining, by circling, by using a flannelboard, or by using any other device that directs the learner's attention to each separate piece of the puzzle.

4 *The teacher shows the learner how the pieces of the puzzle fit together to form a whole.* Once the learner has responded in terms of each separate piece, he can be shown how the pieces fit together to form a whole. Here, he is directed to put the pieces together and to take them apart again—he is shown the relationship among the separate pieces. This is the point where modeling is especially useful because the teacher can demonstrate how the pieces fit together and the child can mimic the teacher's behavior as a first step toward mastery.

5 *The teacher provides diminishing crutches to lead the learner toward mastery.* Once the learner has been shown the relationship among the pieces and has been led by the hand in putting the pieces together and in taking them apart, the teacher requires him to make a series of responses to the task. At first, the response is much like Step 4 in that the learner is provided with elaborate *crutches* that insure a successful response. With each passing successful response, however, the learner is required to respond with fewer and fewer crutches to aid him until he independently performs the skill in its totality. At this point, and not before, the learner is ready for *practice* designed to solidify the response and make it habitual, so that he can retrieve it whenever it is needed.

To assist you in implementing the suggestions in Steps 3, 4, and 5 above, specific teacher directions are provided in the "Model Activity" section of each objective.

Teaching, then, requires the expenditure of considerable teacher effort and energy. It is not simply a matter of demanding a response to a specific task as is the case in testing. Instead, the teacher must analyze the skill, break it down to its separate pieces, highlight these pieces for the learner, show the relationships among the pieces, and lead him through a series of responses in which he is given fewer and fewer aids in performing the task.

The *effective* teacher is aware of the difference between testing and teaching, and applies the above steps in his instruction to make certain of effective learning. The *creative* teacher uses the same steps, but with ingenuity and inventiveness, making each learning situation a unique experience.

APPENDIX G / A MODEL SKILL LESSON: TEACHING OBJECTIVE II B **4** IN CHAPTER FOUR

The material presented in this model lesson will demonstrate how a typical lesson can be expanded and amplified. In this instance, we have used Objective IIB 4 in Chapter 4. Marginal notes call attention to some particular points.

■ THE PERFORMANCE OBJECTIVE Given a spoken stimulus word beginning with either the *m* or *d* sound and a group of three other words one of which begins with the *m* or *d* sound, the learner pairs the two words beginning with the same sound.

The principle of blockage is established, the learner is told what he is to learn, and he is told what he must pay attention to in order to learn.

■ DIRECTING THE LEARNER'S ATTENTION Say to the learner, "Today we are going to do something that is very hard. We are going to learn how to tell when certain words sound the same at the beginning. In order to do this, you must listen very carefully to the sound you hear at the very beginning of words." To help the learner focus on the listening task, direct him to close his eyes as you pronounce the words.

■ THE PRESENTATION, RESPONSE, AND REINFORCEMENT Say a single word and ask the learner to repeat the word, saying, "Say this word and listen carefully to what you say at the beginning of the word." You may find it expedient at this

Modeling techniques are used.

point to exaggerate slightly the beginning sound in the words as you model for the learner, but this should not be continued beyond the first example. When the learner mimics your response, reward him and provide another word, repeating the above process without the modeling. Then direct the learner to say other words one after another, saying, "Listen to the beginnings of these words as you say them. Is the sound the same or different at the beginning? How can you tell it is the same (or different)?"

290

If the learner still cannot match the words having the same beginning sounds, dramatize and simplify the task for him by using contrasting pairs of words in which only the beginning sound is different, as in *mate* and *date*. If further help is needed, use the say-it-slow,-say-it-fast technique, saying to the learner, "Listen carefully as I say this word slowly. M——ate. Now I'll say it fast. Mate." After modeling the activity for the learner in this way, have him repeat the task, directing him to emphasize, but not to isolate, the beginning sound when he says the word slowly, comparing the sound he makes at the beginning of one word with the sound he makes at the beginning of another. Provide other words, gradually reducing the emphasis on the beginning sound and introducing words which are not contrasting pairs.

Techniques become more and more simplified and directed.

Use of contrasting pairs to focus attention on differences at the beginning.

Crutches are gradually diminished.

If he still has persistent difficulty, teach him how the beginning sound of a word is formed with the mouth, having him compare how his mouth forms the sound of *m* as compared to how it forms the sound of *d*.

The learner is rewarded for each correct response according to what turns him on. For one, it might be M&M candy, for another praise, and for another a combination of praise and physical touch, such as a handshake.

The different kinds of reward.

■ PRACTICE Have a large number of magazines in the classroom and direct the learner to cut out pictures that begin with the sound you hear at the beginning of *mouse* or *dog*. A variation of this activity is one in which the learner is given a number of pictures beginning with the *m* and *d* sounds, and he is directed to sort them into two piles. All the pictures the names of which begin with the sound heard at the beginning of *monkey* are placed in one pile and the pictures the names of which begin with the sound heard at the beginning of *dog* are placed in another pile.

The direct relationship between the practice and what was taught.

Still another practice exercise is a form of bingo, in which learners are provided with bingo-like playing cards having pictures in the squares. Say, "Do you have a picture on your card the name of which begins with the same sound you hear at the beginning of *dog*? If you do, you may cover that square with a marker." The first learner to have every picture in a row covered wins the game.

The game is simple and reinforces what was taught.

■ APPLICATION Since this is a readiness skill and the learner does not know how to read yet, it cannot be directly applied in reading a book. However, the skill of listening for the beginning sound in words can be applied in learning the next skill in the sequence, which is connecting the sound of *m* with the letter *m*.

Use is a synonym of apply.

APPENDIX H / A CHECKLIST FOR EVALUATING YOUR SKILL LESSONS

The following checklist has been devised to help you evaluate the effectiveness of your skill lessons. The list is organized according to the major parts of a skill lesson as described in Chapter 3. Under each major heading, read each question carefully. If your answer to each question is *Yes*, you are doing an effective job of teaching skills. If, however, you find one or more questions to which you must answer *No*, you need to improve your skill instruction.

A / Directing the learner's attention   *Yes*   *No*
   1. Have I directed the learner to the attenders cited in the objective?
   2. Have I been specific in directing attention? Does the learner know what the pieces of the skill puzzle are?
   3. Have I used physical as well as auditory cues in directing attention?
   4. Have I taken the "guessing game" element out of the learning experience?
   5. Is the learner able to say to himself, "I know what the teacher is trying to teach me, and I know what I must pay attention to in order to learn it"?
   6. Has the difficulty of the task been established?

B / Presentation
   1. Is my presentation clear and concise?
   2. Is my presentation brief? Is it within the expected attention span of the learners with whom I am working?
   3. Have I proceeded from the simple to the complex in my presentation?
   4. Have I asked questions that force the learner to focus on the concept to be understood?
   5. Have I done less talking than the learner?

6. Have I modeled the relationship between the separate pieces of the skill puzzle?
7. Have I used devices such as color coding to dramatize or graphically illustrate the principle I am teaching?
8. Have I provided the learner with a series of diminishing crutches?
9. Does my presentation lead gradually to an independent learner response?
10. Am I asking the learner to use more than one of his senses in my presentation?
11. At the conclusion of the presentation, does the learner have a model, a strategy, or a principle he can apply in solving similar tasks independently?

C / Response

1. Is the learner provided with opportunities to respond at each step during the presentation?
2. Is the learner effectively involved in the presentation?
3. Does the learner respond with manipulative, visual, and other devices as well as by answering questions orally?
4. Does the learner *do*, as well as listen?
5. Is the learner provided with immediate feedback regarding the "rightness" or the "wrongness" of his responses?

D / Reinforcement

1. Is the reinforcement I use positive in nature?
2. Does the learner receive a reward for responding correctly?
3. Is the form of the reinforcement effective? Is it really a reward for him, or do I just *think* it is?
4. Does the reinforcement encourage the learner to achieve more? Is this the most effective reinforcement for this learner?
5. Do I provide the reward immediately for those learners lacking a sophisticated reward system?
6. Am I spacing my rewards properly for the learners possessing more sophisticated reward systems?
7. Am I making plans to move the learner gradually toward self-motivation where tangible rewards are no longer needed?

E / Practice

1. Is the learner practicing the same skill I taught in the presentation?
2. Is the practice an intensive experience in which the learner retrieves the desired response many times in a brief period of time?
3. Is the practice relevant rather than busy work?
4. Does the practice reflect the reading act by forcing the learner to respond to a visual stimulus, as opposed to

Yes *No*

spelling-type activities in which he responds to auditory stimuli?

5. Does the learner receive adequate instructions regarding how to do the practice exercise?

6. Do I check occasionally to see that he is performing the practice exercise correctly?

7. Does the learner receive immediate feedback regarding the quality of his performance on the practice exercise?

F / Application

1. Have I done more than simply tell the learner that the skill is important?

2. Have I demonstrated how the skill will aid in reading library books, social studies books, etc.?

3. Have I structured experiences to make certain that the learner puts the skill to use in his daily reading?

4. Have I observed the learner reading other materials to make certain that the skill taught in isolation has transferred to the reading act itself?

APPENDIX I/DIAGNOSTIC CHARTS KEYED TO CORRECTIVE SUGGESTIONS

The following charts will aid you in relating the observed reading behavior of learners to specific instructional suggestions provided in this book. Three charts are provided. The first relates to the objectives in Chapter 4, the second to those in Chapter 5, and the last to those in Chapter 6. Each chart is divided in terms of the observed behavior, the possible cause, and the sections in the book that provide helpful instructional suggestions. When you observe persistent learner deficiencies in reading and wish to locate specific corrective measures, check these charts for that particular behavior and refer to the objectives suggested.

You should be aware of several cautions, however, in using these charts. First, it is not possible for such charts to anticipate all the possible behaviors your readers may exhibit. These charts represent, instead, the most common types of problems you will encounter. Second, the cause listed for each chart is a *possible* cause; it is not possible to predict the actual cause without knowing the specific learner. You are urged to use your knowledge of the learner and his environment to supplement the possible cause listed on the chart. Finally, remember that any particular deficiency may exist because the learner has not mastered the prerequisites to that particular skill. Consequently, before using the instructional techniques suggested for a deficiency, check to be certain that the learner has mastered and retained the crucial prerequisite skills.

IF THE LEARNER CANNOT READ AT ALL

WHEN LEARNER SHOWS THIS BEHAVIOR	THE CAUSE MIGHT BE	SEE OBJECTIVE
Fails to learn sight words at a normal rate. Confuses letters of the alphabet.	Poor visual discrimination.	IA 1, Chapter 4.
Cannot remember letter and word shapes.	Poor visual memory.	IA 2, Chapter 4.
Reverses words, says *was* for *saw*, etc. Does not read from left to right and from top to bottom.	Has an orientation problem. Does not know how to look at words and the printed page.	IIA 8, Chapter 4.
Does not hear the differences in sounds. Cannot rhyme. Letters do not have distinguishing sounds for him.	Poor auditory discrimination.	IIB 2 and IIB 3, Chapter 4.
Cannot provide the correct sound for specific letters.	Has not made the sound-symbol connection.	IIB 5, Chapter 4.
Poor oral language. Limited vocabulary. Immature oral language patterns.	Few prior opportunities to express himself. Limited experience background.	IIB 10 and IIB 11, Chapter 4.
Does not use context as a means for identifying unknown words.	Lacks sentence sense. Poor oral language background.	IIB 12, Chapter 4
Does not use the words he recognizes at sight to write sentences and stories.	Does not understand the thinking-writing-reading concept of language communication.	IIIA 10, Chapter 4.
Is not interested in learning to read.	Unfamiliar with books. Has not seen how books can be useful and/or enjoyable.	See suggestions in Chapter 7.

IF THE LEARNER KNOWS SOME WORDS BUT DOES NOT READ FLUENTLY

WHEN LEARNER SHOWS THIS BEHAVIOR	THE CAUSE MIGHT BE	SEE OBJECTIVE
Has a limited stock of sight words.	Poor visual discrimination and/or visual memory.	IA 1 and IIIA 2, Chapter 4.
Has mastered visual discrimination and visual memory prerequisites, but still has a limited stock of sight words.	Needs added practice on learning specific words.	IIIA 6, Chapter 4.
Failure to differentiate words somewhat different in spelling, as *where* and *there*.	Does not attend to the specific discriminator that contrasts the similar-looking words.	IA 2, Chapter 5.
Reads word by word. Lacks fluency and smoothness in his reading.	Poor sight vocabulary.	IIIA 6, Chapter 4.
Reversals in reading. Confuses *p* and *q*, *was* and *saw*.	Left-to-right orientation.	IIA B, Chapter 4.
Complete inability to sound out words. Inability to attack new or unfamiliar words.	Lacks the prerequisites for analyzing words.	IIB 2, IIB 3, and IIIB 12, Chapter 4.

WHEN LEARNER SHOWS THIS BEHAVIOR	THE CAUSE MIGHT BE	SEE OBJECTIVE
Cannot blend together individual sounds or word parts in pronouncing unknown words.	Lacks understanding of how individual letters and word parts combine in pronouncing the word. Does not know how to use the principle of consonant substitution.	IB 7, Chapter 5.
Does not understand the short vowel spelling patterns.	Lacks understanding of common word families and short vowel phonograms.	IB 7, Chapter 5.
Does not understand the long vowel principles.	Has not been properly taught these principles.	IVB 2, IVB 3, IVB 4, VB 1, VB 2, and VB 3, Chapter 5.
Cannot break words into syllables.	Does not know the principle upon which words are syllabicated.	VIB 2, Chapter 5.
Cannot analyze words in terms of word parts or structure.	Lacks understanding of compound words and/or of the root word–prefix–suffix structure.	IB 13, Chapter 5.
Cannot analyze and pronounce contractions.	Does not understand the principle upon which contractions are formed.	IIIB 9, Chapter 5.

IF THE LEARNER PRONOUNCES WORDS BUT DOES NOT UNDERSTAND

Does not know the meaning of content or referent words such as *erosion*.	Does not possess concepts for the words. Lacks experience background.	IA, Chapter 6.
Does not get the meanings signaled by function words such as *if*, *meanwhile*, etc.	Does not know the relationships signaled by such words.	IB, in Chapter 6.
Does not see the relationship among words such as *moon* and *starts*.	Does not know how to look for commonalities in meaning among words.	IIA, Chapter 6.
Cannot classify words in terms of their relationships to each other.	Has not been taught to classify in terms of common characteristics.	IIB, Chapter 6.
Cannot pick out the main idea in sentences and/or paragraphs.	Does not know how to pick out the common thread in sentences or paragraphs.	IIC, Chapter 6.
Cannot pick out the facts in his reading.	Has not been properly directed. Lacks specific purpose for reading. Teacher is asking the wrong questions.	IIIA, Chapter 6.
Cannot infer meanings from what he reads.	Cannot relate his experience to what he reads. Has not been properly guided by teacher questioning.	IIIB, Chapter 6.

APPENDIX J / A MODEL FOR RELATING COMPREHENSION SKILLS TO CONTENT MATERIAL

Teaching your learner to think about and understand what he reads requires that you be an imaginative and flexible teacher. You must accurately assess both what your learner needs to do or know in order to understand a selection and what kinds of thinking operations can best be taught from it. These two considerations should pervade all your teaching efforts.

In the first instance, you are saying that you want your learner to know and understand the content of the selection. If the reading is in a history book, then you want him to know history. Consequently, a portion of your teaching effort is expended in teaching whatever he needs in order to understand history. In the second instance, however, you are saying that you want your learner to think. Now the history book becomes the vehicle by which you show him how to do this. The content assumes a secondary importance while the process of thinking becomes the focus. These two considerations must guide you in planning content lessons.

To illustrate this, we have chosen a short three-paragraph selection about whales, typical of most fourth- or fifth-grade science books. Following this is a description of typical activities appropriate to both learning about whales and developing general thinking skills. The latter involves concept development, classification–organization skills, and fact–inference skills as described in Chapter 6. If this lesson were well taught, your learner would learn how to learn while also learning something about whales. The model provided here can be used by you in planning your own content lessons.

The Largest of All Animals[1]

The largest of all land or water animals is the whale. The great blue whale is sometimes over one hundred feet long and weighs as much as one hundred and twenty-five tons. Our largest elephants do not often weigh more than six tons, so the largest whale weighs more than twenty times as much as the largest elephant. Not all whales are as large as the great blue whale, however. The smallest whale, or dolphin, is seldom over four feet long.

The whale can grow to such great size because it lives in water. The water supports its great weight and provides plenty of food for it. As the whale swims through the water, it sweeps bushels of food into its mouth at one time.

Although the whale is shaped like a fish, it is really a mammal. Its young feeds on the mother's milk. It has lungs instead of gills. It breathes air. The whale usually comes to the top of the water every five or ten minutes, but it can stay under water for forty-five minutes. When it comes to the top of the water, the whale blows stale air from its lungs and takes in a supply of fresh air. Often when fishermen see the cloud of water vapor and air which the whale breathes out, they say, "There she blows."

CONCEPT–WORD MEANING SKILLS

In order to comprehend this selection, a learner would need meaning for many of the words and concepts used in the selection. Several examples follow:

One hundred feet / Not one fifth grader in a hundred has an accurate estimation of the linear measurement of 100 feet. Because size is so important to an understanding of this selection, you would need to devise a teaching tactic to clarify this value. You should have your learners measure the length of the classroom and picture whatever number of rooms it would take to make 100 feet. It would be even better to measure a hall that is at least 100 feet long, or even to pace this distance off on the playground. Some learners might also grasp this concept by directing them to picture a football field in their minds, with 100 feet roughly the distance from the goal to the 35-yard line.

One hundred and twenty-five tons / This is another measurement that needs some kind of description if it is to be understood. You might make an approximation of this weight by directing your learners to the fact that a car weighs about 3,000 pounds. One hundred and twenty-five tons is 250,000 pounds. How many cars piled on top of each other would equal one great blue whale? This could even be extended to the weight of the learners in your room. How many rooms of fifth graders would it take to balance the weight of one blue whale?

Four feet / The contrast between largest and smallest is needed for an understanding of this selection. Again, measurement or comparison

[1] *Atomic Submarine Book*, Building Reading Skills, McCormick-Mather Publishing Co., Wichita, Kansas, 1965, p. 72.

with a learner with a known height of four feet would help create an understanding of this concept.

Dolphin / The important concept here is that the dolphin and the great blue whale are relatives. They are brothers or sisters, so to speak, and whatever qualities of whaleness are inherent in one must be inherent in the other. Television shows with dolphins as main characters ("Marine Land" or "Flipper") could be mentioned for increased recall of dolphin qualities such as size, shape, etc.

Supports / An understanding of this verb is crucial to other questions that will follow. The sentence context should give adequate meaning in this instance. Ask learners to find synonyms for this term. Have them read the sentence and substitute their synonyms.

Provides / Use the preceding technique to create synonyms for this verb.

Sweeps bushels / A discussion of the figurative use of *sweeps* in this sentence would be both interesting and informative. A free association game such as the following would be appropriate. Say, "Listen to me. I am going to say a word. When I point to you, say the first word that comes into your mind. The word is, *sweep*." Point to a learner. A typical response will be "Broom" or "Kitchens" or "Clean." Elicit a number of responses and then guide the class in a determination of why the writer chose to use this word in this selection. The term *bushels* has a quantity connotation in the phrase. Most learners will picture a bushel basket and you could create an interesting and humorous situation by transferring this picture to a literal interpretation of this word. Can you picture a whale with a broom, sweeping bushel baskets into his mouth? The absurdity is apparent and can teach a learner to be careful of the meanings he assigns to figurative language.

Mammal / Meaning for this term can be beautifully illustrated by teaching a classification skill. Direct the learners to read the first sentence in the third paragraph carefully and name what "things" are being compared. (The answer is *fish* and *mammal*.) Make a chart on the board. Have the learners find qualities that belong in each column. *Note:* Some qualities are implied as opposites to what is stated. This will become clear to your learners as they fill out this chart.

Fishness qualities	*Mammalness qualities*
shape of fish	shape of fish
don't feed on mother's milk	feed on mother's milk
gills	lungs
breathes water	breathes air

Stale air / Direct the learner to inhale and hold his breath. Count to 60. Tell him to exhale. Question what happens to air that would change it from "fresh" to "stale." In both the whale and humans the body burns the oxygen to maintain life. The air is replaced with carbon dioxide, and neither the whale nor humans could live on this gas. A science experiment with a bell jar and candle would graphically illustrate this concept.

Gills and lungs / A fish drawing or model would illustrate what gills are and where they are located. Their function is explained as similar to lungs. Again, a human model or demonstration of breathing would illustrate what lungs are, and the comparison would be clear.

Water vapor / To develop the concept, you could ask your learners what happens when you breathe out on a cold winter morning. The warm air from the lungs is condensed by the cold, and we see it in the form of water vapor. This also happens when a whale expels the air from his lungs after diving deep in the cold ocean water.

These are but a few of the possibilities for developing word meaning and concept skills from this selection. You can see that you must be cognizant of both the demands of the material and the resources of your learners. In any case, the above illustrations give you a model for developing your own word meaning exercises in similar lessons.

CLASSIFICATION SKILLS

When using this particular reading selection, you could also teach classification skills. Several examples follow.

Classification skill / By defining the concepts *mammal* and *fish* in the previous section one classification skill has already been taught.

Relationship skills / The following sentence relationships and key words could be examined and used. For example, in the first sentence of the second paragraph, the word *because* signals a cause–effect statement. *Cause*, it lives in water; *effect*, it grows to such a great size.

To show the parallel importance of the two pieces of information contained in the second sentence of the second paragraph, you could chart the sentence structure as follows:

The water ⟨ supports weight.
           provides food.

Finally, in the first sentence of the third paragraph, the word *although* signals a contrasting relationship in the statement, ". . . a whale is shaped like a fish, it is . . . mammal." This relationship can also be developed.

Main idea / The paragraph structures in this selection lend themselves beautifully to a study of topic sentences and supporting details. You could direct the class to underline the most important sentence in each paragraph, perhaps using the triangle technique described in IIC of Chapter 6. This would be followed by a list of the words in each paragraph that supply details about the most important sentence. Next, attach the name *topic sentence* to this first sentence. Finally, have the class make an outline of each paragraph.

FACTS AND INFERENCE

This reading selection also has many possibilities for activities relating to both fact and inference as described in Cluster III of Chapter 6.

Fact / The possibilities for factual questions from this selection are so numerous and so obvious that two or three questions such as the following should be sufficient illustration:
1. In what way are blue whales and dolphins alike?
2. How large is a great blue whale?
3. Do whales have gills?

Inference / Inferential skills can also be taught using this selection. An excellent way to start this would be to use a variation of the SQ3R technique described in Objective IIIA in Chapter 6. Before assigning the selection, put the title on the board and ask a learner to read it. Then say, "This is the title of the selection we are going to study today. I wonder if you can do something that is very hard? I wonder if you can figure out what you might learn in this selection just by reading these five words? Can you make a question that you will be able to answer after you read the rest of the page?" An obvious question would be, "What is the largest animal?" List any other questions the class creates, letting them serve as purpose-setters for their reading. What they are doing is inferring, from a small five-word input, both factual and inferential information that should be found in the selection.

Another possibility for inference is found in the second paragraph, which explains the relationship between the size of a whale and the place that it lives. This offers many possibilities for inferential thinking. For example, the question, Could a whale live on land? would necessarily lead to thinking far beyond the information given in the paragraph. The dialogue might go like this.

Class: No, a whale can't live on land.

Teacher: Why not? They are mammals, they breathe air just like we do.

Class: They need the water to keep their skins wet.

Teacher: All right. I'll water the whale with a fire hose and keep him wet. Now can he live on land?

Class: No. How would he eat?

Teacher: I'll trap tons of food for the whale and pump it into his mouth and down his stomach. Now can he live on land?

Class: No. Whales just can't live on land.

Teacher: Well, why not?

Although this looks like a stalemate, if you push hard enough and refer the class back to the word *supports* in the second sentence of the second paragraph, some learner will grasp the implication of this word, and the dialogue will then continue like this:

Class: A whale can't live on land because water supports it, but land doesn't.

Teacher: What do you mean by "supports it"?

Class: Well, a whale is so heavy that he just collapses on land, while in the water he doesn't collapse.

Teacher: Why not?

Class: Water supports whales.

Once again you need to direct the class to a key concept, that of buoyancy. You could do this with a series of questions such as these:

Teacher: How many of you can swim?

How many of you can float?

What happens when you float?

What does the water do?

With a little planning, you could have a pail of water, a spring scale (fish scale), a brick, and some cord on hand to provide a simple demonstration of the effect of buoyancy on the weight of the brick. This would illustrate the concept, and you could conclude in the following manner.

Teacher: Why can't a whale live on land?

Class: Land won't support his great weight. He probably wouldn't be able to breathe. All his great weight would just squeeze him together and he'd die.

Teacher: Why can he live in the water?

Class: He has lots of food available, and he can catch it in the water. The water also supports his great weight; he doesn't weigh so much in the water (buoyancy). Water allows him to breathe.

Although you might choose to teach inferential skills from this selection in a slightly different manner, you can see that such instruction demands imagination and flexibility on your part and that the success of such instruction is largely dependent upon the types of questions you ask and the kinds of thinking you demand of your learners.

SUMMARY

Hopefully, these pages have stimulated you to see the possibilities for developing thinking skills and content learning with a relatively simple reading selection. *These are possibilities.* You would never attempt to use all these exercises with one selection. Instead, you would look at the selection, look at your class, and say, "What should I use this material for? Should I teach them about whales? Should I teach them some word meaning skills? Should I teach them to classify and organize and outline? Should I teach them to infer the principle of buoyancy?" To do *all* of these would bleed the material dry. You would surely kill it, kill your learners, and kill the whales. Instead, select *a* skill and make your lesson. But please, do something other than saying, "All right class. Turn to page 61 in your science book. Read the first three paragraphs carefully. We will have a little quiz on it when you finish." This kind of behavior is assigning, not teaching, and you want to be a teacher.

APPENDIX K / A GLOSSARY OF TERMINOLOGY USED IN THIS BOOK

The following is a listing of 139 terms used in this book. Although many of these terms have been defined in the book itself, either parenthetically or by the context, you will nevertheless find it helpful to clarify meanings by using this glossary.

Ability grouping / Grouping of pupils in reading on the basis of instructional reading level.

Accent / To give stress or prominence to a syllable or word.

Affective / Refers to the attitude, feelings, and interest learners have regarding reading.

Affix / A letter or syllable at the beginning or end of a word, which changes the meaning; for example, the *un* in *unhappy* and the *ful* in *joyful*.

Analysis / See *Word analysis.*

Antonym / Is the opposite in meaning, for example, hot–cold.

Application / The act of *using* learned reading skills in the daily school program.

Attenders / Those salient features of the learning task (pieces of the skill puzzle) to which the learner must pay close attention in order to achieve mastery.

Auditory discrimination / Listening to and discriminating between sounds.

Auditory memory / Listening to and remembering sounds.

Aural / Refers to learning through listening; learning by attending with your ears rather than with your eyes.

Basal reader A sequential series of reading textbooks, developmental in nature and designed for use with specific grade levels.

Behavioral objectives / Instructional goals stated in terms of what the learner will do or accomplish.

Blends / The fusion of two or more consonant sounds in a word without loss of identity of each sound; for instance, *bl*ack, *pl*an.

Blockage / A condition in which the task to be performed cannot be done by the learner. Because it cannot be done, it is a "block" to the desired behavior change.

Buffer / A learner who assists with routine questions and problems while the teacher works with other individuals or small groups.

Classification / The skill of discriminating likenesses and differences between concepts and grouping them according to their likenesses and differences.

Classifying / See *Classification.*

Closed syllable / When the only vowel letter in a word or accented syllable is any place but at the end of the word or syllable.

Cluster / A group of skills; used to divide the skills contained in Chapters 4, 5, and 6; such division is arbitrary and is done for ease of management rather than for any pedagogical reason.

Compound words / A word composed of two free morphemes or their derivatives; for example, *blueberry* (*blue berry*) and *fireplace* (*fire place.*)

Comprehension / Reading a passage with various degrees of understanding.

Concept / An understanding of a particular phenomenon; a mental image of what it should be; usually depends upon the amount of experience one has with the phenomenon.

Conceptual / See *Concepts.*

Configuration / The general form or shape of a word.

Consonant / A partially or completely closed or obstructed phonetic sound other than *a, e, i, o, u.*

Consonant substitution / See *Substitution.*

Content words / Those English words that have a definite referent in the culture; for example, *erosion, skeleton, knife,* and *Christmas* are content words.

Context / The known words surrounding an unknown word that are indicative of the meaning or pronunciation of the unknown word.

Contextual / See *Context.*

Criterion level / The number of items on a test that the learner must complete correctly to achieve mastery.

Decode / The process of identifying the sound value of printed symbols; being able to look at the printed symbol *cat* and say (or pronounce) the word *cat.*

Dialect / A nonstandard way of pronouncing English words; usually rooted in the geographical backgrounds of the speaker.

Digraph / Two successive letters representing a single speech sound; for example, *ch* in *child.*

Diphthong / When there are two adjacent vowels each contributing to the sound heard (blending); for example, the *oi* in *oil.*

Directing the learner's attention / The first step in an instructional episode; directs the learner's attention to the specific task. Incorporates two aspects: with what (looking, listening, feeling) and to what (skill focus or pieces of the skill puzzle).

Discriminator / The crucial aspect of a word that serves to contrast it with other similar words; the part of the word the learner must focus on particularly; can be either visual or aural.

Drill / See *Practice.*

Experience approach / The development of beginning reading instruction through the use of learner-written materials based on learner experiences as shared or discussed in oral situations.

Experience background / The amount of contact one has had with various phomemena in the culture; these contacts can be either direct or vicarious.

Extrinsic motivation / External, material, or tangible reward, such as raisins or tokens.

Family words / A group of words, such as *hat, sat, fat, mat*, containing identical phonemic elements.

Flash cards / Small cards on which letters, words, or phrases are printed and exposed briefly for rapid recognition.

Function words / Words that signal relationships, such as chronology or cause–effect, among the other words in a sentence; includes words such as *the, and, into, under, meanwhile, if*.

Functional literacy / A level of reading ability deemed necessary to function in society; defined by various sources as being between fourth- and seventh-grade reading levels; defined by this book as fourth-grade level.

Generalization / A principle of reading that is applicable in most situations; a rule.

Grade equivalent / The grade level for which a given score is the real or estimated average; for example, the grade-equivalent score of 4.1 means that the learner is performing at a level comparable to an average learner in the first month of the fourth grade.

Independent activities / Those reading-related tasks that learners perform when they are not directly involved in a teacher-led skill group.

Individualized reading / An approach to reading instruction in which the learner reads material (usually trade books) of his choice while receiving individualized skill help from the teacher as he needs it.

Individualization / An attempt to adapt instruction to individual differences.

Instructional episode / A period of intensive skill instruction roughly equivalent to a lesson, but usually briefer and more tightly organized and efficient.

Instructional level / The level of reading material at which a learner pronounces no less than 95 percent of the words, comprehends no less than 75 percent of the material, and at which no evidence of tension is present.

Inferential reading / The ability to comprehend meaning that is not stated; to think what is implied; reading between the lines.

Intrinsic motivation / Inward or internal reward, such as a good self-image or achieving well simply for the satisfaction it brings.

Key objectives / An objective in Chapters 4, 5, and 6, similar to other objectives taught later in the book, which serves as the basic reference for all such objectives.

Kinesthetic / Connecting sensations with body movements; learning through the sense of touch.

Language experience approach / Emphasizes that the oral language background of each child is a basic ingredient in word recognition; similar to the *experience approach*.

Learner / The term used by this book to refer to students and pupils.

Left-to-right progression / The skill of inspecting words from left to right and of reading lines of print from left to right.

Letter-sound correspondence / See *Sound–symbol connection.*

Lower case / The small form of a letter; the form of the letter other than its capital-letter form.

Main idea / The general idea of a sentence, paragraph, or selection; the common thread that holds it together.

Management / That set of teacher behaviors that determines how smoothly, routinely, and efficiently the learning situation functions from day to day.

Manuscript / The *printed* form of a word, as opposed to a written or cursive form.

Mastery / Demonstrated performance on a pretest or posttest that meets or surpasses the established criterion level.

Medial / The middle sounds or letters in a word.

Model activity / The instructional activity for each objective in Chapters 4, 5, and 6 that describes the most thorough way to teach that particular skill.

Modeling / A technique for developing understanding during the presentation step of an instructional episode in which the learner mimics, or models, your behavior as you demonstrate the task to be learned.

Motivation / A need or desire that causes a person to act; an inducement by another person to act.

Nonreader / A person who has not been properly exposed to the reading process and therefore is unable to read.

Open syllable / When the only vowel letter in a word or accented syllable is at the end of the word or syllable.

Orientation / Skills relating to the learner's ability to orient himself in terms of the printed page; to inspect words from left to right, to read pages from top to bottom.

Paraprofessionals / Persons not having a teaching certificate who are employed to assist regular classroom teachers.

Performance objective / See *Behavioral objective.*

Performance terms / Noting the overt behavior of learners as a means of determining whether the instructional objective has been achieved; see also *Behavioral objectives.*

Phoneme / A minimum distinctive sound unit in speech or a group of variants of one speech sound, such as the /g/ in *go,* or /che/ in *ache*

Phonemics / The study of sound–letter relationships in reading and spelling.

Phonetics / The study of classification of sounds used in human communication.

Phonetic analysis / The analysis of the sound units in an unknown word as a means of identifying the word.

Phonics / An imprecise term used by teachers to describe the process of analyzing the sound units of an unknown word; the correct term to use is *phonetic analysis.*

Phonogram / The endings of words used in teaching word families; for example, *ing* in *sing, ring, thing.*

Posttest / An informal means of evaluating the learner's terminal behavior.

Practice or drill / The fifth step in an instructional episode, which emphasizes drill on a specific skill as a means of making that response a habitual one.

Prefix / Letters or a syllable at the beginning of a word that changes or modifies its meaning; for example, the *un* in *unlike*.

Prerequisite / Those skills, concepts, or understandings that the learner must have mastered previously in order for him to succeed in a particular task.

Pretest / An informal means of evaluating a learner's entering behavior.

Presentation / The second step in an instructional episode, which develops an understanding of the specific skill to be mastered.

Readability / The objective measure of the difficulty of a book or article; usually involves the use of a specific formula with the results reported in terms of a grade level.

Readiness / The period of reading instruction that precedes the formal reading instruction; emphasizes the development of the prerequisites to successful reading achievement.

Reading / Meaningful interpretation of printed or written symbols.

Recognition / The term given to that primarily visual memory aspect of reading in which a learner instantly identifies words.

Recreational reading / Reading for the fun of it; recreational reading programs develop the habit of reading for pleasure.

Reinforcement / The fourth step in an instructional episode, which rewards the learner for a correct response.

Relevancy / The descriptive term associated with independent reading activities that the learner considers to be worthwhile; the opposite of busy work.

Remedial reader / A learner not achieving in reading at a level commensurate with his general ability.

Response / The *third step* in the instructional episode, which provides for learner response to the instruction.

Retention / Learning that permits later recall or recognition.

Reversals / An inaccurate perception of symbols or words; for example, *was* for *saw*, *p* for *q*, *b* for *d*; caused by examining letters and words from right to left, rather than from left to right.

Root / An original word form from which other words have been developed by the addition of affixes; for instance, *happy* is the root of *unhappy*.

Safety-valve activities / A variety of ongoing independent activities that the learner can use whenever his regularly assigned work has been completed.

Schwa / The sound heard in the vowel position of an unaccented syllable; for example, the vowel sound heard in the second syllable of *bedlam* is a schwa.

Sequencing / The process of reading the printed page from left to right and from top to bottom; also involves concepts of first–last, front–back, etc.

Sight word / A word instantly recognized by the reader without his needing to resort to word analysis techniques.

Silent letter / A letter or letters that are not pronounced in a word; for example, the *gh* in *right*.

Skill grouping / Grouping pupils for instruction on the basis of specific skill needs.

Sound–symbol conection / The ability to associate a letter sound with a letter symbol; for example, associating the sounds heard at the beginning of *mouse* and *man* with the letter *m*.

Sound–symbol correspondence / See *Sound–symbol connection.*

Sound units / A term used in this book to mean syllable.

Stimulus–response learning / A low-level type of learning in which the learner, primarily through repetition, learns to associate one thing with another; learns to pair a response to selected stimuli.

Stimulus word / A word to which a learner must make a response or a word that serves to elicit a response from the learner.

Storehouse of techniques / An extensive list of instructional activities and practice exercises provided as a part of each Key Objective in this book.

Structure / See *Structural analysis.*

Structural analysis / Seeing the parts of words that signal meaning in order to identify words; for example, recognizing the *s* in *boys*, the *ing* in *falling*, etc.; *not* synonymous with syllabication, because the latter is concerned with sound units and not meaning units.

Substitution / The skill of replacing one letter element of a regular spelling pattern with another to form a new word; for example, changing *hat* to *bat*, *bat* to *bag*, *bag* to *beg*.

Suffix / Letters or syllables added to the end of the word to change or modify the meaning; for example, *ful* in *harmful*.

Supportive activities / Those classroom activities not directly related to the teaching of reading skills but which support the learner's general development as a reader.

Syllabication / Division of words into syllables, usually for pronouncing; for example, de-light-ful; is a part of phonetic analysis; is not synonymous with structural analysis.

Synonym / Words that have similar or same meanings.

Syntactic / See *Syntax.*

Syntax / The way words are put into English sentences in order to make meaning.

Systematic instruction / A planned program moving through a hierarchy of reading skills, insuring that each prerequisite skill is mastered before subsequent skills are introduced; emphasizes a test-teach-test strategy.

Tachistoscope / A device that provides rapid exposure of letters, words, or phrases; used heavily as both a testing and a practice device for sight words; not useful for word analysis because the brief exposure leaves little time to analyze the word.

Tactile approach / See *Kinesthetic approach.*

Trade books / Books published for sale as other than textbooks; books usually referred to as library books.

Transfer / The process of using a learned task in a situation different from the one in which it was first learned.

Upper case / The large form of a letter; its capital letter form.

Vicarious experience / Secondary experiences with phenomena in the culture; experiences other than direct experiences; experiencing a phenomenon by reading about it, by viewing a film about it, etc.

Visual discrimination / Looking at and noting a likeness and/or difference between printed symbols.

Visual memory / After visual exposure, the ability to remember and/or reproduce sequenced symbols or shapes.

Vocabulary / Refers to the words the learner encounters in his reading; in this book, the term refers specifically to the *meaning* attached to words.

Voiced sounds / Phonetic sounds that cause the vocal cords to draw together and vibrate when they are produced.

Voiceless sounds / Phonetic sounds that cause the vocal cords to remain open so that they do not vibrate when they are produced.

Vowel / An open, unobstructed sound; for example, *a, e, i, o, u.*

Vowel digraph / When there are two vowels together in a word or accented syllable and the first has a long sound and the second is silent; the *oa* in *boat.*

Word analysis / The techniques used by a reader to survey an unknown word, analyze it, and identify its sounds; the most common techniques of word analysis include context, structural analysis, phonetic analysis, and/or a combination of these.

Word family / See *Family word.*

Word form / See *Configuration.*

Word meaning / The concept attached to any particular label; for example, the four-legged, hairy, barking, domestic pet that is usually associated with the label *dog.*

Word recognition / Identifying a word as previously known; pronouncing it; decoding it; includes both sight word recognition and word analysis techniques.